D0148308

RESTRUCTURING *the* PHILADELPHIA REGION

IN THE SERIES *Philadelphia Voices, Philadelphia Visions*
EDITED BY DAVID W. BARTELT

Richardson Dilworth, ed., *Social Capital in the City: Community and Civic Life in Philadelphia*

HARVARD UNIVERSITY
GRADUATE SCHOOL OF EDUCATION
MONROE C. GUTMAN LIBRARY

RESTRUCTURING *the* PHILADELPHIA REGION

Metropolitan Divisions and Inequality

Carolyn Adams, David Bartelt, David Elesh,
and Ira Goldstein
With Joshua Freely and
Michelle Schmitt

TEMPLE UNIVERSITY PRESS
Philadelphia

#X89285

HN
80
.P5
R47
2008

HARVARD UNIVERSITY
GRADUATE SCHOOL OF EDUCATION
MONROE C. GUTMAN LIBRARY

TEMPLE UNIVERSITY PRESS
1601 North Broad Street
Philadelphia PA 19122
www.temple.edu/tempress

Copyright © 2008 by Temple University
All rights reserved
Published 2008
Printed in the United States of America

∞ The paper used in this publication meets the requirements of the American National Standard
for Information Sciences—Permanence of Paper for Printed Library Materials,
ANSI Z39.48-1992

Library of Congress Cataloging-in-Publication Data

Restructuring the Philadelphia region : metropolitan divisions
and inequality / Carolyn Adams . . . [et al.] ; with Joshua Freely and Michelle Schmitt.
p. cm. — (Philadelphia voices, Philadelphia visions)
Includes bibliographical references and index.
ISBN 978-1-59213-896-8 (cloth : alk. Paper)
ISBN 978-1-59213-897-5 (pbk. : alk. paper)
1. Philadelphia Metropolitan Area (Pa.)—Social conditions.
2. Philadelphia Metropolitan Area (Pa.)—Economic conditions.   3. Sociology, Urban—
Pennsylvania—Philadelphia Metropolitan Area.   4. Philadelphia Metropolitan Area (Pa.)—
Politics and government.   5. Equality—Pennsylvania—Philadelphia Metropolitan Area.
I. Adams, Carolyn Teich.
HN80.P5R47 2008
307.1'4160974811—dc22

2008006408

2 4 6 8 9 7 5 3 1

October 30 2008

CONTENTS

LIST OF FIGURES AND TABLES

Figures

Tables

ACKNOWLEDGMENTS

This book expands the focus on inequality that defined our earlier book on the central city, titled *Philadelphia: Neighborhoods, Division, and Conflict in a Postindustrial City* (Temple University Press, 1991). In that earlier volume, we portrayed the deindustrialization that had transformed the city during the latter half of the twentieth century, and we interpreted the consequences of that shift for the labor force, housing markets, and politics in Philadelphia. Since that earlier book, we find ourselves in a new century and a new urban environment—one in which many of the most important questions about economic, social, and political inequality must be addressed at the regional level. With this book, we attempt to do just that.

The work that went into this book was made possible by the rich data resources that Temple University has assembled through its Metropolitan Philadelphia Indicators Project (MPIP). Since 2003, MPIP has collected, analyzed, and mapped information from dozens of data sources at the local, state, and federal levels to measure conditions and track changes across metropolitan Philadelphia. The project has assembled comparable information for all 353 municipalities included within this region, overcoming the obstacles created by differing geographical boundaries, definitional approaches, and data collection methods used by its many data providers. A particular challenge in this region spanning two states has been to harmonize data sets obtained from state agencies in Pennsylvania and New Jersey. MPIP tracks over a dozen different dimensions of the quality of life in the region's hundreds of communities, from health and housing to education, employment, arts and culture, and

environmental quality. You may see the breadth of the project's work at www
.temple.edu/mpip/. The MPIP project—and in turn this book—owe a profound debt to The William Penn Foundation, whose leaders saw the need for a
systematic regional database to undergird policy debates and action across the
region. The foundation's vision of evidence-based civic development inspired
the MPIP project, and the foundation has generously supported MPIP for five
years. We wish particularly to acknowledge the encouragement and guidance
to MPIP provided by the foundation's former president, Kathy Engbretson,
and current president, Feather Houstoun, and by Houstoun's associates, Gerry
Wang, Shawn McCaney, Helen Davis Picher, and Patrick Sherlok. The authors
would also like to thank Jeremy Nowak, president and CEO of The Reinvestment Fund (TRF). Mr. Nowak drew upon both his academic and extensive
practical experiences to offer critiques to earlier versions of this manuscript.
Those critiques helped to ground this work in the reality of social, political,
and economic life in Philadelphia. At TRF, Al Parker provided important geographic information system assistance.

Within the MPIP, two critical contributors to this book are Joshua Freely
and Michelle Schmitt, each of whom has served as MPIP project coordinator
at different times managing the data collection, cleaning, and analysis to produce the many tables and maps in the volume. We thank them both for their
excellent judgment, skill, patience, and unwillingness to accept anything less
than the right number in the right column. Temple's Institute for Survey Research (ISR) partnered with MPIP to conduct three annual surveys of atti-
tudes expressed by the region's households. Findings from those surveys are
reported in this volume. At ISR, we especially thank Leonard LoSciuto for his
vision in conceiving the multiyear survey and Peter Mulcahy for his outstand-
ing stewardship of every detail of the project, from constructing the questionnaire and training interviewers to cleaning and reporting findings.

We extend our deepest appreciation to our colleague Mark Mattson, the
incomparable cartographer and graphic designer who created all the maps and
graphs for both the MPIP and this volume. His ability to convert masses of
numbers into engaging, informative graphics has provided the visual "signa-
ture" for both MPIP and for the book.

Finally, we wish to acknowledge Janet Francendese, the editor in chief at
Temple University Press. She marshaled the talented staff of the press to both
support and push us to accomplish our best work She secured constructive
suggestions from a number of anonymous reviewers, whose advice we appreciate. Her gentle prodding helped us to correct many, if not all, of the manuscript's gaps and errors. Those that remain are the responsibility of the authors
alone.

Restructuring *the* Philadelphia Region

INTRODUCTION

Expanding the Focus

～

Yesterday's cities are today's metropolitan areas. Not only have cities grown beyond their early municipal boundaries, but the rapid expansion of suburban areas after World War II generated a seismic shift in the way people live and distribute themselves in urban areas and in the ways that we think about current and future urban issues. With over three-quarters of the U.S. population living in urbanized areas, this new urban reality concerns the entire nation.

While some cities in the United States have the ability to expand their boundaries as their population grows, Philadelphia, like most older cities, does not. The dynamics of urban development have spilled across the boundaries that made political sense in the nineteenth century. These dynamics have erased the easy distinctions between cities and suburbs defined by earlier boundaries. Our contemporary sense of the city has changed how we think about metropolitan regions. Today, both in Philadelphia and in metropolitan areas nationally, more than 70 percent of the population live and work in the suburbs. The problems of job loss, physical deterioration, affordable housing, development and redevelopment, racial segregation, inadequate school quality and funding, high tax levels, and the unresponsiveness of government now trouble suburbs as well as the cities. The appearance of these problems in the suburbs emphasizes the need to understand the larger metropolitan processes that affect both city and suburb. For those living and working in the greater Philadelphia area, the persistent social and economic divisions, even as they map themselves differently across the regional landscape, continue to shape public institutions and private lives.

Our earlier work, *Philadelphia: Neighborhoods, Division, and Conflict in a Postindustrial City,*[1] was about the life chances of city residents with respect to jobs, income, education, and housing. Inequalities in life chances remain central to our concern here. In this book, however, our consideration of those inequalities expands to encompass the entire metropolitan area, and we ask how those issues have evolved in the 1990s by examining them regionally and in relation to trends elsewhere. The decade of the 1990s and the first half of the current decade have brought with them a dramatically changed political and social environment, including significant differentials in municipal fiscal and organizational capacity, a new diversity of population across the region, and increasing questions over the feasibility (or rationality) of expanding limited transportation and public utility (e.g., water and sewer) infrastructures.

Our work departs from regional analyses that stress a strong central development engine. There is no easy metaphor that incorporates the co-occurrence of sprawl and gentrification or vacant land and edge cities. Even the notion of uneven development does not capture the diversity of conflicting pressures that influence many local communities. The combination of regional economic restructuring—from industry to service sector, heavy industry to information-driven enterprises, and urban agglomeration to decentralized, multiple nodes—has been accompanied by residential decentralization, making a Philadelphia-centered focus both incomplete and inadequate. Adopting a regional perspective means more than simply changing the spatial scale of the analysis. In the last decade, both academic paradigms and public policy debates have shifted away from seeing metropolitan regions as territories dominated by centrally located clusters of commerce, industry, and transportation toward a view of regions as having dispersed and "thinned out" patterns of development. That changing conception of how metropolitan space is organized has prompted intense debates about the future role that central cities will play in regional economies. We have been influenced by the work of other urbanists who have sought to understand the future of cities within their metropolitan contexts, as well as by scholars who have challenged traditional models of urban ecology and opposed orthodox city-suburban dualities.

Within the academy, a group of urban analysts centered in the Los Angeles area has systematically challenged the field's traditional model of how urban space is organized—sometimes termed the "Chicago School" of urban ecology. In that traditional approach to understanding how inequality is distributed across urban space, a city's commercial center was taken to be the primary driving force behind urban expansion—and in more recent years, behind urban decline as well. For most cities the large urban marketplace and the manufacturing districts close to transportation nodes were the major organizing forces that generated employment and profits, aligning factories and other workplaces, as well as communities, along class, race, or ethnic identities. The traditional urban narrative, at least through the beginning of the dramatic suburban shift after World War II, emphasized the centrifugal movement of people outward from the center as the normal result of economic progress and the market.

The self-named "LA School" stresses a different dynamic that is regionally focused, with multiple loci of growth exerting their own influence over the distribution of opportunity and inequality. Extensive highways and growing electronic linkages make lengthy and distant commuting patterns a taken-for-granted reality. Rather than dominating the region, the central city is incorporated into the region's evolution. Ultimately rooted in Harris and Ullman's polycentered view of the city,[2] the LA School sees industrial, commercial, and other economic growth centers as distributed across an ever-widening spatial scale, a trend that is facilitated by the development of roads versus rails and by the disaggregation of the production and distribution processes that traditionally shaped urban centers. In central cities that once housed manufacturing industries, we now see residents living in refurbished factories, we see galleries and offices occupying warehouses, and we see city leaders making calculated efforts to attract transient visitors (tourists, students, patients, and connecting passengers).

While the LA School's polycentered model more easily fits Sunbelt cities than those of the Rustbelt, its emphasis on the region is now shared by analysts concentrating on how to revitalize urban regions of the Northeast and Midwest. A significant literature has sought to distinguish between cities that have rebounded or prospered over the past decade and those that have not, linking the cities' differing fortunes to their regional contexts. Analysts as diverse as Myron Orfield,[3] David Rusk[4] and Bruce Katz[5] have found a common theme in looking for revitalization strategies. Simply put, they observe that successful revitalization depends on how cities and their surrounding areas are able to link to one another's resources, assets, and governance structures to address ongoing issues of employment, education, and housing quality. While each writer sounds a somewhat different tone in identifying key factors producing revitalization, their common focus on the region has helped change the national debate about the urban future.

Although there are substantial differences between the views of Orfield, Rusk, and Katz and the LA School in how they describe urban issues, they see a common set of forces shaping metropolitan change: location decisions by firms that deny some communities easy access to jobs, transportation modes that both link and separate communities from each other, differential streams of migration and immigration to urban areas, the persistence of race and ethnicity (as well as gender) in forming community identity, the importance of local "growth machines" in determining how and where urban areas expand and revitalize, and state and federal policies that shape metropolitan options.

Another academic influence driving us to examine the regional scale is one that emerges from a substantial literature in the architectural and planning fields that blurs the conventional understandings of urban and suburban places. The movement for a "new urbanism" has stressed the need for a more community-focused approach to suburban development. Seeking to re-create the strengths of urban neighborhoods, the new urbanists advocate a higher density model to develop residential spaces, surrounded by common areas in which automobile traffic is severely restricted. In what many see as a restatement of traditional "garden city" concepts, the new urbanism is now guiding an important—albeit a small—portion of suburban development in the United States and seeks to have its work replicated in revitalizing city neighborhoods as well.

In works that are not as prescriptive as new urbanist writing, recent historical scholarship[6] cautions that the development of suburban communities was neither as linear as urban expansion models would have it nor was it driven solely by economic privilege, as some critics contend. These scholars suggest that we differentiate suburbs by time period, construction style, and the dispersed regional economy. We have taken that suggestion seriously, creating our own typology to differentiate the suburbs surrounding Philadelphia and using that typology throughout this work. (Later in this chapter we will present that typology.) If we differentiate among suburban types, we see clearly that revitalization is not just an issue for core cities; it is a task confronting many suburban communities as well. Municipalities in all eight of the suburban counties surrounding Philadelphia seek substitutes for the loss of manufacturing jobs, restoration of commercial districts facing competition from malls, and renewal of aging housing stocks—even as commercial and residential growth are driven into high gear in nearby communities.

Our earlier book portrayed Philadelphia as the beleaguered core of the metropolitan region. While it remains beleaguered, our focus here is on the region's shifting organization of employment, commerce, and development—and on the city's role within this dynamic. In fact, parts of Philadelphia have shown a degree of economic resilience attributable to the same forces that are restructuring the region as a whole. Even while jobs are decentralizing, the value of some land within the urban core has increased, due to its access to arts and culture, corporate and legal headquarters, and a form of urban, cosmopolitan life that appeals to many but that can scarcely be found in suburban communities.

The uneven development pattern experienced within the city and across the region has meant that some city neighborhoods now resemble suburban places more than they resemble nearby sections of Philadelphia. In several inner-city neighborhoods, for instance, affordable housing has been built recently in suburban styles at lower densities than the city's historic row houses. These new developments have given each home its own side yard and driveway. The downtown district is now full of stores one would see in suburban malls. One such retailer, a gourmet food discounter named Trader Joe's, built a downtown store whose ground plan so closely duplicates its suburban outlets that the store's main entrance is not located on the side fronting Market Street—arguably the most important commercial street in the entire city—but rather in the rear of the building, closest to the parking lot.

While the city shows signs of suburbanizing, some suburban officials have begun to emphasize their communities' urban features—including commercial main streets, walkable neighborhoods, and public transportation options—in order to appeal to future residents. In some of the more affluent suburbs, condominium developments now constitute an important fraction of residences. Thus distinguishing between only two traditional categories of city versus suburbs no longer makes sense because of the increasing differentiation in the characters of both. In this volume we highlight the fragmentation of the city into increasingly divergent districts while recognizing the strong parallels between this segmentation and what is happening in the increasingly diverse suburbs.

Privatism, Regionalism, and the Third Sector

We build our discussion of the region around the idea that "place matters"—that geographic patterns of privilege and disadvantage confer very different opportunities on communities and households trying to make the best of their place in the region. Like other U.S. metropolitan regions, greater Philadelphia is balkanized into hundreds of separate communities, each electing its own local officials to make decisions about land development, tax rates, local schools, garbage pickup, police and fire departments, and dozens of other public services. Many observers see the proliferation of these small local governments as the embodiment of privatism in our public life, because they enable each community's residents "to pursue their own self-interest regardless of the impact on their neighbors," creating "a privatized conception of the boundary lines between the central city and its suburbs—and between the suburbs themselves."[7] Sam Bass Warner, in his celebrated history of the "city of brotherly love," argued that from the beginning, Philadelphia's political culture (and by extension, that of other U.S. cities) assumed "there would be no major conflict between private interest, honestly and liberally viewed, and the public welfare."[8] That assumption led to a view of the city as an arena in which private individuals and families pursued opportunity and prosperity; a community became "a union of such money-making, accumulating families."[9] Today, metropolitan Philadelphia represents a similar conception of privatism imprinted on the region as a whole.

Observing the tendency toward fragmentation across many U.S. metropolitan areas, researchers have renewed calls for regional strategies to address the resulting problems of uneven development, social inequality, and uncoordinated planning. As noted earlier, Myron Orfield, David Rusk, and Bruce Katz have all urged urban revitalization strategies that connect central cities to their surrounding suburbs. All have advocated strong governmental action to require regional tax base sharing, fair share laws to provide affordable housing in the suburbs, and regional growth management. In greater Philadelphia, such calls for coordinated action among local governments—although they have inspired many civic conferences, appeals by media commentators, and publications by public interest organizations—have gained little political traction.

In 1995 Neal Peirce was commissioned by the *Philadelphia Inquirer* to bring to Philadelphia his insights on regional political cooperation—insights that Peirce had elaborated in his book *Citistates*.[10] The newspaper devoted a special section to the so-called Peirce Report, and a few months later the Chamber of Commerce sponsored a call to action conference at which 2,000 people heard Neal Peirce urge local leaders in the city and suburbs to forge more cooperation for the most practical of reasons: to help this region compete in the global economy. Although released in a barrage of optimistic publicity in 1995, the Peirce Report disappeared from public view with amazing speed. No civic or governmental coalition emerged to champion its recommendations.

Two years later, the Pennsylvania Environmental Council commissioned another national expert, Myron Orfield, to apply his methods of mapping and analyzing regional inequities in greater Philadelphia. The council published Orfield's findings and brought him to town to explain his views on regional tax sharing as the solution to the problems he identified. He showed civic leaders that the intense fragmentation of the land area into hundreds of small jurisdictions offered people the chance to opt out of paying many of the costs of their location choices. In Orfield's words, "The increase of property wealth in outer suburbs and the stagnation or decline of central city and inner-suburban values represents, in part, an interregional transfer of tax base."[11] Orfield's radical proposal of tax sharing was greeted with skepticism to say the least. One Delaware County politician observed, "I think it borders on the unthinkable."[12] Despite that reception, in the following year the Delaware Valley Regional Planning Commission brought Orfield back to Philadelphia to discuss regional tax base sharing, hoping to stimulate new thinking about a regional agenda. Since then, Orfield has returned numerous times to the region, his visits sponsored by foundations, policy think tanks, and other organizations. Yet the region's political establishment seems no closer to accepting tax base sharing. We hold out little hope for this approach.

Urbanists have been debating the advantages and the feasibility of regionalism for more than fifty years, starting in the early twentieth century, when proponents saw regional cooperation among local governments as a way to make service delivery more effective and tax burdens more equitable. Although some idealists advocated consolidating cities and suburbs into unified metropolitan governments, the more pragmatic voices argued for federated, or two-tier governmental arrangements in which specific services (e.g., water and sewer services) and functions (e.g., land use planning) would be assigned to a regional government while other services (e.g., schools and policing) would remain in the hands of local governments. The early metropolitan reformers emphasized the ability of regional authorities to gain economies of scale in delivering public services and to spread the cost of services across the wealthiest and poorest communities. They offered a progressive, good government rationale for broader metropolitan institutions to consolidate services and share tax revenues.[13]

Toward the end of the twentieth century, however, advocates for regionalism shifted their focus away from efficiency and equity in public services and toward competitiveness in the global economy. Advocates for the "new regionalism" began urging voluntary cooperation among suburbs and cities to achieve economic success: "What is different about the new regionalism compared to earlier debates is that the focus has shifted from the effects of fragmentation on public goods consumption to the effects of fragmentation on production, or economic growth."[14] Proponents of the new regionalism like Neal Peirce have urged city and suburban leaders in Philadelphia and other metropolitan areas to cooperate as a matter of self-preservation. Regions without unified strategies, they predict, will lose in competition against regions that are operating in greater harmony.[15]

Observers in this region are hard pressed to find signs of either the old or the new variety of regionalism. Neither voluntary intergovernmental cooperation nor coordination coerced from above by the state government is a feature of the public realm. Instead, regional politics are marked by fragmentation and competition among localities. Greater Philadelphia exemplifies the pattern of intergovernmental politics that is typically found in the northeastern United States. The central city is surrounded on all sides by long-established suburban townships that zealously defend their separation from Philadelphia. The last time that Philadelphians managed to persuade the state government to allow the city to annex adjacent territory was 1854, and no one expects that to happen again. State laws make it difficult for suburban officials to consider merging their townships with one another; such a move would require placing the question on the ballot in all of the communities involved. Moreover, this particular metropolitan region spans two states, creating even greater obstacles to formal cooperation.

Not only the jurisdictional boundary lines divide communities but also the dramatically different conditions prevailing within their borders. Research has shown that regional cooperation is more likely to occur among homogeneous units of government. Yet, as this book shows, the gaps between communities are widening, in terms of the opportunities and quality of life available to residents in various parts of the region. Where social needs are greatest, the resources to pay for services are the most constrained. This divergence creates an irony: cooperation is most needed under conditions of extreme inequality, yet cooperation is less likely to occur under those unequal conditions than where conditions are similar.

Race is a factor as well. Studies of regional efforts in other metropolitan areas in the United States have documented the challenge of establishing intergovernmental arrangements between central cities dominated by African American political elites and suburbs dominated by Whites.[16] Greater Philadelphia shares some racial dynamics with the U.S. cities studied by John Powell, who offered this observation about the role of race in regionalism:

Those of us who advocate regionalism are troubled by the resistance to it, not only from the developing suburban communities, but from the communities of color as well. While the suburban resistance may be shortsighted, the reluctance to embrace something that will have a short-term negative consequence appears to make sense. What is more surprising, at least initially, is resistance from minority communities at the urban core. This resistance is often based on non-economic concerns: the loss of political control and cultural control or identity.[17]

The traditional tendency for separate municipalities to "go it alone" has been exacerbated by neoliberal policies adopted after 1980 by the federal government. Drastic cutbacks in federal funding for urban areas, along with the devolution to the states and localities of responsibility for many federal programs, pushed local governments to compete against each other for the tax revenues needed to pay for services.[18] That intense competition continues to dominate their interactions far more than any impulse toward cooperation.

Philadelphia is not alone. The policy debates concerning regionalism have produced relatively little action on the ground anywhere in the United States. A special volume of the *Journal of Urban Affairs* titled "Regionalism Reconsidered" surveyed almost a century of interest expressed in the idea of regionalism. The conclusion reached by the volume's coeditor, at least for U.S. metropolitan areas, was disappointing:

> Regardless of their respective contributions to the debate, the arguments of neither the metropolitan reformers nor the new regionalists have succeeded in producing much change . . . the politics of metropolitan reform are decidedly stacked against significant structural change.[19]

So long as we confine our focus to intergovernmental arrangements, we are forced to conclude that little is happening. However, if our gaze shifts away from local government to encompass a wider set of actors and projects, we draw a different conclusion. A major lesson emerging from this book is that regionalism is alive in greater Philadelphia, but it flourishes largely outside the institutions of local government.

In writing this book, we have been less interested in debating what *should* be happening in the regional realm and more interested in what *is* happening on the ground, particularly the ways that people are working to overcome the geographic inequalities that divide the communities of the region. We have been attentive to the individuals and groups that have been most active during the 1990s in addressing uneven development in greater Philadelphia. One must look beyond local governments to find them. In case after case, we observe that local governments are relinquishing authority, either to state government agencies or to organizations operating in the "third sector" of the region's institutional landscape. Third-sector organizations are nonprofit agencies or quasi-governmental authorities that pursue public purposes, yet operate outside the bounds of formal government. They often work in partnership with each other, with government, and with for-profit entities, shouldering a large and growing share of responsibility for addressing the problems that arise from metropolitan economic restructuring. To a great extent, the third sector is driving regional efforts to cope with the uneven development that is the hallmark of the evolving regional landscape.

One reason for their increasing prominence is that the neoliberal policy climate favors withdrawing direct government management over the public sector and giving nongovernmental organizations responsibility for managing public services. National discussions of urban issues assume an ever more limited role for direct government intervention in community development, but they assume a growing role for the nonprofit sector along with profit-making enterprises. We see evidence of the tendency toward privatization, for example, in the way that some school districts rely on nonprofit as well as profit-making organizations to administer publicly funded schools. Philadelphia is arguably the nation's leading examples of outsourcing public education, as we will see in Chapter 4.

Another reason for the rise of the third sector is simply that the scope of local government authority does not match the geographic scale of the issues that need to be addressed. Some of those issues are far larger than the territory encompassed by any one, or even several, local governments. But the scale of problems needing urgent attention may also be far smaller than a local government jurisdiction, requiring customized solutions that are difficult for general-purpose government to fashion. As we will see in coming chapters, the greater Philadelphia region has spawned a network of third-sector agencies dedicated to purposes both larger and smaller than local government boundaries. The brand of regionalism adopted in this metropolitan area fits the definition offered by Neil Brenner, that is, "Strategies to establish institutions, policies or governance mechanisms at a geographical scale which approximates that of existing socioeconomic interdependencies within an urban agglomeration."[20] The reader will notice Brenner's use of the term "governance" rather than "government," as a signal that formal government does not always dominate public efforts to solve regional problems. Traditional dynamics of city versus suburbs are giving way to a more decentered model that incorporates new sources of private investment (both for-profit and nonprofit) and new models of local governance that emphasize performance and efficacy.

In our earlier book, *Philadelphia*, we used a framework of distributive justice to address the issues facing the city and region. While social justice (defined here as equal access to opportunity) remains a key concern, we recognize that the terms of public debate have shifted during the recent decade. These days, in addition to concerns about unequal access to opportunity, one hears an increasing emphasis on strengthening the capacity and efficacy of public and community agencies. Decisions made by government and the independent sector about how to invest in communities are increasingly driven by concerns over returns on investments, rather than redressing distributional inequities.

Plan of the Book

This book is about how the trends of the 1990s in metropolitan Philadelphia, particularly the growing differentiation among its many communities, have affected the structure of opportunity for residents. This study relies on an information base whose comprehensive coverage has rarely been available for the study of any U.S. metropolitan area. The Metropolitan Philadelphia Indicators Project (MPIP) monitors social and economic conditions in over 350 municipalities located within the greater Philadelphia metropolitan area. Using the data resources of MPIP, we have been able to undertake a systematic analysis of trends and issues across the region, including every community in both the Pennsylvania and New Jersey suburbs. The data we have used come from a variety of state and federal data sources, as well as an original household survey administered in three separate waves, in the autumns of 2003, 2004, and 2005.[21]

In the first chapter, we describe the region in some detail, laying out the geographic patterns of development across nine counties. In subsequent chapters, we focus on three kinds of opportunity that shape the quality of people's lives: employment, housing, and education. Each chapter considers the geographic scale at which people seek opportunities, from the immediately surrounding neighborhood to the region. We document the trends in employment, housing, and education that have exerted unequal effects on the region's local communities.

These chapters pay special attention to the impacts of uneven development on the region's low-income communities. Considerable space in each chapter is devoted to analyzing the policy efforts that have been made to address the disadvantages that development patterns have created for low-income populations. We divide the region's efforts to increase opportunities into two main policy options. The first option is to increase investment in the communities where disadvantaged residents are living. From the 1960s through the 1980s, advocates for disadvantaged urban communities concentrated mainly on increasing the cities' share of public investments in housing, transportation, and economic infrastructure, as well as schools and social services. During the 1980s, that focus on public investments was expanded when urban activists began working to entice private investors into the inner cities, through such means as the Community Reinvestment Act and Low Income Housing Tax Credits, both programs enabling community organizations to find private investment partners for their development efforts. A desire to improve opportunities for jobs, housing, and education has led to an array of investments in the declining communities of the region.

However, we will also give attention to another option that has gained popularity during the 1990s, particularly in a political climate that assumes a decreasing role for direct government intervention in cities. That alternative strategy is to provide greater mobility to disadvantaged households so they can seek opportunities on a wider geographic scale.[22] In an impassioned essay, Paul Dimond has explained his preference for mobility strategies this way: "Voting with their feet about where to live, learn, and work is how families most powerfully choose to build a better life for themselves and their children."[23] Since other Americans often pursue opportunities in this way, the argument goes, low-income and other disadvantaged citizens should also be given this chance. Thus, in our chapters on jobs, housing, and education, we devote attention to policies that promote choice and mobility.

Chapter 1 describes the region and its recent development in terms of its demographic composition, migration patterns, and its social and economic diversity. We take some time to develop a typology to help orient the discussion of these diverse communities, a typology that will be used as a background for discussions in the later chapters.

Chapter 2 analyzes employment patterns at the regional scale because the region functions as an economic unit within which employers, investors, and workers move readily across geographic boundaries. Many high-wage workers choose to reside in suburbs but work inside the city, while suburban firms employ many workers who commute from homes in Philadelphia. Increasingly, employment has dispersed from Philadelphia into the suburbs, not into a limited number of job centers but in a pattern defined by the region's road network. Chapter 2 presents some challenges to the prevailing assumptions about the "spatial mismatch" hypothesis. That line of research has focused on the increasing distance between residential neighborhoods in the urban core and suburban locations where employment is expanding, on the theory that geographic distance is the most significant barrier to employing city residents. Our findings in Chapter 2, however, call into question the significance of geographic proximity; they cast doubt on the assumption that living close to well-paying jobs necessarily improves the incomes of nearby households. The chapter assesses policy efforts to bring more employers into Philadelphia and other older urban centers of the region, while at the same time creating more mobility for residents of these core communities to travel to jobs in the suburbs.

The second arena of opportunity, housing, is discussed in Chapter 3. It describes the patterns by which housing is geographically subdivided into distinct submarkets characterized by different ages of construction, price levels, housing types, and neighborhood characteristics. Chapter 3 shows that low-income and minority citizens have far more constrained choices than other residents seeking housing. It further explores the problems faced by low-income residents seeking mortgage loans to buy or improve properties in older neighborhoods. We consider policy strategies to rebuild housing within older core communities, along with efforts to insert more affordable housing into the suburban landscape. Social researchers have shown the social disadvantages of concentrated urban poverty, leading many observers to ask this question: should we continue to emphasize rebuilding housing in inner-city neighborhoods, or instead offer inner-city residents more opportunities to move to other communities with less poverty, less crime, better schools, and better services? Federal housing policies of the past decade have increasingly emphasized spatial deconcentration of urban poor populations. In fact, spatial deconcentration has been called "the country's most recent antipoverty strategy."[24] Chapter 3 shows that spatial deconcentration of the poor has not progressed very far in this region.

Educational opportunities, the subject of Chapter 4, have traditionally been determined by residence. Those opportunities differ dramatically across different types of communities. The majority of students attend schools close to home, tying educational opportunities to housing opportunities. To portray the educational opportunities available to families across the region, we have chosen to measure school district performance by using standardized test scores. Then we ask how student characteristics correlate with that measure of school performance. We also describe the different levels of spending for schools across the region's districts, and we investigate how spending per pupil correlates with the measures of school performance. A particularly interesting aspect of educational opportunity within the greater Philadelphia region is the unusually high percentage of school-age children who attend private schools in both the core cities and the suburbs. The historic strength of the private school sector may be one reason why political support for school choice is high, as reflected in large enrollments in charter schools.

In Chapter 5 we follow up our discussion of jobs, housing, and education by considering whether the people who choose to live in the most desirable communities—defined as those that provide the greatest opportunities in the three realms of jobs, housing, and education—are paying a premium to enjoy those advantages. Recognizing the different kinds of opportunities provided by the employment profiles, the housing markets, and the school systems of different communities, some observers interpret these differences as the natural, inevitable result of mobility choices that Americans enjoy. More affluent households, they assume, will use their greater resources to "buy" the locations that give them better access to employment, higher-quality housing, and better schools. In this view of the metropolitan area as a marketplace of choices, households in different economic circumstances can afford different levels of expenditure, which is why we see households at different economic levels clustered in different communities. This "value proposition" affects both households and communities, most of which are dependent on property tax revenues to fund public services, including the local contribution to school budgets. Chapter 5 examines the operation of this value proposition in the greater Philadelphia region, focusing particularly on how the level of taxes that residents pay in different communities is associated with differing levels of opportunity within those communities.

Finally, in Chapter 6 we examine the governance implications of the increasing divergence among the communities of the region. We consider how some traditional responsibilities carried by local governments have shifted upward to state government and outward to nongovernmental institutions like nonprofit housing developers, special services districts, regional development agencies, and so on. We ask whether the emergence of new institutions at the community and regional levels, along with the state's increasing role in the cities' fortunes, signals a "hollowing out" of local government. We detect an emerging pattern of governance that relies less on formal government and more on other institutions that are working to address the inequalities of place that pervade this region.

1

EXPANSION, DECLINE, AND
GEOGRAPHIES OF INEQUALITY

~

The narrative of the Philadelphia region's transition into the twenty-first century is a tale of mixed themes. The metropolitan area has expanded dramatically, developing a complex spatial pattern of inequality that defies conventional categories of city and suburb. The timing of growth and decline has affected the kinds of communities we find in different locations in the region. At the most basic level, the emergence of elite suburbs in the late nineteenth century and the emergence of middle-class suburbs in the early- to middle-twentieth century created patterns of housing and land use that in turn affected the subsequent transformations that took place after World War II.

The diverse development trajectories of the region's communities suggested to us that we need more complex categories for thinking about these patterns than "city" and "suburb." Relying on the simple distinction between city and suburbs does not capture the dynamics of regional development in a decentered region. As a consequence, we have created a typology of the region's communities that emerges from a cluster analysis of the population, socioeconomic, and housing differences among communities. Access to jobs, housing, and educational opportunities is markedly different in the resulting five community types: Urban Centers, Stable Working Communities, Established Towns, Middle-Class Suburbs, and Affluent Suburbs. Accordingly, we use this chapter to begin the discussion of several geographies that affect access to income, wealth, and opportunities for mobility.

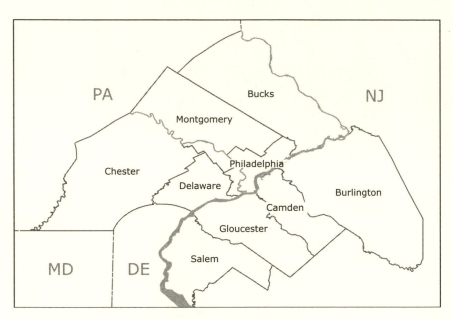

FIGURE 1.1   The region: Philadelphia and eight surrounding counties.

Simultaneous Growth and Decline

The metropolitan region surrounding Philadelphia covers a nine-county area that stretches from immediately below Trenton, New Jersey, in the north down to rural Salem County, New Jersey, in the south and from the far western reaches of Chester County, Pennsylvania, to the farmland in the eastern portion of Burlington County, New Jersey. Different parts of this region have experienced dramatically different development trajectories during the past sixty years, as Table 1.1 shows. The table portrays population changes during that period. The city of Philadelphia, whose government serves as both a local authority and a county, lost over one-fifth (21.4 percent) of its population from 1940 to 2000. Among the eight suburban counties, the rates of growth experienced during those sixty years differed widely, from a low of 52 percent to a high of 455 percent. Overall, the population growth and simultaneous decline in different parts of the region resulted in a net loss of population during the 1980s, followed by an improved picture (3 percent gain) during the 1990s.

Rapid growth in some communities combined with population loss in others suggests a region that "churns" its population across locations. This is most strongly seen in census information on recent migration (since 1995). The 2000 census collected information on where residents over the age of five had

TABLE 1.1   COUNTY AND REGIONAL POPULATION CHANGE, 1940–2000

	Population, 1940	Population, 2000	Change, 1940–2000 (%)	Growth Decade*
Philadelphia	1,931,334	1,517,550	−21.4	1940s
Bucks	107,715	597,635	454.8	1950s
Chester	135,626	433,501	219.6	1980s
Delaware	310,756	550,864	77.3	1960s
Montgomery	289,247	750,097	159.3	1970s
Burlington	97,013	423,394	336.4	1960s
Camden	255,727	508,932	99.0	1950s
Gloucester	72,219	254,673	252.6	1960s
Salem	42,274	64,285	52.1	1950s
Region	3,241,911	5,100,931	57.3	1950s

Sources: U.S. Census, U.S. Census of Population and Housing, 1940; U.S. Census, Summary File 3, 2000.
*This is the decade of greatest increase in number of residents.

TABLE 1.2   MIGRATION BY RESIDENTS OF THE REGION, 2000

Migration	Percentage Aged Five or Older
Lived in the same house in 1995 and 2000	62.1
Moved into current house since 1995	37.9
Moved from within the same county	55.6
Moved from out of county, same state	54.0
Moved from within the MSA	73.6

Source: U.S. Census, Summary File 3, 2000.

been living in 1995. As Table 1.2 indicates, the majority of people living in the region in 2000 had not moved since 1995. Of those who had moved, almost three-quarters (73.6 percent) had moved from someplace within the region.

This pattern varied across the region. Table 1.3 examines the same classification on a county-by-county basis but adds one more piece of information: the percentage of recent movers who had come from outside the metropolitan area

TABLE 1.3   VARIATION IN MIGRATION WITHIN THE REGION, 2000 (PERCENT)

County	Same House	Moved, Same County	Moved, Same State	Moved within Metropolitan Area	Moved from Other Metropolitan Area
Burlington	60.0	47.7	48.8	66.0	28.2
Camden	63.0	60.0	48.2	80.3	14.8
Gloucester	65.4	50.4	59.2	80.0	17.5
Salem	67.2	59.5	63.1	75.5	19.3
Bucks	63.2	51.5	57.6	74.1	20.8
Chester	58.6	43.2	56.1	66.1	27.9
Delaware	64.4	55.1	59.0	75.8	18.4
Montgomery	61.2	48.1	65.7	71.9	21.3
Philadelphia	61.9	66.5	40.1	74.7	16.6

Source: U.S. Census, Summary File 3, 2000.

(MSA). With the exception of Chester County, more than 60 percent of residents in all counties in 2000 were living in the same home they had occupied in 1995. If we look only at those who had recently moved into their present home, we see that Burlington and Chester counties show the largest percentage of people who had come from outside the county and the highest percentage who had come from outside the MSA. Focusing on Philadelphia alone, instead of the entire region, we see that a large percentage of the people who had moved into their Philadelphia home between 1995 and 2000 had come from elsewhere within Philadelphia County (which has identical boundaries with the city). This is further evidence that mobility patterns are dominated by churning of the region's existing population as opposed to attracting newcomers.

Shifting population numbers have been accompanied by shifting patterns of affluence and disadvantage. By 2004 the households in Chester County, the richest of the region's suburban counties, had achieved a median income of $72,288, a growth of more than 20 percent since 1990. (By comparison, the national median household income in 2004 was $44,684.) That placed Chester County as the twelfth richest county in the United States; the county had a median household income fully 68 percent higher than the state average. Both Montgomery and Bucks counties had incomes about 50 percent higher than the state's. By contrast, the city of Philadelphia in 2004 had a median household income of only $30,631. Adjusting for inflation, Philadelphia's median household income actually declined from 1990 to 2004.

It would be a mistake, however, to assume affluence prevails throughout the suburban counties. In fact, the Census Bureau's 2005 American Community Survey showed that virtually every suburban county in the region experienced a rising share of families living in poverty from 1990 to 2004, particularly in older suburbs where the housing stock and population were aging. After gaining population and jobs from 1945 to 1970, many suburban communities found themselves in a downward spiral as their housing stock lost appeal in competition with the region's new subdivisions. When middle-income households moved out, the tax base stagnated even as the price tag for schools and other public services increased. These older communities found it hard to compete for new commercial development, both because they typically lacked large, inexpensive parcels of undeveloped land and because higher taxes made them less attractive than the rapidly developing suburbs on the fringes. A disproportionate number of these older, poorer towns and boroughs sit along the banks of the Delaware River, reflecting the earlier geographic influence of the region's main commercial waterway and the continuing impact of the loss of manufacturing firms that lay along it.

A Region of Increasingly Diverse Communities

Focusing at the county level masks important variations within counties. In a region where European settlers arrived during the seventeenth century, a number of communities in the Philadelphia suburbs are as old as the city of Philadelphia; they existed long before national economic forces began shaping our modern metropolitan areas. Some suburbs share Philadelphia's industrial heritage, their initial growth stemming from manufacturing plants in the nineteenth century. In the twentieth century, suburban development after World War II consisted of at least two waves—one that was concentrated in the immediate postwar era, and one that has been concentrated during the 1980s and 1990s. Local histories tend to resist integration into a metropolitan whole. Community leaders and organizations struggle to maintain their identity, even while old market towns, factories, and farms are increasingly merged with town houses, McMansions, and office parks—all of which can be easily witnessed in the space of a twenty-minute journey through the region. Within the city, as well as the suburbs, a variety of community types exists. Portions of Philadelphia have more conditions and problems in common with parts of the suburbs than they do with other sections of the city. The city is differentiated and must be treated that way, as we illustrate in our discussion in Chapter 3 about the city government's efforts to apply different strategies for revitalizing housing in different types of neighborhoods.

If we examine the changes taking place in the communities within each of the nine counties, we gain a stronger sense of the disparate and uneven ways in which the overall pattern of slow growth was experienced. The typology of five kinds of communities that we have created is a means of recognizing these differences and classifying all 353 municipalities within the greater Philadelphia metropolitan area (defined as the nine counties in Table 1.1). The typology derives from a two-stage cluster analysis of thirteen variables from the 2000 census describing each community's housing, socioeconomic, and household characteristics. (We provide detailed information about the method of constructing the typology in Appendix 1). Our typology divides the communities of the region into the five general types described below. Figure 1.2 shows the distribution of community types within the metropolitan area.

Urban Centers

Beyond the boundaries of Philadelphia, the region contains about thirty other municipalities that developed as high-density centers around commerce and manufacturing. The most prominent is Camden, the city located directly across the Delaware River from Philadelphia. Once the industrial home to major manufacturers like Campbell's Soup Company and the Victor Talking Machine

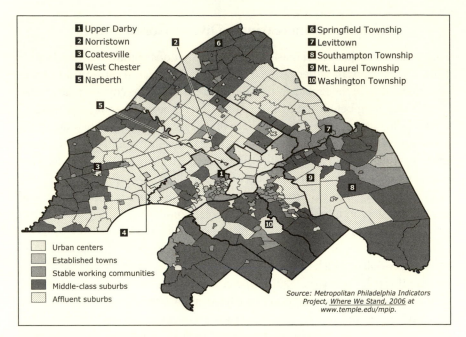

FIGURE 1.2   Community types in the metropolitan Philadelphia area.

Company (later RCA Victor), Camden achieved its peak population of 124,000 in 1950. The subsequent flight of both firms and residents, which by 2000 had brought the population down to only 80,000, left the city vulnerable to all manner of unwanted incursions, from a sewage plant and garbage incinerator to a prison on its waterfront and an interstate highway cutting through the city's fabric. The city gradually came to symbolize the physical blight and public neglect that have challenged urban centers across the nation.[1]

Our category of Urban Centers also includes other former centers of manufacturing strength now on the decline. These towns contain populations with lower incomes and lower education levels than the rest of the region, with as many as one-fourth of residents not having completed high school. Although these communities have significantly more female-headed families than the rest of the region, a very high proportion of householders no longer have children under eighteen, so these communities are not as "child-centered" as many suburbs. Large shares of the housing stock were built before 1940, while few housing units were built within the last decade. These communities have steadily lost population since 1960.

An example is Coatesville, an old community in western Chester County where Lukens Steel Company once employed 6,000 workers. From its heyday as a booming steel city in the 1950s and 1960s, Coatesville's economy was dev-

Row housing is the traditional building style of Philadelphia.

Recent affordable housing in Philadelphia resembles the suburbs.

Urban Center: Coatesville was rated Pennsylvania's poorest city in 2000 after it had been abandoned by Lukens Steel Company.

Urban Center: Norristown is a county seat with many social service agencies.

Stable Working Community: Levittown still retains modest subdivisions built in the 1950s and 1960s to house industrial workers at nearby steel plants.

Stable Working Community: Upper Darby, located at the city's edge, is home to an ethnically diverse group of residents and business owners.

Established Town: Narberth is a typical Main Line community with a walkable town center served by a rail line connecting it to downtown Philadelphia.

Established Town: Like other suburbs boasting historic architecture, West Chester is developing a cultural district as a destination point for recreation and shopping.

Middle-Class Suburb: Southampton's transition from farmland and wooded areas is evident as the backdrop for its newer housing construction.

Middle-Class Suburb: At the outer edge of the region, Springfield Township in Bucks County built many housing developments for the middle class.

Affluent Suburb: A McMansion in Mt. Laurel, New Jersey, a community accused of exclusionary zoning in lengthy lawsuits.

Affluent Suburb: Termini Bro's, a well-known Italian bakery in South Philadelphia, followed its Italian American clientele to suburban Washington Township.

astated when its one industry declined. After three decades of contraction and decay, by 2000 it was the poorest city in Pennsylvania (ironically, located in the richest county in Pennsylvania). City officials are promoting redevelopment projects that include offices, apartments, retail, entertainment, and a new parking garage, much of it on the abandoned grounds of a steel mill.

Norristown, the county seat of Montgomery County, had been a relatively prosperous community of homes ranging from row houses to old Victorians, shops, theaters, and even hotels well into the 1960s. Textile mills and light manufacturing, along with the county government, had provided jobs for a population that historically had included a large African American component, as well as immigrants from Italy, Ireland, and Germany. In the 1970s, however, the borough lost about one-third of its manufacturing jobs. Furthermore, the state government's actions to deinstitutionalize the mentally ill led to the discharge of more than 1,500 patients from Norristown State Hospital. Many of them stayed in Norristown. As homes in the community were subdivided into unregulated group homes, housing authorities began to concentrate Section 8 tenants in Norristown, which rapidly became the location of more than half of all affordable housing units in Montgomery County. A recent news story about Norristown began its coverage of the "ragged Montgomery County seat" this way: "Within its 3.2 square miles are at least nine shelters, five drug treatment clinics, and 1,350 section 8 rental units."[2]

Stable Working Communities

This category includes dozens of the region's oldest towns nestled along the banks of the Delaware River, both upriver and downriver from Philadelphia, but it also includes some working-class boroughs at greater distances from Philadelphia. High percentages of housing units in these towns were built before 1940, with relatively little new construction in the past decades. Compared to the Urban Centers, these Stable Working Communities have greater proportions of their housing stock in single-family detached units (as opposed to multifamily units) and higher levels of home ownership. On average, less than one-fifth of their residents have college degrees, a lower percentage than any other type of community except the Urban Centers. Female-headed families, while they comprise only half as large a percentage of the population as in Urban Centers, exceed the proportion of such households in the remaining three types of communities.

Perhaps the best known example of a working-class suburban development is Levittown, a planned suburb constructed by a single builder in 1958. With over 17,000 homes and churches, schools, swimming pools, and shopping centers, Levittown was marketed to blue-collar families, especially steel workers employed at U.S. Steel's Fairless Works, which in the 1950s was the second largest integrated plant on the East Coast. Although it was built at relatively high density, compared to recent suburbs, Levittown has spread across four different municipalities in lower Bucks County. It never had an identifiable town center, and its boundaries cannot be easily detected in the suburban developments that subsequently engulfed it.

A different kind of working-class suburb is Upper Darby, a very old town west of Philadelphia that rapidly expanded after 1907, when the Philadelphia Rapid Transit Company extended an elevated rail line from the city out to 69th and Market streets. By the 1920s, the shopping district that grew up around the 69th Street terminal had become the second busiest shopping area in the region after downtown Philadelphia. Like other aging shopping districts, Upper Darby found it difficult to compete against retail malls and deteriorated during several decades. In the 1970s its modestly priced housing began to attract African American residents and immigrants. The township is now home to a tremendously varied ethnic mix, including newcomers from Liberia, Korea, Haiti, Vietnam, and Kosovo. Asian Americans now own many businesses in the 69th Street shopping district, as local planners are struggling to redefine and reenergize this bustling location.

Established Towns

While the towns in the prior category are working to create a sense of place, the region contains fifteen Established Towns that already possess that asset. Many of these older towns, centered on commercial main streets, are desirable locations because their townscapes connote solid, established communities and they are well served by transportation. Although significant proportions of these municipalities consist of pre-1940 housing stock, their age is not associated with economic decline. Their populations are among the best educated in the region. Even though the levels of home ownership are about the same as in the Urban Centers, their residents are more affluent than those residing in the Urban Centers. More of these Established Towns are located on the Pennsylvania side than on the New Jersey side of the Delaware River.

This category includes a number of towns along the "Main Line," the ribbon of development that grew up when the Pennsylvania Railroad built a suburban route through Montgomery County in the 1850s. An example is Narberth, a tree-lined residential borough cut in half by the Pennsylvania railroad tracks that divide the town into north and south sides. The roughly one-half square-mile town, which celebrated its centennial in 1995, has a traditional town center with shopping, recreational facilities, religious organizations, a library, school, and playgrounds, all within comfortable walking distance.

Another example is West Chester, the county seat of Chester County, lo-cated twenty-four miles west of Philadelphia. About two square miles in area, the 200-year-old town is densely developed with buildings laid out in a rectan-gular pattern of streets. In the early 1900s, West Chester earned the reputation of being the "Athens of Pennsylvania" because of its educational institutions, its Greek Revival architecture, and its cultural assets, including a library com-pany and both medical and natural history societies. By the 1970s, the town's commercial base had begun to erode in the face of competition from nearby shopping malls. The town responded by establishing a historic district in the late 1980s, a move that encouraged building repairs and drew specialty shops and restaurants.

Middle-Class Suburbs

Of all the community types, the eighty-nine suburbs in this category have the highest share of their housing stock in single-family detached housing. Com-pared to the populations in the Affluent Suburbs, twice as many residents in these communities have only a high school degree or less. Only about half as many have earned a college degree. Compared to the Affluent Suburbs, a somewhat smaller percentage of families have children at home. These sub-urbs experienced their most dramatic population gains from 1960 to 1980, af-ter which their gains leveled off or even reversed. While one can find some examples of these communities within the inner suburban ring, the majority of them are located toward the outer edge of the region.

For example, Southampton Township in Burlington County originated as a rural community in south-central New Jersey. Since almost three-quarters of the township is located in the Pinelands Preserve, it maintains much of its rural character. The town's Web site boasts that of only four remaining dairy farms in Burlington County, three are located in Southampton Township. Its recent de-velopment reflects a mix of upscale and more moderate new housing, including several retirement communities. These farms and wooded lands and these newer developments are in contrast to the small town of Vincentown, which now pres-ents itself as a town center for the larger township.

Another good illustration of this community type is Springfield Township in Bucks County, which grew up as a village of mills, churches, a tavern, a store, and a cluster of homes and was surrounded by some of the best farm-land in the area. In the early twentieth century, its population actually de-clined when Philadelphia and other manufacturing centers began drawing residents away. With suburbanization in the 1960s and 1970s, Springfield Township began regaining population, although it experienced a slight de-crease between 1990 and 2000.

Affluent Suburbs

These suburbs are mostly located in the middle ring of the region, giving residents easier access to central Philadelphia than the communities farther out. Numbering slightly over 100, these Affluent Suburbs are well served by transportation, and they are growing rapidly. Of all the community types, they show the largest percent of housing units built within the last decade. They are developing at higher densities than the outer suburbs, which explains why they show a larger share of housing built as town houses, condominiums, and options other than single-family detached homes. The residents are well educated, reflecting a higher percentage of college graduates than in the other community types. Fewer families are headed by females than in all other types of communities.

Mt. Laurel in Burlington County is a highway-oriented suburb that grew rapidly with the opening of the New Jersey Turnpike in 1951. Its population doubled between 1950 and 1960, and it had doubled again by 1970. The suburb became famous when a coalition of civil rights groups sued the township in the 1970s, claiming it was practicing "exclusionary zoning" in order to exclude affordable housing. (We will have more to say about the Mt. Laurel litigation in Chapter 3.) The community was overtaken by a second wave of development that rolled through western Burlington County in the 1990s, bringing more office parks and residential developments. These days, officials are estimating that the township will be built out entirely by the end of the decade.

Another New Jersey community, Washington Township in Gloucester County, also illustrates the growth of the affluent communities in this category. Known to some in the region as "South Philly South," this township sits twenty minutes away from the city across the Walt Whitman Bridge and has become home to many households leaving the Italian neighborhoods of South Philadelphia during the 1960s. A South Philadelphia builder named Esposito successfully marketed his new construction to groups of residents who transplanted their family and social networks to Washington Township. The population of this township, which has no real town center, grew more than ninefold between 1960 and 2000. In 2000, about one-third of the suburb's population remained of Italian descent.

Figure 1.2 is instructive with respect to several generalizations often repeated by policymakers and urbanists. First, it shows that the frequent characterization of "inner-ring" suburbs as troubled communities fails to acknowledge a considerably more complex reality: some of these inner suburbs are among the most affluent in the region. Hence, the map casts doubt on the "contagion" model, which assumes that the decline of inner suburbs is due to problems spilling over from central cities. Second, socioeconomic status of the suburbs does not increase with distance from the city, as the most affluent communities tend to fall in a broad band that begins quite close to the city limits. Third, the majority of the Middle-Class Suburbs lie at the farther reaches of the metropolitan area; these are the most rapidly growing parts of the region. Fourth, what we have called Stable Working Communities are scattered throughout the region.

The fortunes of these different types of communities have changed significantly over recent decades. Documenting income and housing value data from the 1970 and 2000 decennial census, Table 1.4 shows that the communities of the region have had markedly different experiences with the economic shifts of the past several decades depending upon where they fall within our typology. For instance, the Urban Centers have seen the average household income rise by a factor of 4.27, while in the Affluent Suburbs the increase was by a factor of 6.69. (By comparison, the Consumer Price Index rose 4.54.) The income of a household in one of the region's urban centers would have on average almost kept pace with inflation, while in Affluent Suburbs growth in household income outpaced inflation by a factor of 1.5. The discrepancy between Urban Centers and Affluent Suburbs accelerated during this time, with the average Affluent Suburb income being 1.5 times that of Urban Centers in 1970, increasing to 2.4 in 2000.

TABLE 1.4   HOUSEHOLD INCOME AND HOUSING VALUE CHANGES BY COMMUNITY TYPE, 1970–2000

Typology	Average Household Income		
	1970 ($)	2000 ($)	2000/1970
Urban Centers	9,415	40,199	4.27
Established Towns	13,858	71,076	5.13
Stable Working Communities	10,689	55,028	5.15
Middle-Class Suburbs	10,936	66,697	6.10
Affluent Suburbs	14,281	95,474	6.69
Region	11,082	62,654	5.65
Hi-Low Ratio	1.52:1	2.38:1	
	Average Housing Value		
	1970 ($)	2000 ($)	2000/1970
Urban Centers	11,092	75,155	6.78
Established Towns	15,922	209,178	13.14
Stable Working Communities	14,937	122,288	8.19
Middle-Class Suburbs	14,216	160,919	11.32
Affluent Suburbs	22,793	234,380	10.28
Region	15,929	147,186	9.24
Hi-Low Ratio	2.05:1	3.12:1	

Source: Geolytics and the National Neighborhood Indicators Partnership, Neighborhood Change Database, 1970–2000,

Housing values display even more striking differentials across communities, as gaps widened from 1970 to 2000. The region's average housing value increased by more than twice the inflation rate, with the average home in 2000 valued at $147,186, or more than nine times the average value in 1970. As was the case when examining income differentials, the ratio of Urban Center to Affluent Suburb housing values increased from a ratio of 2 : 1 to 3 : 1. The most striking pattern, however, was the extremely high increase in housing values in the Established Towns category, where the ratio of 2000 to 1970 housing values was over thirteen to one, almost doubling the increase seen in Urban Centers, at 6.78 times 1970 values. These two key indicators of economic well-being—income and housing values—suggest the increased differentiation that is emerging among these communities.

Growth Centers in the Region

Looking at the changes in Philadelphia's downtown district during the past decade, many local commentators boast about its "comeback" from the overwhelming pessimism that prevailed in the early 1990s. The 2000 census showed that during the 1990s Center City (as locals refer to their downtown district) grew by 9 percent, while the city as a whole lost 4 percent of its population. Center City gained enough new residents during the 1990s to make it the third largest downtown residential population in the United States, behind only Manhattan and Chicago, a trend that has continued since 2000. According to population estimates released in 2005 by the U.S. Census Bureau, downtown Philadelphia has added another 9,000 residents since 2000—the result of building about 6,400 new housing units in Center City. The downtown residential revival of the 1990s was accelerated in 1998 when the city government adopted a ten-year abatement of property taxes on new construction. Much of the new housing is aimed at young, college-educated professionals, many of whom prefer to live and work in urban environments rather than working in suburban office parks. A senior vice president of one of the region's largest developers of office and industrial space explained in 2001 that the firms leasing space in his developments had begun expressing a need for more space in urban centers in order to accommodate younger workers; he predicted that "companies will become increasingly sensitive to creating vibrant environments that attract the best and brightest workers."[3]

A significant share of the new housing has been created by converting old, under-utilized office buildings into apartments and condominiums. These conversions benefit from the city's tax abatement just as new construction does; the city forgives property taxes on the value that developers add to buildings when they are converted. But with only a limited supply of vacant office buildings to convert, developers began in 2002 constructing brand new housing, particularly in the form of condominiums. So eager had builders become to find locations for these projects that one developer risked the wrath of historic preservationists and well-organized residents of the upscale Society Hill neighborhood with his proposal to make way for a fourteen-story $25 million condo tower by demolishing the house built in 1957 by former mayor Richardson Dilworth. Outraged opponents argued that this house, built by Dilworth as a sign of his personal confidence that the revitalization of Society Hill would succeed, has too much historic significance to be swept away by the current wave of condominium construction. When the Philadelphia Historical Commission denied permission to demolish the house, the architects redesigned the project to preserve its façade and front portion as part of the new high-rise.

These positive population changes mask some underlying structural weakening of Philadelphia's downtown, relative to suburban developments. Although it retains the single largest concentration of white collar jobs, Philadelphia's central business district increasingly competes with other employment centers. Office jobs in Philadelphia did not experience significant growth during the 1990s, when most new office construction occurred in the suburbs. During the 1990s, downtown Philadelphia only added 1.2 million square feet of office space, compared to cities like Boston, which added 9.7 million, or Atlanta, which added 4.5 million. While downtown Philadelphia made only modest gains in office space during the decade, the suburbs on the Pennsylvania side grew rapidly. Consider that in 1993, downtown had accounted for 41 percent of the region's commercial office space, but by the end of 2004 downtown's share had declined to 28 percent, six points below the national average. Noting this fact, the head of the civic organization that takes the leading role in promoting downtown development observed that as a result of this suburbanization of office employment, "The region is beginning to look more like Atlanta (with a 25% market share of office space in the Central Business District) or Houston (22% share) than Boston (38%), Chicago (58%) or New York (63%)."[4]

The city's biggest competitor is the suburban center known by the name of its central feature, the King of Prussia shopping mall. Located at the intersection of routes 202, 422, I-76, and the Pennsylvania Turnpike, this enormous agglomeration of 3 million square feet of retail space is surrounded by offices and affluent residential development. King of Prussia comes as close as any suburban development to qualifying as the region's second downtown, with about 40 percent (16 million square feet) of the office space located in Center City Philadelphia.[5] The mall occupies the center of a huge concentration of commercial growth shaped, not by careful municipal planning, but by state highway engineers. Spreading outward from the intersection of expressways where the mall sits, massive new development stretches down the Route 202 corridor toward West Chester and along Route 422 toward Pottstown. (See Figure 2.2 in Chapter 2.) From 1994–1995 to 2001–2002, the number of jobs in King of Prussia grew by an amazing 47 percent, compared with only 2 percent growth in Center City jobs. This westward growth is generating the best-paying and fastest-growing white collar employment hub in the region, without the political or civic infrastructure that normally accompanies such economic activity. Like other malls across the United States, King of Prussia is operated by a private developer—in this case the region's largest retail property manager, Kravco. Its leaders do not invest much effort in the public life of the community. It is a growth center whose geographic boundaries do not conform to any political jurisdiction. There is no town of King of Prussia, nor any mayor or local council.

Other economic centers have grown up across the Delaware River in New Jersey. Cherry Hill (also identified in Figure 2.2), an area that once carried the name "Delaware Township," acquired its new identity in 1961 with the opening of the Cherry Hill Mall, the first major enclosed shopping center in the region. Built at the intersection of major traffic arteries, the mall so dominated the area that it prompted the name change. From 1960 to 1970, Cherry Hill's population more than doubled, even as it changed from a bedroom community to a bustling commercial center, attracting retailers of all kinds, car dealerships, fast food businesses, office parks, a hospital, and a college. Cherry Hill now contains the corporate headquarters of Subaru of America and Commerce Bank. These days, however, the rapid growth of recent decades has subsided, as the land area has been almost completely built out. The population is increasingly diverse, including many immigrants from India and China, and it is aging. Upscale retailers in other regional malls are drawing shoppers away, and the post–World War II housing stock is wearing out. After about forty years of rapid growth, Cherry Hill's leaders find themselves focusing on redevelopment issues. Political leaders in Cherry Hill and other growth areas across the Delaware River are oriented toward New Jersey state government, which involves an entirely different cast of political characters and substantially different laws and regulations governing economic development, land use, and taxation than are found in Pennsylvania. This orientation to a different state capital makes it hard to incorporate the New Jersey suburbs into regional coalitions operating in greater Philadelphia.

Philadelphia also competes against the Route 1 corridor in New Jersey between Princeton and New Brunswick, which has become a hot spot for high tech companies. In the late 1980s, the New Jersey government began discussing the idea of developing the corridor along Route 1 as a prime location for technology companies, coining the name "Silicon Alley." Up and down the Route 1 corridor, pharmaceutical companies, manufacturers, start-up companies, and high-tech firms have clustered, most located within a mile of Route 1. This boom has been fueled by the presence of several institutions of higher education, particularly Princeton University. Quite a number of start-up companies have originated around Princeton technologies, and Princeton graduates have founded firms in the area. The latest effort to bolster this economic node is a campaign to rename the corridor "Einstein's Alley" in order to improve its visibility at the state and national levels. If the campaign to expand the Route 1 corridor is to succeed, planners will have to tackle the problem of traffic congestion that plagues the artery. By the year 2020, planners expect traffic volumes to increase by as much as 55 percent, while average roadway travel speed will drop by nearly one-third. This snarled New Jersey corridor is considered by many transportation engineers to be the worst commuter nightmare in the state.

Population Differences

The region's differentiation is evident not only in the characteristics of its places, but in its people as well. Rather than distributing themselves evenly across the metropolitan area, people who possess different incomes, education, and assets cluster in different communities. This is a well-known pattern in American life, and there is a large amount of literature exploring the reasons for economic stratification in metropolitan areas. We can see the income differences among the communities in our five types by looking at the percent of households with incomes over $75,000 living in each type of community in 2000. Table 1.5 shows that whereas only 12 percent of all households in the Urban Centers had incomes exceeding $75,000, fully one-half of all households in the Affluent Suburbs did.

In addition to economic differences, race is a critical factor driving residential stratification. Between 1990 and 2000, the percentage of the region's African American population residing in the suburbs increased from 27 to 32. Regionally, the picture is one of declining but still substantial residential seg-

TABLE 1.5   PERCENTAGE OF HOUSEHOLDS WITH INCOMES
OVER $75,000

Urban Centers	12
Established Towns	32
Stable Working Communities	23
Middle-Class Suburbs	33
Affluent Suburbs	50

Source: U.S. Census, Summary File 3, 2000.

regation. While African Americans were 19 percent of the region's population in 2000, they were only 11 percent of the suburban population. Across the suburbs, they were both broadly distributed—being now at least nominally present in all but one of the suburban municipalities—and concentrated—five municipalities contain 31 percent of the total. In only twenty-three of the region's suburban municipalities did African Americans comprise more than 10 percent of the population and at least 2,500 persons. The locations of these concentrations are shown in Figure 1.3.

Geographies of Inequality

In this book, we link the differences we observe in places to the differences in the opportunities they provide for their residents. This work contributes to an emerging interest among urban scholars in the ways that place of residence affects social inequality.

Academic researchers are showing increasing interest in the geography of opportunity within metropolitan areas. In their book, *Place Matters: Metropolitics for the 21st Century*, Peter Dreier and his coauthors observed that while scholars and public figures have vigorously debated the reasons for the rising inequality in the United States, they have paid little attention to the spatial

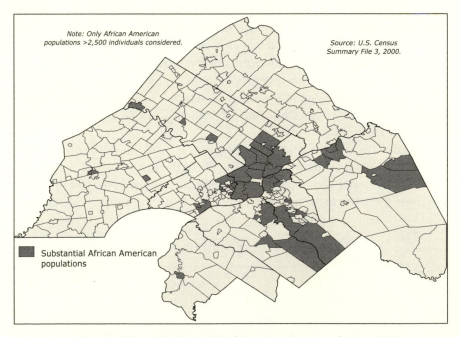

FIGURE 1.3   Communities with substantial African American populations, 2000.

dimension of inequality.[6] Dreier's work makes a compelling case that place matters because it exerts a strong influence on our choices and our quality of life, affecting access to jobs and public services (especially education), access to shopping and culture, level of personal security, and many other dimensions of our quality of life.

Other recent work focuses specifically on how place differentially affects different races' access to opportunity. For example, one collection of papers examined how housing choices in metropolitan areas shape opportunities for racial and ethnic groups, a topic the editor said is "all but invisible on the public agenda as well as in the nation's intellectual life."[7] Acknowledging the significant and still growing literature on the role of race in limiting housing choice, Xavier de Souza Briggs noted that little research had focused at the metropolitan level. He brought together authors who discussed not only the causes but also the consequences of uneven housing opportunities for the social and economic prospects of racial and ethnic minorities.

The message from such researchers is that place creates opportunity. Economic and racial segregation are not just the *effects* of people having differential access to opportunity. Geographic separation actually *causes* people to have different opportunities. And the results are especially strong for the poor. Compared with family effects, place effects appear to be greatest for the families with the fewest resources.[8] The most obvious examples are high-poverty neighborhoods in inner cities where the environment can actively work against the families who live there, making it even more difficult than their household circumstances would suggest for them to achieve a decent education, find and hold a job, and stay away from drugs and crime. In both poor and working-class neighborhoods, residents may lack the social networks that would help them connect to jobs and other opportunities, and they may have no reliable transit to get to work. Even the air people breath is often a function of place.[9]

Locally, a study by the Brookings Institution documented that Philadelphia families who support themselves by low-wage work often pay higher prices than more affluent suburban families for a variety of everyday goods and services.[10] Focusing on working families earning less than $30,000, the researchers reported that such families pay more than affluent households pay to buy automobiles (through higher loan rates), and they pay higher insurance rates. They spend more to buy groceries nearby, because the stores where they shop tend to be two or three times smaller than the typical store where more affluent families buy food. Using check-cashing shops in neighborhoods with inadequate banking services costs a low-wage family hundreds of dollars in extra fees every year. When they own their homes, these families are more likely than affluent families in the region to pay high security deposits for utilities, to pay more for home loans, home appliances and furniture, and real estate taxes. The researchers concluded that altogether, low-wage families are charged thousands of dollars per year in higher prices that are not charged to better-off families who buy the same necessities. In large part, these discrepancies hinge on the places where families live.

A perverse structure of incentives built into our pattern of local government has created and continues to widen place differences. The fragmentation of government into hundreds of small, independent communities has multiplied the opportunities for households to pursue social advantages by geographic mobility. Politically subdividing metropolitan areas as we have done encourages people to use location decisions to differentiate themselves from other residents of the metropolis. Moving to a "better" community is a way to secure more opportunities of many kinds, as we have outlined above. It is also a way to put social distance between one's own family and the social problems that impose costs on all members of the community in which they occur. The suburban governmental pattern helps protect residents' advantages by assuring that their own resources will not be channeled to pay for another community's social problems. In short, the governmental fragmentation in our metropolitan areas establishes incentives that exaggerate social and economic inequalities.

Beyond this age-old pattern of fragmented local government, some newer influences are exacerbating place differences. During recent decades, local differences that have existed for a long time have acquired greater significance because of the federal government's tendency to push governmental functions down to the state and local levels.[11] As local communities and states gain increasing responsibility for taxes and services within their boundaries, access to public goods may depend even more on where people live. Another national trend affecting place differences is the sprawling pattern of suburban growth, because sprawl makes it more difficult to channel public investments into core areas of metropolitan regions, where decaying infrastructure is diminishing the quality of life for residents. The need to spread public investments over an ever-widening territory raises the overall cost of public services and introduces inefficiencies, all of which reduces the resources available for disadvantaged communities. The sprawl that is evident in greater Philadelphia is a recurrent theme in this book.

Comparing Philadelphia to Other Metropolitan Regions

A Brookings report, *Back to Prosperity*[12] identified sprawl as the major development problem facing the region. To gain a perspective on how the region's experience of sprawl during the 1990s compared to other metropolitan areas, let us examine regional trends alongside eight other metropolitan areas that we have chosen to reflect three kinds of comparisons: (1) two older industrial centers whose industrial past is similar to Philadelphia's (Cleveland and Detroit), (2) four flourishing regions that may serve as models (Boston, Chicago, Minneapolis, and Phoenix), and (3) two regional competitors (Baltimore and Pittsburgh).

With its pattern of churning in the housing market, one might assume that Philadelphia would exhibit a high level of residential sprawl compared to other urban regions. One would be wrong. When Smart Growth America compared levels of sprawl in eighty-three metropolitan regions across the United States, Philadelphia ranked seventy-second, close to the bottom of the list, meaning it exhibits a very *low* level of sprawl, at least with regard to housing densities.[13] Table 1.6 shows the residential density scores assigned by those researchers to our comparison metros; the only one with a more compact housing pattern than Philadelphia is Chicago.

With respect to job sprawl, however, Philadelphia's problem appears to be more serious. Chapter 2 describes a region in which economic opportunities are increasingly dispersing. That dispersal is more pronounced in this region than in many others. Table 1.7 shows that, with the exception of metropolitan Detroit, Philadelphia exhibits the highest percent of jobs located over five miles out of the central business district (CBD). That dispersal of jobs is accompanied by a widening gap in incomes between the central city and the suburbs. Table 1.8 shows that the central cities of the Philadelphia and Detroit regions lost the most ground from 1980 to 2000, when compared to their surrounding suburbs.

Racial segregation remains a serious problem in the region's housing markets. Compared with other metropolitan areas listed in Table 1.9, the Philadelphia region falls near the middle. The table measures African American and White segregation using an index of dissimilarity, a number that represents the percentage of either racial group that would have to move to a different

TABLE 1.6   RESIDENTIAL DENSITY SCORES, FROM MOST TO LEAST SPRAWLING

Pittsburgh	90.4
Minneapolis	94.7
Detroit	97.3
Cleveland	99.7
Phoenix	106.8
Boston	113.6
Philadelphia	114.7
Chicago	142.9

Source: R. Ewing, R. Pendall, and D. Chen, *Measuring Sprawl and Its Impact.* Washington, D.C.: Smart Growth America, 2002, pp. 15–16.

TABLE 1.7   PERCENTAGE OF REGION'S JOBS LOCATED OVER
FIVE MILES FROM CBD, 2000

Baltimore	73
Boston	62
Chicago	77
Cleveland	75
Detroit	92
Minneapolis	79
Philadelphia	81
Phoenix	69
Pittsburgh	64

Source: M. Stoll, *Job Sprawl and the Spatial Mismatch between Blacks and Jobs.*
Washington, D.C.: Brookings Institution, February 2005.

TABLE 1.8   CENTRAL CITY INCOME AS A PERCENTAGE OF SUBURBAN INCOME, 1980–2000

Metropolitan Area	1980	1990	2000
Boston	76	78	77
Chicago	71	67	73
Cleveland	63	53	60
Detroit	67	54	55
Minneapolis	90	86	85
Philadelphia	73	66	61
Phoenix	95	90	85
Pittsburgh	87	88	88

Source: T. Swanstrom, C. Casey, R. Flack, and P. Dreier, *Pulling Apart: Economic Segregation among Suburbs and Central Cities in Major Metropolitan Areas.* Washington, D.C.: Brookings Institution, October 2004.

TABLE 1.9   AFRICAN AMERICAN AND WHITE DISSIMILARITY INDEX (*D*), 1990 AND 2000

Metropolitan Area	*D*, 1990	*D*, 2000	Change in *D*
Baltimore	.709	.666	−.043
Boston	.677	.629	−.048
Chicago	.836	.778	−.058
Cleveland	.848	.766	−.082
Detroit	.873	.840	−.033
Minneapolis	.612	.561	−.051
Philadelphia	.751	.687	−.064
Phoenix	.444	.343	−.101
Pittsburgh	.713	.682	−.032

Source: E. Glaeser and J. Vigdor, "Racial Segregation: Promising News," in *Redefining Urban and Suburban America: Evidence from Census 2000, Vol. I,* eds. B. Katz and R. Lang. Washington, D.C.: Brookings Institution Press, 2003, pp. 227–233.

census tract in order to distribute African Americans and Whites evenly
throughout the metropolitan area. A higher number indicates greater racial
segregation.[14] Philadelphia displayed about the same degree of African American and White segregation in 2000 as Pittsburgh and Baltimore, but was significantly less segregated than Chicago, Cleveland, or Detroit.

TABLE 1.10   PERCENTAGE OF THE POOR WHO LIVE IN HIGH-POVERTY CENSUS TRACTS, 1990 AND 2000

Metropolitan Area	No. of High-Poverty Tracts	Concentrated Poverty Rate, 1990 (%)	Concentrated Poverty Rate, 2000 (%)	Change in Poverty Rates, (%)
Baltimore	33	22.5	13.5	−9.0
Boston	13	5.0	4.2	−0.7
Chicago	114	26.4	13.7	−12.8
Cleveland	52	21.7	15.3	−6.4
Detroit	53	36.0	10.4	−25.6
Minneapolis	15	17.3	8.6	−8.7
Philadelphia	67	23.0	19.6	−3.4
Phoenix	30	15.2	10.5	−4.7
Pittsburgh	26	13.3	8.5	−4.7

Source: P. Jargowsky, "Stunning Progress, Hidden Problems: The Dramatic Decline of Concentrated Poverty in the 1990s," in *Redefining Urban And Surburban America: Evidence from Census 2000, Vol. II*, eds. A. Berube et al. Washington, D.C.: Brookings Institution Press, pp. 160–166.

Poverty is concentrated within the Philadelphia region to a higher degree than in other metropolitan areas. Table 1.10 shows the percent of poor people in nine metropolitan areas residing within high-poverty neighborhoods (defined as census tracts where 40 percent or more of the population is poor by federal poverty standards). In 2000 the poor were more concentrated in the Philadelphia region than in the other eight metropolitan areas. Although Philadelphia had not ranked the highest among these nine metropolitan areas in 1990, all of the other regions had made enough progress reducing their concentrations of poverty to pull ahead of Philadelphia by the end of the decade. Philadelphia showed only weak improvement, reducing its concentrated poverty by only three percentage points.

Taken together, these numerical comparisons between Philadelphia and eight other urban regions show that greater Philadelphia has recently witnessed particularly high levels of job sprawl and concentrated poverty, accompanied by an increasingly unfavorable income gap between the city of Philadelphia and its suburbs. Addressing these deeply entrenched inequalities requires understanding and addressing three main sources of opportunity: employment, housing, and education. In the next three chapters, we consider each of these in turn.

2

EMPLOYMENT OPPORTUNITY

~

A t the close of World War II both the United States and the Philadelphia region were known for their manufacturing prowess. Yet both already had seen manufacturing's share of employment begin to decline. Although in 1950 manufacturing held a larger job share in the Philadelphia region than in the nation as a whole, improvements in communication and transportation, technological shifts, differences in labor costs, and other factors allowed production to relocate elsewhere and soon caused the economic paths of the region and the nation to diverge. By the late 1980s, manufacturing in both the city and suburbs of the Philadelphia region fell below its role in the nation.[1] Since that time, the gap between the region's and the nation's industrial profiles has continued to widen. The changes in Philadelphia resemble those experienced by other older metropolitan regions as manufacturing there faced similar challenges and managers continued to seek new markets and lower-cost sites in the United States and abroad.

This chapter explores some of the implications of these changes for the metropolitan economy and their consequences for regional workers' earnings and economic prospects. It begins with a brief overview of the structure of the regional economy, showing that greater Philadelphia duplicates many national trends: the decline of manufacturing and the rise of economic activities based upon education, health care, biomedicine and tourism. Then we look at the geographic patterns created by these economic shifts, especially the growing spatial diffusion of the metropolitan economy, as decentralized and often private decision making has trumped coordinated governmental efforts to shape development. While spatial deconcentration has characterized urban areas since at least the mid-nineteenth century, federal housing policies, the widespread adoption of the automobile, and federal highway construction promoted the rapid suburbanization of both population and jobs after World War II. Understanding where jobs are located is important for understanding regional economies because the ability of workers to commute to jobs depends upon the location of the employers, and different industrial sectors have historically had different locational requirements. Today, more than 70 percent of the Philadelphia region's jobs sit in the suburbs, often in areas accessible only by automobile and often in areas distant from housing affordable to their workers. Thus the spatial organization of the regional economy has real consequences for workers' lives.

The New Regional Economy

If the nation has moved into the postindustrial era, the Philadelphia region has moved more swiftly. Table 2.1 shows that, relative to the nation, the region's jobs are even more concentrated in wholesale, finance-insurance-real estate, advanced technology services, business services, consumer services, and nonprofit organizations, and regional jobs are less involved in agriculture-mining-construction, transportation-communication-utilities, retail, advanced technology manufacturing, and other manufacturing.[2] The nonprofit sector—which includes medical care organizations, hospitals, clinics, social

TABLE 2.1   PRIVATE SECTOR EMPLOYMENT BY INDUSTRY, UNITED STATES AND PHILADELPHIA METROPOLITAN AREA, 2004 (PERCENT)

Industry	United States	Philadelphia Metropolitan Area
Agriculture-mining-construction	7.0	5.8
Advanced technology manufacturing	3.4	2.7
Other manufacturing	9.8	7.2
Transportation-communication-utilities	5.7	5.6
Wholesale	5.6	5.8
Retail	22.7	20.6
Finance-insurance-real estate	7.8	8.4
Advanced technology services	5.1	6.2
Business services	8.8	11.5
Consumer services	14.9	15.7
Nonprofit organizations	9.3	10.5
Total	100.0	100.0
(N)*	(115,323,983)	(2,326,017)

*Zip Code Business Patterns does not give detailed employment by industry totals; totals were estimated by multiplying medians of establishment size categories by number of establishments in the categories.
Source: U.S. Census, Zip Code Business Patterns 2004, 2005.

service agencies, institutions of higher education, and arts organizations—is particularly prominent in Philadelphia. Although the region has long been recognized as a center for medical care and research, with five medical schools, the Fox Chase Cancer Center, and eighty-five nonprofit hospitals, it has only recently begun to acknowledge the economic and social significance of its more than sixty colleges and universities. As a center for higher education, the Philadelphia metropolitan area has few competitors. Higher education and medical institutions are frequently grouped together with other economic organizations in related activities as the "meds and eds" sector.

Finance-insurance-real estate is another broad sector that plays a larger role in greater Philadelphia than nationally. Although the region is home to the nation's largest mutual fund company, the Vanguard Group, and the nation's third-largest health insurer, CIGNA, its strength in this sector comes from the diversity of its enterprises rather than these specific companies' domination of their markets. Nonetheless, questions exist about the future of the sector because each of the industries in it has been subject to increasing forces of consolidation and dispersion. Since the early 1980s the financial sector has seen, and is likely to continue to see, significant consolidation as deregulation, foreign investment, and global competition lead to fewer and larger entities. Sassen[3] has suggested that the consolidation of firms may lead to their concentration in fewer and fewer places, but the growth of electronic trading lowers the cost of transactions and allows traders and financial managers to work from almost anywhere. Further complicating the future picture is the fact that the technologies that enable greater consolidation of financial enterprises also create new businesses capable of sustaining and growing local economies and of upsetting the fortunes of firms tied to more traditional ways of conducting business in traditional financial centers.

These changes also are evident in the region's industrial shifts during the 1990s, which Table 2.2 displays.[4] Between 1994 and 2004, total employment in the metropolitan area expanded by over 18 percent, and Table 2.2 displays the changing industrial profile of the region. The most dramatic change is clearly the decline in manufacturing. Consistent with national trends, the shares of both advanced technology and other manufacturing dropped by almost one-third. Absolute manufacturing job losses in the region totaled more than 68,000 or 22 percent of their 1994 base. At the same time, business services, advanced technology services, and consumer services increased their presence in the regional economy. In short, the 1990s saw a continuation of the postindustrial shift away from manufacturing and toward service employment. Lest one infer from Table 2.2 that the nonprofit sector is on the decline in this region, we note that it actually added about 10,000 jobs during this period, but its share declined because, in contrast to the national case,

TABLE 2.2 PRIVATE SECTOR EMPLOYMENT BY INDUSTRY, PHILADELPHIA METROPOLITAN AREA, 1994 AND 2004 (PERCENT)

Industry	1994	2004
Agriculture-mining-construction	5.2	5.8
Advanced technology manufacturing	4.1	2.7
Other manufacturing	11.6	7.2
Transportation-communication-utilities	5.1	5.6
Wholesale	7.6	5.8
Retail	20.8	20.6
Finance-insurance-real estate	8.3	8.4
Advanced Technology Services	4.9	6.2
Business services	7.0	11.5
Consumer services	13.4	15.7
Nonprofit organizations	12.1	10.5
Total	100.0	100.0
(N)*	(1,963,997)	(2,326,017)

*Zip Code Business Patterns does not give detailed employment by industry totals; totals were estimated by multiplying medians of establishment size categories by number of establishments in the categories.
Sources: U.S. Census, Zip Code Business Patterns 1994, 1994; U.S. Census, Zip Code Business Patterns 2004, 2005.

nonprofit employment grew more slowly than for-profit employment. Despite that reduced share of the region's employment during the 1990s, the nonprofit sector in this region still retains a competitive advantage, compared to the nation.

By far the largest employers among the nonprofits are Philadelphia's institutions of medicine and higher education.[5] Despite increasing attention to the role of these sectors in urban futures,[6] analysts differ on why they are important to urban economies. A Brookings report focused on the contributions made by these institutions in anchoring urban neighborhoods and facilitating redevelopment.[7] Other researchers and planners have drawn attention to the function of these institutions and related enterprises in creating new knowledge that fosters new economic activity and in providing the kinds of skills required for growing economies.[8] But few researchers have examined the role played by these nonprofit enterprises in promoting growth when they bring income into an area by selling goods and services to consumers elsewhere; industries that bring much of their revenue into an area from outside of it are called export industries.[9] Many elements of the meds sector are export oriented, such as pharmaceutical manufacturers, health insurance companies, and major university medical schools and hospitals. The four academic health systems (Drexel University, Jefferson Health System, University of Pennsylvania, and Temple University), the Children's Hospital of Philadelphia, and the Fox Chase Cancer Center all attract patients from outside the region. In the mid-1990s, an SRI International study estimated that 44 percent of the output of the region's health services was exported.[10]

Occupationally, the meds sector is extremely diverse; work varies from daily patient care to basic research in genetics, incorporating elements from manufacturing to insurance to patient care.[11] Taken together, these jobs provide 14 percent of regional employment, a figure exceeded only by retail and consumer services as reported in Table 2.1. The sector also incorporates much of what remains of the region's manufacturing through its inclusion of pharmaceuticals, medical devices, and biotechnology. Philadelphia's history in the pharmaceutical industry dates to 1830 when John K. Smith opened the drugstore that evolved into the modern GlaxoSmithKline company. The pharmaceutical manufacturers Wyeth and Warner Lambert also have nineteenth-century origins in Philadelphia. Today, the pharmaceutical industry represents more than 9,700 jobs in the region. According to the Harkavy and Zuckerman study, 80 percent of the world's largest pharmaceutical companies have a presence in the Philadelphia metropolitan area, and employment in the industry is second only to the New York metropolitan area. Yet these numbers actually underrepresent the true impact of the pharmaceutical industry, since they include only direct employment by pharmaceutical firms. If, for example, a chemical factory sells all of its output to a pharmaceutical firm, the connection to pharmaceutical manufacturing is downplayed because its jobs are counted as part of chemical manufacturing.

The meds sector often has close connections to the eds sector, and that is clearly the case in Philadelphia. Philadelphia has four university-based health systems, each of which includes a medical school as well as health service delivery enterprises. By themselves, the more than 60 colleges and universities in the region contribute only slightly over 1 percent to total employment, but their impact on the economy is quite large. A 1998 study found that Temple University and its associated health systems alone put more than $1 billion annually into the city's economy and another $600 million into the region.[12] A 1997 PricewaterhouseCooper study for the University of Pennsylvania (Penn) and its associated health system found that it contributed $1.5 billion annually to the city's economy and more than $4.3 billion to the state's economy.[13] Taken together, the two schools and their health systems generated more than 80,000 jobs locally. But since the late 1990s, both the universities and their health systems have grown significantly with commensurately larger economic impacts on the city and region. A 2006 Econsult study for the University of Pennsylvania and its associated health system found that it contributed more than $6.5 billion annually to the city's economy, almost $9.8 billion to the region, and more than $9.6 billion to the state;[14] Penn is the largest private employer in the city and region and second largest private employer in Pennsylvania. A more limited 2004 Econsult study for Temple University, which excluded its substantial health system and the New Jersey side of the region, found that it added $1.5 billion to the city's economy, $2.7 billion to the region, and $3.1 billion to the state.[15] Directly and indirectly through their purchases and the purchases by their staffs and students, these institutions create more than 115,000 jobs within the region—further testimony to their strategic place in the regional economy.[16] Educational institutions are even being used as keystones for urban renewal: across the Delaware River from Philadelphia, Rutgers University-Camden and Camden Community College are at the center of redevelopment efforts, as we will see in Chapter 3.

Hidden in these figures for higher education is the fact that many of the colleges and universities attract students from outside the region—in effect, exporting their educational services. The University of Pennsylvania, Villanova University, and Swarthmore, Bryn Mawr, and Haverford colleges have long served national and international student populations. And recently, Temple University, the region's largest school with an enrollment of more than 34,000, has successfully sought to diversify its undergraduate student body; from 1999 to 2005, its enrollment grew by 26 percent with 60 percent of that growth from out-of-state students.[17] Similarly, St. Joseph's University, with more than 7,200 students, has moved from serving a local to an increasingly national population. In the last few years, following a strategy Boston has long used and building upon the initial efforts of the city of Philadelphia, nineteen of the region's most prominent schools, working through the Knowledge Industry Partnership, a collaboration of nonprofits, foundations, state and city government, and business leaders, have marketed the region's schools as a group to increase the area's national visibility and attractiveness as a place to attend college.

But there are questions about the sector's ability to continue to serve as an engine of growth. The sizes of college-age birth cohorts are stabilizing after several years of growth—increasing the competition for these students nationwide. While in recent years urban schools have attracted an increasing share of the traditional college-age cohorts, they will have to increase their share even more to maintain enrollments in the face of stabilizing cohorts. They may also seek to increase their efforts to draw older, continuing education students, although they face growing competition from for-profit schools in this area.

Another effort to stimulate the regional economy has been a drive to increase tourism. The Philadelphia area is shaped by its history as the cradle of the nation, with Independence National Park and the National Constitution Center downtown and suburban sites like Valley Forge National Park. As manufacturing has declined, federal, state, and local leaders have vigorously sought to increase tourism and have met with some success. According to the *2004 Inbound Travel Report* of the U.S. Department of Commerce's Office of Travel and Tourism Industries,[18] Philadelphia is now one of the top ten U.S. destinations for travelers from western Europe and since 2000 has risen from twenty-first to tenth among all travelers to the United States. Another measure of Philadelphia's success as a tourist destination is the fact that since 1993 occupancy rates in downtown hotels have remained essentially constant despite an 82 percent increase in the number of hotel rooms. These trends are particularly impressive, given the fact that for much of the U.S. eastern seaboard, a trip to Philadelphia is easily managed within one day and does not necessarily require an overnight stay. In 2002, tourism accounted for 12 percent of the region's jobs. As positive as these figures are, the tourism and hospitality industries are not the strongest urban economic foundations because the wage structure is sharply pyramidal—it has relatively few middle- and upper-income jobs and large numbers of poorly paid ones.

Spatial Deconcentration in the Regional Economy

After decades in which business decisions, consumer preferences, and public policy from the national to the local level made the motor vehicle the primary shaper of metropolitan space, the dispersal of jobs and population in the Philadelphia area—as in other metropolitan regions—continues apace. Locally and nationally, the revitalization of downtowns has not significantly slowed the deconcentration of work and residence. Improvements in communication, computing, and transportation have permitted firms to lower costs by separating functions and relocating them geographically—trends that have been reinforced by the drive to improve organizational efficiency and lower costs by outsourcing what had previously been internal firm functions. Lower land and congestion costs in the suburbs, reduced commuting times, lower regulatory burdens, lower taxes, and municipal incentive packages also contribute to decentralization within metropolitan areas.

We can see how dramatically these trends toward job decentralization have affected commuting patterns by looking at Figure 2.1. Only in Philadelphia and some immediately adjacent suburbs do more than one-quarter of all workers hold jobs in Philadelphia. A modest 10 percent to 25 percent of all workers in the mid-distance suburbs commute to Philadelphia, while less than 10 percent of the workers living in the outer suburbs hold jobs in the city.

The trend toward job dispersal is more pronounced in Philadelphia than in many other metropolitan areas. One recent study[19] ranked Philadelphia sixteenth in the level of job sprawl among all metropolitan areas with populations of 500,000 or more. Its 353 municipalities are spread over two states that place almost all responsibility for land use regulation on municipalities and, until quite recently, actively discouraged municipalities from coordinating their urban planning. Philadelphia's metropolitan growth has occurred along major highways rather than concentrating in the core city or in "edge cities."[20]

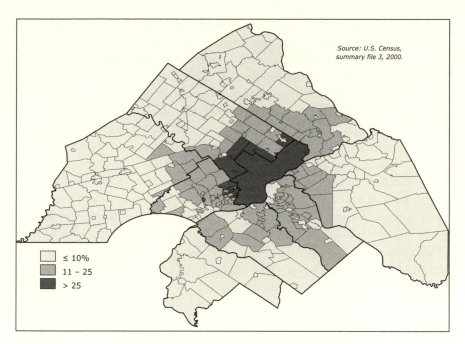

Source: U.S. Census,
summary file 3, 2000.

≤ 10%
11 – 25
> 25

FIGURE 2.1   Percentage of workers with a Philadelphia workplace, 2000.

The regional political fragmentation, one of the most extensive of any metro-politan area, significantly distinguishes Philadelphia from larger urban re-gions like Chicago, Los Angeles, and New York and has historically put its suburban communities in severe competition for jobs with each other and with Philadelphia.[21] Please note that in this chapter, we focus on *job* sprawl, not *residential* sprawl. Although readers might be tempted to equate these two patterns, they are not the same. With respect to employment, this chapter documents a pattern of broad dispersal. However, in Chapter 3, where we will turn our attention to housing patterns, we will see that the Philadelphia region is less marked by sprawl than other metro areas. Galster and colleagues[22] have developed a sophisticated conceptualization of residential sprawl and mea-sured it in thirteen urban areas including Philadelphia.[23] According to that measure, the Philadelphia urban area has relatively little sprawl. In general, residential sprawl is correlated with office sprawl, but Lang[24] notes that Philadelphia is the solitary exception to this pattern.

In the early 1990s Joel Garreau saw the shift away from central cities result-ing in polycentric development patterns. His 1991 book, *Edge City*, celebrated "new urban centers" emerging from normal market forces that were simply developments "blown out to automobile scale."[25] In Philadelphia, he found three such suburban centers—King of Prussia and Willow Grove–Warminster in Pennsylvania and Cherry Hill in New Jersey. While Garreau's definition involved more than just concentrations of jobs, jobs were central to it.

Now, more than a decade later, it is worth examining whether Garreau's vision of the polycentric metropolis still applies to greater Philadelphia. In Figure 2.2, which depicts the spatial concentrations of private sector jobs in the nine county region from 2003 to 2004, Garreau's edge cities of Willow Grove–Warminster, Pennsylvania, and Cherry Hill, New Jersey, have receded into the broader suburban landscape.[26] Only King of Prussia stands out from its surroundings as a job center. Clearly, concentrations of employment are more volatile than Garreau imagined. Instead of his pattern of edge cities, the distribution of jobs in the metropolitan area appears to involve a variant of Lang's "edgeless cities,"[27] a new form of sprawl arising as developers seek to avoid high land prices and the costs of congestion emerging from the growth of edge cities.[28] In the evolving metropolitan landscape, the suburban job centers that Garreau saw as edge cities appear to be only temporary phases preceding a more dispersed spatial organization, as developers continually seek lower land and development costs and developers, businesses, and residents continually seek less congested sites. The rise of "big box" stores like Wal-Mart and Home Depot leads to further deconcentration; these stores seldom seek mall locations, preferring to create their own retail environments at stand-

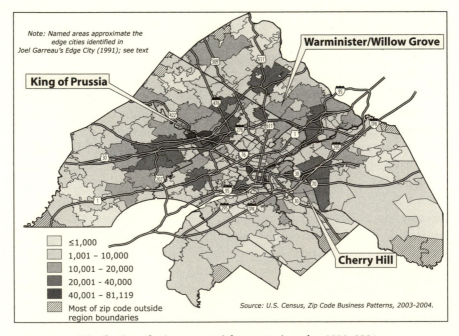

FIGURE 2.2 Distribution of private sector jobs across zip codes, 2003–2004.

alone locations. While a few edge cities such as Tyson's Corner in suburban Washington, D.C., and King of Prussia in suburban Philadelphia are likely to remain important centers, Lang's analysis points to the fact that office, retail, and institutional locations are increasingly spreading along roadways rather than sharing space in malls or on Main Streets.[29]

Edgeless cities are office complexes in places difficult to reach without a car and therefore places that do not encourage mixed use or nodal concentrations. For the Philadelphia metropolitan region, Lang found that 54 percent of all office space was located in edgeless cities, a figure only exceeded among the thirteen areas he studied by Miami with 66 percent. Lang characterized Miami as "the Edgeless Metropolis," and Philadelphia as "the Edgeless Metropolis of the North." But Figure 2.2 suggests that the dispersal of jobs in the Philadelphia suburbs goes well beyond just office jobs. The suburban "edge cities" Garreau sought to describe have given way—at least in the Philadelphia region—to continuous ribbon developments that follow major roadways.

One reason for the edgelessness of job clusters in the Philadelphia metropolitan area is its governmental fragmentation—the fact that it has 353 municipalities spread over two states. These two states have placed almost all responsibility for land use regulation on municipalities and have only recently begun encouraging municipalities to coordinate their urban planning. Although Galster and colleagues[30] question whether fragmentation is a cause of sprawl generally (because there are examples of metropolitan areas with unified governments that exhibit sprawl), we believe it has been a factor in Pennsylvania and New Jersey. Until 2000, the Pennsylvania Municipalities Code, which governs planning within the state, did not allow municipalities to jointly plan the development of land within their boundaries or even have legal standing before each other's planning and zoning boards. While New Jersey's municipalities currently cooperate and coordinate their plans far more than Pennsylvania, this situation has only existed since 1975. When New Jersey adopted its current constitution in 1948, it joined the "strong home rule" states, granting health, welfare, public safety, and zoning authority to its municipalities. This meant that from 1948 to 1975—the period of greatest suburbanization—each municipality determined its own land uses independently of those of its neighbors.[31] This history does not prove that fragmentation facilitates sprawl, but it does suggest that it has been a factor in the Philadelphia metropolitan area, and it raises the general issue of how state law shapes metropolitan development in the context of broader economic and social forces.

A case in point is the recent redevelopment of the roadways serving the King of Prussia area. King of Prussia lies at the junctions of Interstate 276 (the Pennsylvania Turnpike), Interstate 76 (the Schuylkill Expressway), Interstate 422, and U.S. Route 202, but it is the latter road along which much of the development sits. As King of Prussia grew, congestion on 202 became an increasing impediment to further development, and in 1999 the state began a project to relieve the congestion by widening the roadway to six lanes and reworking the connections to other roads. But the state's capacity to improve the situation was significantly impeded by the fact that King of Prussia sits on the boundary between two municipalities, Upper Merion and Tredyffrin townships. Because of this situation, development along 202 followed very different paths in the neighboring municipalities. (In Pennsylvania, municipalities have the power to decide the width of road rights-of-way as well as setbacks required for development.) Upper Merion Township in Montgomery County, the home of much of the existing King of Prussia development, established as early as 1953 a right-of-way of 100 feet and a setback of 35 feet for Route 202, and it has changed little despite the enormous development the area saw in the ensuing decades.[32] Tredyffrin Township in Chester County, in contrast, required a much wider setback of 300 feet. Widening Route 202 in Upper Merion Township would therefore have meant condemning many existing properties sitting only 35 feet back from the roadway, whereas widening the stretch of the same route in Tredyffrin Township would not. As a result, the widening project largely by-passed one township, while relieving congestion in the other. The project clearly improved traffic flow in the area, but it also had the effect of accelerating growth along 202 in Chester County, while doing little for 202 in Montgomery County. In effect the congestion in Montgomery County limited further development and pushed development elsewhere.

The pattern of development in Upper Merion and Tredyffrin townships is fairly typical of the region as a whole. It is a pattern essentially driven by the many local government decisions to accommodate private developers. Public policies at the state and local levels have mainly encouraged private development, with individual municipalities often competing for investment and unwilling to take actions that might discourage developers. Again, Upper Merion is illustrative: its zoning code has been essentially unchanged since 1953 because, over the years, the township commissioners believed that the best policy was to leave development issues to private entrepreneurs.[33]

The Distribution of Jobs by Industry

The degree to which jobs disperse depends on their industry. Retail and many consumer service jobs have always had the widest geographic distribution because they serve dispersed residential populations. Other sectors are more place oriented. For example, manufacturing has often depended on space, energy, or transportation in ways that favor certain locations over others. Or consider legal services (a part of business services), which have often concentrated in urban centers because that is where the state and federal courts are located.

In this section, we examine the spatial distribution of significant economic sectors in the region. While jobs in *all* these sectors are dispersing, Figures 2.3, 2.4, and 2.5, showing the number of jobs in each zip code, reveal some differences in the extent to which particular industries tend to congregate in particular parts of the suburbs. We begin with sectors that show a stronger tendency to cluster. Employment in information-driven businesses and business services is concentrated along Route 202, which runs across the region from southwest to northeast above the city of Philadelphia. While advanced technology services like software engineering (shown in Figure 2.3) require higher skills than conventional business services like accounting (Figure 2.4), their geographical distributions overlap considerably. Employment in finance-insurance-real estate (Figure 2.5), appears similarly concentrated, as has long been characteristic of this sector. The finance elements are particularly concentrated in downtown Philadelphia and King of Prussia—the latter the home of the Vanguard Group, the large mutual fund company noted earlier. But there is a scattering of other suburban sites that are home to financial giants like the Advanta Corporation (Horsham), a major credit card issuer.

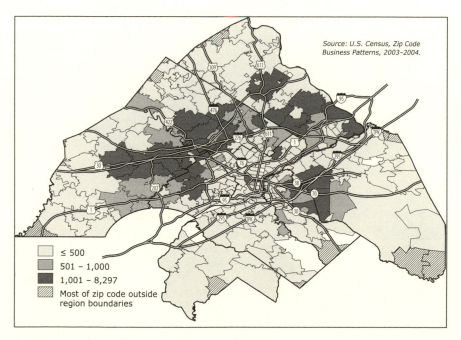

Source: U.S. Census, Zip Code Business Patterns, 2003–2004.

≤ 500
501 – 1,000
1,001 – 8,297
Most of zip code outside region boundaries

FIGURE 2.3   Advanced technology services jobs, 2003–2004.

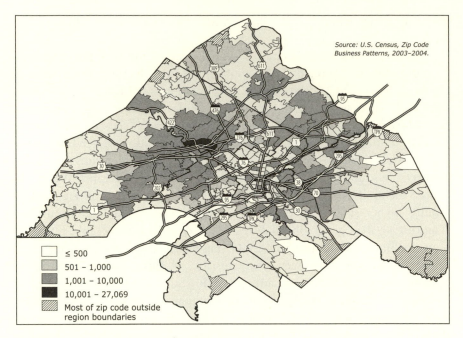

Source: U.S. Census, Zip Code Business Patterns, 2003–2004.

≤ 500
501 – 1,000
1,001 – 10,000
10,001 – 27,069
Most of zip code outside region boundaries

FIGURE 2.4   Business services jobs, 2003–2004.

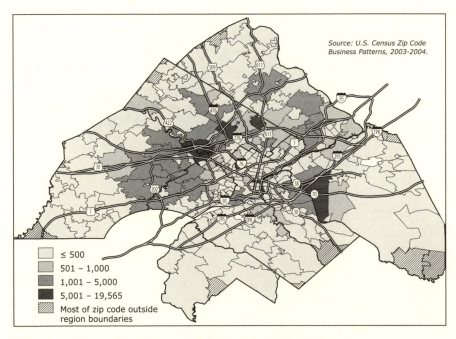

Source: U.S. Census Zip Code Business Patterns, 2003-2004.

≤ 500
501 – 1,000
1,001 – 5,000
5,001 – 19,565
Most of zip code outside region boundaries

FIGURE 2.5   Finance, insurance, and real estate jobs, 2003–2004.

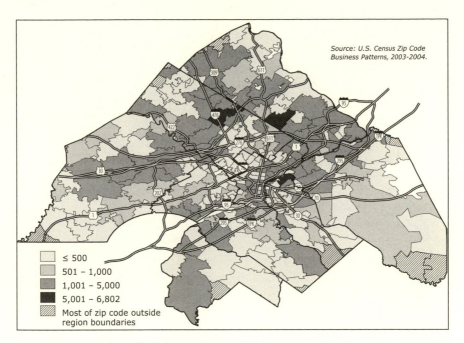

Source: U.S. Census Zip Code Business Patterns, 2003-2004.

≤ 500
501 – 1,000
1,001 – 5,000
5,001 – 6,802
Most of zip code outside region boundaries

FIGURE 2.6   Manufacturing jobs, 2003–2004.

In comparison with those business services, manufacturing appears more widely dispersed (Figure 2.6). Four decades ago Delaware County was an important manufacturing center, but it now retains just a shadow of its former strength. Similarly, southern Bucks County, another historic manufacturing site, has lost much of its base; the larger concentrations have moved toward the upper end of Bucks County. The largest concentrations of the region's remaining manufacturing jobs are now in central Montgomery County in areas with ready access to Interstate 476 and in central Chester County, along Interstate 276.

Still more widely dispersed are several sectors that provide many jobs for entry-level workers—namely, retail and consumer services and tourism and hospitality. The retail sector (Figure 2.7) and consumer services (Figure 2.8) illustrate fairly similar, broad distributions of jobs. Retail has more nodes where employment exceeds 5,000, but the reach of the two sectors across the zip codes overlaps considerably. Retail jobs tend to be low-wage jobs, and many jobs in consumer services, like those in hotels and restaurants and building maintenance, also pay poorly. Many of the jobs in both sectors are located in suburban places distant from public transportation. And even though Philadelphians usually identify their tourist attractions as being concentrated in the historic central core of the city, Figure 2.9 shows

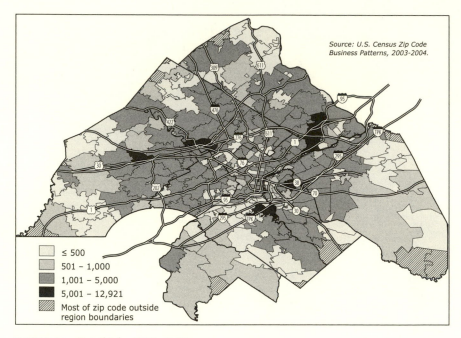

FIGURE 2.7 Retail jobs, 2003–2004.

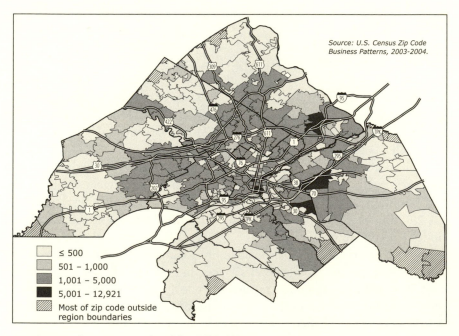

FIGURE 2.8 Consumer services jobs, 2003–2004.

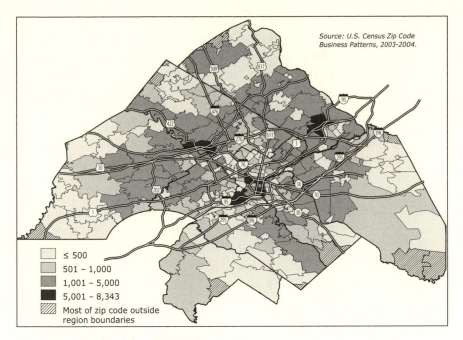

Source: U.S. Census Zip Code Business Patterns, 2003-2004.

≤ 500
501 – 1,000
1,001 – 5,000
5,001 – 8,343
Most of zip code outside region boundaries

FIGURE 2.9   Tourism jobs, 2003–2004.

that employment in tourism is almost as widely dispersed as retail and con-sumer services.

Comparing those maps portraying the geographic concentrations of the relatively well-paying employment in business services with the pattern of manufacturing jobs and the distribution of relatively low-paying employment in retail and consumer services and tourism, we see that the better-paying jobs show a greater tendency to cluster geographically, while the lower-paying jobs are the most broadly scattered across the regional landscape. This observation prompts us to consider the issue of how people get to work, particularly entry-level workers in the widely scattered low-wage jobs.

Who Gains, Who Loses? Bearing the Costs of Job Dispersal

A half century ago, many workers walked or took public transportation to their jobs. Today, the vast majority—84 percent in the Philadelphia area—drive to work and willingly accept the higher costs of doing so for the other benefits of automobile ownership.[34] However, for those without access to a car to reach the jobs increasingly dispersed across the metropolitan area, there are often substantial costs in transportation, time, and—for those with small children—child care involved in getting and holding a job. Journey-to-work data from the 2000 Census reveal that the longest commuting times are often borne by those least able to afford them. Analysis of populations whose one-way commute takes at least an hour shows that these commuters are concentrated within the city of Philadelphia, principally in low-income sections of North, West, and South Philadelphia (see Figure 2.10). Commuters in these areas are typically paying significant amounts to commute to highly dispersed retail and consumer service jobs that pay relatively little. Outside of the city, there is another cluster in Camden and a few scattered in Bucks and Burlington counties.

Public transportation in the Philadelphia metropolitan area, as is typically the case nationwide, is primarily organized to bring workers from the suburbs to the city and to help them move about within the city. Public transportation in the Philadelphia suburbs is limited to several regional rail lines and buses. Rail lines are far more effective at bringing workers to Center City jobs than taking them from Center City to distant job sites. Buses are far from serving most suburban job locations and, for many users and potential users, require long commutes and often frequent transfers. When one considers that a quarter of working Philadelphians commute to jobs outside of the city,[35] it is clear that the issue is not trivial for many.

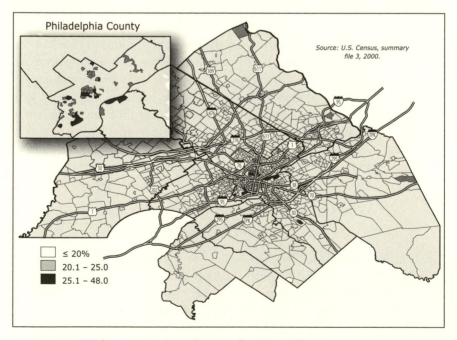

FIGURE 2.10 Workers commuting at least one hour to work, 2000.

It appears therefore that having access to a working motor vehicle is crucial to one's job prospects. Our analysis confirms that a relationship exists between vehicle ownership and household income, but its meaning is ambiguous. While the lack of a vehicle limits job opportunities, it is also true that lack of income limits the ability to own a vehicle, and the available data do not clearly reveal which line of causality is stronger.[36] According to the U.S. Census data for 2000, 13 percent of households with a householder under 65 and not enrolled in school in the metropolitan area lacked a vehicle.[37] There is, however, wide variation by ethnicity. Only 6 percent of White households lacked a motor vehicle, but the percentages of African American and Latino households without vehicles were 35 and 28, respectively. Table 2.3 shows the percentages of households with incomes in the lowest 20 percent of all household incomes, differentiated by three characteristics: (1) whether they owned a motor vehicle, (2) ethnicity, and (3) residence in the city or suburbs. Residence is controlled because the greater accessibility to public transportation within Philadelphia presumably makes access to a vehicle less necessary.

The table reveals that in every ethnic category in both city and suburbs, a half or more of those households that lack an automobile fall into the lowest income quintile. In the city, 50 percent of Whites, 65 percent of African Americans, and 74 percent of Latinos without a car fall into the lowest quintile. In the suburbs, the comparable percentages are 49 percent, 64 percent, and 70 percent—only modestly different from the city figures. Thus, for those with-

TABLE 2.3   PERCENTAGE OF CAR OWNERS AND NONOWNERS FALLING INTO
THE REGION'S LOWEST INCOME QUINTILE, 2000*

	Percentage in Lowest Income Quintile	No. of Persons
City of Philadelphia		
Among Whites with cars	17	140,743
Among Whites without cars	50	35,255
Among African Americans with cars	30	93,499
Among African Americans without cars	65	73,940
Among Latinos with cars	43	19,235
Among Latinos without cars	74	12,323
Philadelphia Suburbs		
Among Whites with cars	9	779,80
Among Whites without cars	49	25,584
Among African Americans with cars	20	75,533
Among African Americans without cars	64	17,551
Among Latinos with cars	26	24,159
Among Latinos without cars	70	4,904

*Householders under the age of 65 and not enrolled in school.
Source: U.S. Census, 5% Public Use Microdata Sample (PUMS) File, 2000.

out a vehicle, living in the suburbs gives an ethnic group little advantage over their urban counterparts in staying above the lowest income category.

But suburban residence does matter for households that *do* have access to an automobile. Regardless of ethnicity, Table 2.3 shows that for households with access to a vehicle, suburban residence reduces the probability that household incomes will fall into the lowest quintile, compared with the same ethnic group in the city. While the result is evidence that ownership offers critical access to the more numerous suburban jobs, it does not explain why a higher fraction of city vehicle-owning households fall into the lowest quintile. One might suppose that because householders in the suburbs are somewhat better educated than those in the city, they may be better able to translate their vehicle access into higher-paying jobs. However, a further analysis (not shown) revealed that house-holders' education does not materially affect the findings in Table 2.3.

Another possible explanation flows from the substantially lower levels of residential segregation in Philadelphia's suburbs than in the city—even when measured at the block level—and the possible relationship between less segregated neighborhoods and more heterogeneous social networks.[38] Lower levels of segregation suggest that minorities in the suburbs may have social networks that vary more in terms of socioeconomic status and minority group membership than minorities in the city. Existing research has shown that most people find their jobs through their social networks, that networks are critical to finding jobs that pay well, and that the character of networks varies by socioeconomic status and place.[39] Granovetter[40] found that persons of lower socioeconomic status tend to have smaller social networks, which are largely composed of relatives and friends with whom they have strong relationships. But as socioeconomic status rises, individuals' social networks become larger, more diverse, and more comprised of persons with whom ties are often weak. Somewhat paradoxically, however, these weak and diverse social networks are more effective for finding higher-paying jobs than strong ones. The paradox arises from the homogeneity of the lower socioeconomic status person's network; those with whom he or she has strong ties are likely to have similar occupations and thus have limited knowledge of jobs that would pay more.[41] The lower level of suburban residential segregation fosters the development of more diverse social networks, thus allowing vehicle-owning suburban minorities to leverage their ownership into better-paying jobs.

These data also suggest that the oft-mentioned "spatial mismatch" of suburban jobs and minority job seekers would not be resolved by simply moving the latter to the suburbs. The diffuse locations of jobs in the Philadelphia suburbs—and probably in the suburbs of many other metropolitan areas—means that having a motor vehicle is critical. Clearly, Whites are considerably less disadvantaged by the lack of a vehicle than minorities; inspection of the sample sizes in Table 2.3 shows that a far larger fraction of Whites own motor vehicles than is true for minorities, especially in the suburbs. But Whites, if they do not own a vehicle, share the same handicap as minorities: the disadvantage of not having a car, if less severe, exists for them as well.

Our findings also challenge the spatial mismatch thesis by showing that in numerous locations around the region where disadvantaged people live near well-paying jobs, they do not benefit from their location. We could see this clearly when we classified zip codes according to the average earnings for jobs within them. For this purpose, those zip codes offering the "best" jobs are those where average earnings rank in the top 20 percent of all zip codes in the metropolitan area. Those where the "worst" jobs are located are those where average earnings rank in the lowest 20 percent of all zip codes in the region. Figure 2.11 shows that some of the areas where employers offer the best paying jobs, such as the western areas of Chester and Montgomery counties, are largely home to populations with only modest incomes. This juxtaposition of high-paying employment alongside of low- and moderate-income residential populations suggests that many of the residents in the less well-off communities lack the ability to gain access to the better paying jobs nearby and must commute to jobs elsewhere. Thus while spatial separation from jobs may be one factor dampening the job prospects of disadvantaged workers, it is not the only limitation on their employment.

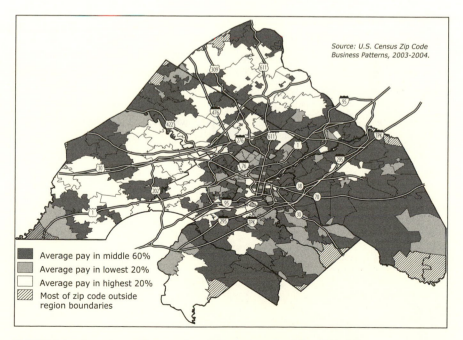

FIGURE 2.11   Locations of best-paying and worst-paying jobs, 2003–2004.

Who Gains, Who Loses? Bearing the Costs
of Industrial Change

It takes more than physical access to take advantage of employment opportunities. Most importantly, it takes education. The industrial shifts of the past several decades have raised the educational credentials demanded for all but the most menial of jobs. Manufacturing traditionally gave many who lacked education a chance for a middle class lifestyle, but most of today's factories seek a more educated workforce than in the past. Semiskilled factory work is rapidly being replaced by either automation, outsourcing to lower-cost sites abroad, or both. Where automation can preserve some jobs, those that remain tend to require substantial literacy. And the better paying jobs in the rest of the new economy also require more education than previously. Table 2.4 provides evidence of the current situation. The contrast between the highly automated advanced technology and other manufacturing jobs in terms of the education level of their workers is quite marked: fewer than 5 percent of the advanced technology workers have less than a high school education while almost 19 percent of the other manufacturing jobs do. Those with limited educations are increasingly found in the two industries that pay the least and often offer only part-time employment, retail and consumer services. The highest concentrations of poorly educated persons are in construction, other manufacturing, retail, and consumer services. Recall that Table 2.2 revealed that construction and retail jobs grew slowly and other manufacturing clearly shed jobs during the 1990s, despite expanding national and local economies. So opportunities for poorly educated workers are shrinking. Of those sectors having a sizeable fraction of their workforce with less than a high school education, only con-

TABLE 2.4   PERCENTAGE WITH LESS THAN A HIGH SCHOOL EDUCATION AND MEDIAN EARNINGS BY INDUSTRY, PHILADELPHIA METROPOLITAN AREA, 2000*

	Less than High School (%)	Median Earnings ($)
Agriculture-mining-construction	21.0	32,000
Advanced technology manufacturing	4.7	48,000
Other manufacturing	18.6	32,000
Transportation-communication-utilities	8.4	39,000
Wholesale	11.8	33,000
Retail	17.0	20,000
Finance-insurance-real estate	3.5	35,000
Advanced technology services	3.1	44,000
Business services	7.6	30,000
Consumer services	12.6	21,900
Nonprofit Organizations	4.7	32,000
Government	4.6	39,000

*Persons under the age of sixty-five and not enrolled in school.
Source: U.S. Census, *1% Public Use Microdata Sample (PUMS) File,* 2000.

sumer services expanded, but even in consumer services more than half of the jobs went to those with more than a high school diploma.

The consequences of limited education also are readily seen in its effects on the percentage of persons of prime working age who are unemployed or out of the labor force. We define the prime working years as ages twenty-five to fifty-four; the former figure eliminates most students and the latter excludes virtually all those who are retired or whose search for a job may be complicated by age discrimination. To further focus the analysis, we restrict attention to males because female labor force participation is more likely to be affected by child-rearing responsibilities. We examine the effect of education for male Whites, African Americans, Latinos, and Asian Americans separately in Figure 2.12, since, as already evidenced in Table 2.3, these groups face different labor market situations.

What Figure 2.12 shows is that (1) while increased education improves the employability of all four groups, differences remain among them; (2) the biggest difference in all four groups' employability is between those who failed to finish high school and those who did finish high school; (3) at every educational level, Whites fared better than African Americans, Latinos, and Asians; (4) while African Americans with no more than a high school education are more likely than Latinos and Asians to be unemployed or out of the labor force, this difference disappears among those with more advanced education;

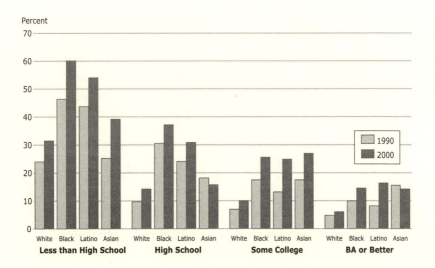

Source: U.S. Census, Public Use 5% Microdata Files, 1990 and 2000.

FIGURE 2.12   Percentage of males aged 25–54 unemployed or not in labor force, 1990 and 2000.

and (5) the labor market situation of all groups at all educational levels either stagnated or deteriorated between 1990 and 2000, despite, as noted, a growing economy during the period. Given that the labor market has required greater educational attainment, it is not surprising that those with the least education are either more likely to be unemployed or out of the labor force. What is more surprising is that the percentage of prime working-age males unemployed or out of the labor force grew at all educational levels and among all ethnic groups. This last finding may be part of the national decline in prime working-age male labor force participation long seen but little explained, and its observation among all educational groups suggests a pressing concern for future research.[42] The rise in unemployment and departures from the labor force at all educational levels during the 1990s suggest that the growth in jobs in the emerging economies of both the region and the nation are less capable of improving life chances than in the past.

As noted at the outset of this chapter, the trends involving industrial change, the dispersal of jobs, and the changing economic fortunes of workers are linked. Industrial change creates a dispersal of jobs as the spatial needs and desires of firms change and the dispersal of some jobs fosters the dispersal of others. Played out in the context of the highly fragmented Philadelphia metropolitan area, the dispersal is probably greater than it would be in a metropolitan area with a more politically consolidated character.

Who Gains, Who Loses?
The Issue of Earnings Inequality

But education does not fully buffer the consequences of industrial change. For more than a quarter century, the nation and region have witnessed the decline of manufacturing jobs that pay earnings in the middle of the distribution, accompanied by the growth of jobs at the two ends of the distribution. An inevitable consequence is growth in earnings inequality between the top and bottom of the distribution. Recent research[43] has shown that much of the rise in inequality is the result of an increasing share of income taken by the top of the distribution. The jobs that are replacing those lost in manufacturing simply provide less of the earnings pie to the vast majority of workers.

One way to describe these changes is to see how industries' growth and decline in jobs relates to the shape of their distributions of earnings. A simple measure of the distribution of earnings in an industry is the ratio of workers' *average*, or mean, earnings to their *median* earnings. The higher the ratio, the greater the amount of total earnings has been captured by those best paid. In Table 2.5, these ratios of mean to median earnings are shown for the region's industries portrayed in Table 2.2, categorized by whether their employment

TABLE 2.5   EARNINGS INEQUALITY BY EMPLOYMENT TREND AND INDUSTRY,
PHILADELPHIA METROPOLITAN AREA, 1994–2004

Industry	Employment Trend*	Ratio of Mean to Median Earnings
Agriculture-mining-construction	Gain	1.14
Advanced technology manufacturing	Loss	1.25
Other manufacturing	Loss	1.24
Transportation-communication-utilities	Gain	1.11
Wholesale	Loss	1.35
Retail	Stable	1.92
Finance-insurance-real estate	Stable	1.48
Advanced technology services	Gain	1.28
Business services	Gain	1.52
Consumer services	Gain	1.59
Nonprofit organizations	Loss	1.21
Total (N)	Gain	1.32

*A gain or loss of 0.3 percent or less is categorized as stable.
Sources: Zip Code Business Patterns 1994, 1994; Zip Code Business Patterns 2004, 2005; 1% Public Use Microdata Sample (PUMS) File, U.S. Census, 2000.

shares grew, shrank, or were stable from 1994 to 2004.[44] Since the data reveal earnings inequality (i.e., the mean is greater than the median) in every industry, we call attention to how the pattern of inequality relates to the pattern of job change during the 1994–2004 period. A useful approach is to compare the inequality for a specific industry to the inequality for all industries. If we look at the four industries with job stability over the period, we find that three of the four had greater earnings inequality than the average for all industries. If we examine the five industries that gained jobs, three had higher inequality. In other words, the region has been losing jobs in industries with more equal earnings distributions and gaining jobs in industries with less equal distributions. In 2004, the jobs in growing industries with above average inequality represented more than 27 percent of all private jobs; the percentage of jobs in the shrinking industries with below average inequality was a bit more than one-fifth.

The pattern of inequality, taken together with the rise in unemployment and departures from the labor force at all educational levels during the 1990s, suggests that emerging regional and national economies are less capable of improving life chances for many—and, perhaps the majority—than in the past. While industrial transformations are clearly improving aggregate incomes, the benefits have largely accrued to the top earners. The rest have seen their shares of the earnings pie shrink or stagnate. The patterns of industrial change, dispersal of jobs, and the economic fortunes of workers also are linked. Industrial change promotes a dispersal of jobs as the spatial needs and desires of firms change, and the dispersal of some jobs fosters the dispersal of others. And, as we have seen, the dispersal of jobs makes it increasingly difficult for those without access to a motor vehicle to find and keep employment. Responding constructively to these patterns will require better ways to both persuade firms to locate more jobs in established areas and allow workers to access the more widely dispersed jobs.

Economic Development Strategies

In an effort to increase job opportunities for residents of Philadelphia, Camden, and other communities in the region that have lost employment over several decades, economic development specialists have adopted strategies that divide roughly into two types: (1) reinvesting to bring jobs back into older communities, and (2) investing in mobility to connect residents in older communities with economic opportunities throughout the region, especially the suburban job centers that provide entry-level jobs. In the following section, we consider the first of these strategies, paying particular attention to creating employment opportunities for workers with limited education and skills.

Bringing Jobs Back to Older Communities

Revinvestment strategies designed to bring new jobs to older communities have been broadly similar regardless of where the communities are located in the region, but they also have been tailored to each community's assets and liabilities. Communities' location, size, physical infrastructure, amenities, and housing, economic, and population profiles all influence the strategies they have pursued to create jobs and redevelopment.

Redeveloping the Region's Central Business District
By far the largest investments in job creation have targeted Philadelphia's downtown. As early as the 1950s, the city's business and political leaders began to fear the central business district would be eclipsed by the suburbs. They mobilized to replace the remains of the manufacturing city with new facilities for the emerging service and information economy.[45] Downtown factories and warehouses, old railroad tracks and stations, narrow streets and alleys were replaced by skyscrapers surrounded by broad plazas, modern office buildings, and new retail outlets. Economic development efforts during the 1960s and 1970s were aimed at building the white-collar employment base. In line with the goal of refitting downtown for the information and service economy, the city's leaders began to bolster downtown residential areas in the 1950s and 1960s. Redevelopment officials worked to increase Philadelphia's White middle-class population to balance its poor, unemployed, and minority residents. Slums and skid rows were demolished. Deteriorated colonial housing

was refurbished and new high-rise apartment buildings were constructed to accommodate educated professionals, who were seen as the backbone of downtown's revival.

Subsequent retail development benefited a broader segment of the population by providing entry-level jobs. In the mid-1970s, a joint venture by the city and the developer James Rouse produced the first major new retail development in Center City since 1931, a multilevel mall of 125 shops and restaurants anchored by major department stores at each end. The Gallery, as it was named, opened in 1977 and proved such a success that it was followed by an adjacent companion project, the Gallery II, which opened in 1983. Additional employment at the entry level came in the form of hospitality jobs. In 1994, after a decade of planning, negotiating for state aid, and coordinating a complex construction project, Philadelphia opened a massive new convention center in the heart of its downtown, replacing a prior civic center that had been located at a distance from the central business district. Mayor Ed Rendell used its opening as the lynchpin of a relentless eight-year campaign to bolster the downtown hospitality industry. The mayor and his economic development team enabled the construction of new hotels, eventually bringing 10,000 hotel rooms into walking distance from the convention center. Tourists, as well as conventioneers, became an economic development target. In 1996, in partnership with the state government and a major foundation, the city established the Greater Philadelphia Tourism Marketing Corporation (GPTMC), a public-private partnership to promote the hospitality industry in the five-county region within Pennsylvania (Bucks, Chester, Delaware, Montgomery, and Philadelphia). Because GPTMC placed such strong emphasis on the cultural and historic tourist attractions in downtown Philadelphia, the city council dedicated a 1 percent increase in the hotel sales tax to support it.

In addition to tourists and conventioneers, the city has, since the 1990s, increasingly worked to make the city more hospitable to suburban visitors— for example, by promoting major retail developments in locations that serve large numbers of customers driving in from the suburbs. A case in point is the massive IKEA home goods store that opened in 2004 next to the Delaware River in South Philadelphia with easy highway access. The Swedish furniture retailer had proposed to open a superstore on twenty-one acres at the edge of downtown that would anchor a much larger retail complex of big box stores. Because the site had been a former railroad yard in a district devoted to port-related industries, IKEA's proposal required rezoning the land from industrial to commercial use. When some advocates protested that the land should be maintained for port-related industries, IKEA responded that this site, which gave the store access to suburban as well as city customers, was the only city option the company would consider. Had the zoning change been denied,

IKEA would have built its store instead in Cherry Hill, New Jersey. Philadelphia's government quickly approved the zoning change. The city made other similar decisions during the 1990s to accommodate visitors—for example, by choosing to enhance a massive professional sports complex housing baseball, football, basketball, and hockey teams at the southern tip of the city—in ways that maximized the convenience of motorists, especially suburban motorists. Nor did the city overlook the interests of suburbanites in its cultural planning. In 1996 Mayor Rendell initiated a major addition to the downtown cultural scene: a massive new performing arts center for the Philadelphia Orchestra to share with other performing groups. The site chosen for the project was on one of the broadest and fastest-moving traffic arteries in the downtown area— Broad Street—again, to make it attractive to motorists.

This emphasis on culture, professional sports, and hospitality followed similar efforts by Chicago, Boston, and other Northeastern and Midwestern cities to revive their cores over the past several decades, catering to suburbanites or to affluent professionals who have moved into downtowns in increasing numbers. A recent study estimated that Philadelphia's downtown population exceeds the downtown residential populations of all other major U.S. cities except New York and Boston. According to that study, "The success of the past 10 years has deep roots. It is the fruit of more than 5 decades of sustained attention to downtowns."[46] Like downtown residents in cities across the United States, Philadelphia's downtowners are more affluent, more highly educated, and more White than city dwellers overall. Middle- and upper-middle-class Whites now have more opportunities to live in or near Center City, and the increase in high-wage, white-collar jobs in Center City has drawn ever more affluent workers into the downtown housing market. On the other hand, African American, Latino, Asian and White working-class neighborhoods close to the center of the city have eroded, either through demolition (as in Society Hill and along South Street) or through gentrification (as in Spring Garden and Northern Liberties).

However, the downtown renaissance has also created some benefits for less affluent Philadelphians. Growth in tourism and hospitality, like the related sectors of consumer and retail services, has created large numbers of jobs that require only modest educational credentials. Lower skill demands, combined with easy access to downtown by public transit, make the burgeoning employment in restaurants, hotels, and retail establishments available to a large part of the inner-city workforce. Unfortunately, the majority of these jobs are poorly paid.

Reviving Neighborhood Retail Centers

Retail businesses are the main source of employment in many residential communities, yet even these relatively low-paying jobs have become scarce, as suburban malls and big box discount stores have undermined shopping districts in the region's older communities. In 1974, Philadelphia responded to the decline in neighborhood shopping by establishing the Philadelphia Commercial Development Corporation (PCDC), whose mission is to bolster the city's aging retail corridors. PCDC targets its loans and technical assistance to small businesses in some of the city's most distressed neighborhoods. An example is a business corridor in North Philadelphia running along 22nd Street, a commercial area that originally grew up around Connie Mack Baseball Stadium. Dominated by Irish, Italian, and Jewish immigrants during the 1940s and 1950s, the neighborhood surrounding the ball park began gaining African American residents in the 1960s and now is predominantly African American. After the stadium disappeared, the commercial base declined, and PCDC provided business loans and technical assistance to this commercial district over several decades to rebuild it. Its work was assisted by one of the first community development corporations in Philadelphia, the Allegheny West Foundation (AWF). Beginning around 1970, the neighborhood's largest employer, Tasty Baking Company, launched AWF as a vehicle for the company to invest in the surrounding neighborhoods. In addition to developing hundreds of units of housing units to stabilize the area, AWF contributed to acquiring and rehabilitating a block of properties on North 22nd Street for mixed use—with commercial businesses on the ground floor and upper floors for residential use.

During the 1990s, PCDC achieved its most dramatic impact in another neighborhood: West Philadelphia, adjacent to the University of Pennsylvania. Like many urban universities, Penn's campus is located near heavily blighted blocks. PCDC began working in 1997 to revitalize the 40th Street business corridor near the campus. The street added an upscale grocery store, a multi-screen movie complex, new restaurants, medical offices, a bookshop, and large chain drugstore. Other streets nearby also added furniture stores, professional offices, realtors, and other goods and services. Like the North Philadelphia example above, this West Philadelphia effort was bolstered by a nonprofit group—in this case, the University City District created by the University of Pennsylvania, Drexel University, and local businesses in 1997. Following the pattern of other business improvement districts, property owners funded the nonprofit to keep the area clean and safe, improve streets, and advocate for the area with the city and state. (See Chapter 6 for more discussion of business improvement districts.)

While PCDC focuses mainly on commercial districts located in low-income areas, even middle-class neighborhoods have suffered from deteriorating retail districts. However, they typically have organized and funded their own revitalization. Some of the commercial strips hardest hit by suburban competition are located at the edge of Philadelphia, where residents find it

convenient to drive outward to suburban malls instead of patronizing their local stores. In Roxborough, a residential neighborhood on the northwest edge
of Philadelphia abutting suburban Montgomery County, a 1960s era shopping district had once provided nearby residents with groceries, appliances,
notions at Woolworth's, and a movie theater, all on a walkable main street
known as "the Ridge" (officially, Ridge Avenue). By the 1990s, the original
stores, however, had been gradually replaced by pawn shops, pizza parlors,
and other low-end retailers. In the early 1990s, concerned businesspeople
formed a nonprofit organization, the Roxborough Development Corporation,
to stimulate redevelopment. Throughout the 1990s, the group provided help
to individual business owners and worked to recruit new services to vacated
properties. After a decade, the group decided more ambitious collective action
was needed. Ultimately, the group formed a nonprofit business improvement
district to collect fees from individual business owners to fund advertising,
cleaning and greening of sidewalks and lots, new lighting, and other street repairs. Although the proposal initially faced stiff opposition from some business owners who did not want to pay the additional 1 percent "tax," in 2003 its
supporters ultimately prevailed.

Reviving Suburban Area Retail Centers

Older suburban towns are not immune from these same competitive forces.
Ambler, an older working class borough in Montgomery County dating from
1888, had historically relied on heavy industries like an asbestos plant. Suffer-
ing from industrial abandonment, Ambler had lost population for decades
and watched its central shopping district deteriorate before embarking on a
makeover of its Main Street during the 1990s. The initial project was a $2 mil-
lion restoration of a seventy-five-year-old movie theater to refurbish its
Moorish terra-cotta façade. The new theater sparked renovation of adjoining
storefronts, including restaurants, an art gallery, and a fitness center.

While Ambler redevelopers focused on its well-defined main street, other
suburban officials have faced the challenge of redeveloping "edgeless cities,"
to use Lang's term. The highly fragmented nature of Philadelphia's suburbs
often means that a single retail district spills across community boundaries as
it flows along a highway or street. If it should decline, the effects of the decline
may spread among all of the places it touches. Yet because communities typically view themselves as competitors, responses to the deterioration are typically separate and distinct. A notable exception occurred in 2004 when twelve
older towns along a fifteen-mile stretch of Route 130 in Burlington County,
New Jersey, collaborated to revive an ailing retail strip. In a move that openly
acknowledged their common dependence on a shared highway to sustain their
economies, officials in a dozen towns decided to join forces to revive the

numerous vacant properties and run-down strip malls dotting their stretch of highway. While county development officials worked to lure a new Home Depot and Wal-Mart to open along Route 130, the townships pooled their money to hire a public relations firm to create a new logo to "brand" this fifteen-mile length of roadway as the "Burlington County River Route—Gateway to Opportunity!" Their goal was to create a sense-of-place that would help attract both businesses and shoppers.[47]

Attracting Investment to Declining Industrial Areas

Given that manufacturing firms usually pay higher wages than retailers, it is no surprise that many communities have fought to sustain a manufacturing base. The extreme political fragmentation described earlier in the chapter puts communities into fierce competition for a limited pool of such jobs. Ironically, state government policy sometimes fuels this competition. A case in point is Pennsylvania's 1999 program allowing local governments to designate economically distressed parts of communities as "Keystone Opportunity Zones" (KOZs). Businesses that choose to locate within those designated areas are relieved of paying both state and city taxes on property and business income until at least the year 2010. Since 1999, this incentive has frequently become a weapon in competitive struggles between municipalities to keep firms that might flee or to attract new employers.

For example, in 1999 a North Philadelphia company that cut rolled paper from paper mills and resold it to printing companies already had decided to move its 130 employees to a suburban industrial park in Falls Township, Bucks County, when the company realized it could take advantage of the new KOZ that encompassed its location in the Kensington section of the city. The company decided to stay: "Without the Keystone Opportunity Zone, staying in the city would not have made any sense economically."[48] The Bucks County town that lost that paper company in 1999 has itself used the KOZ program to help U.S. Steel. A year-long conflict in Falls Township delayed U.S. Steel from gaining the tax benefits it wanted through zone designation. U.S. Steel intended to advertise the KOZ tax breaks in order to lure new manufacturing companies to locate on its sprawling, idle site—the former home of the now-closed Fairless Works. Township officials initially resisted the idea of foregoing tax revenues on this property for fifteen years, but ultimately the county commissioners overrode local opposition and approved the zone designation.[49]

Other suburban towns have also used the KOZ program to reinvigorate their lagging economies. In Montgomery County, the older communities of Pottstown and Norristown have designated large KOZs. In Delaware County, the economically depressed city of Chester used a KOZ to persuade developers to buy a vacant electricity-generating station and turn it into a modern office center. Chester County officials looked at the deal as an unmitigated plus: "We had to ask if we were cheating ourselves of potential tax revenue . . . Our take was, there was nobody here and there was nobody coming."[50] Yet it is uncertain that the KOZ designation actually was critical to the developer's decision. It is difficult to attribute this or any other KOZ project directly to the tax breaks, since companies typically take advantage of multiple local and state incentive programs.

Within Philadelphia, companies have been especially attracted to KOZ sites in the northeastern section of the city because of its access to the region's highway network. For example, the Byberry East Industrial Park has attracted businesses ranging from firms selling computer services or facilities management to wholesale distributors of electronics, appliances, and even beer. It is worth noting, however, that a number of these companies moved to the KOZ from other Philadelphia locations, raising concerns that by foregoing taxes, the city's KOZ program had merely enticed companies to trade places.[51]

Paradoxically, these government incentive programs sometimes operate at cross purposes. For example, if we examine the grants that state governments give businesses to bring jobs into the greater Philadelphia region, we find that the overall pattern of grants favors companies locating in newer suburban sites rather than in the older communities that are the target of KOZs. A classic example was Pennsylvania's willingness in 2000 to provide $55.5 million in tax breaks and other incentives so that Vanguard Group, a financial services company, could build a new corporate home on a 245-acre dairy farm in Chester County. Vanguard, the largest employer in Chester County, was threatening to move across the state line into Delaware. The farm that Vanguard favored was located just off an exit ramp from the Pennsylvania Turnpike, giving the company access to workers across a large geographical area. One township supervisor spoke for the defeated "smart growth" forces favoring an urban location when he asked, "Why couldn't that go in West Chester or one of our other towns? . . . Why in the middle of a farm?"[52] Under the conditions of the $55.5 million state grant, Vanguard promised to spend $500 million on its new facility and add 6,000 jobs within a decade. But four years later, Vanguard acknowledged it had not yet broken ground on the converted dairy farm, nor had it met its interim target for adding jobs. Still hopeful that the project would proceed, the state scaled back—but did not withdraw—its payments to Vanguard.

A study of economic incentives by Keystone Research Center shows the state of Pennsylvania systematically subsidizes sprawl within metropolitan Philadelphia. The researchers calculated the grant dollars per capita going to businesses locating in the older cities and towns of the region from 1998 to early 2003 by the three business assistance programs that gave out the most money[53] and compared those amounts with the grant dollars going to businesses in the outer (newer) portions of the metropolitan area. They found that ratio was only 0.39 : 1, i.e., for every dollar of state grants supporting business expansion in the outer suburbs, only 39 cents were being spent in the older cities and towns.[54] We performed a similar analysis for New Jersey's distribution of dollars under its Business Employment Incentive Program (BEIP). This state program gives grants to businesses that expand or relocate in New Jersey. Our tally of BEIP grants made to New Jersey municipalities in the greater Philadelphia area shows that during a similar period (from 1998 to early 2003), the ratio was strikingly similar to the Pennsylvania side. For every dollar of state grants supporting businesses in the outer suburbs, only 42 cents were being invested in the older cities and towns.[55]

In early 2002, New Jersey's Governor James McGreevy tried to counter this imbalance by establishing a Smart Growth Policy Council to implement a Blueprint for Intelligent Growth (BIG), which would have discouraged developers from building on environmentally sensitive land while simultaneously encouraging development in established towns. Developers protested loudly, and the governor retreated, but not for long. Only a year later he introduced changes in the rules governing BEIP awards to emphasize smart growth principles; he increased the percentage of any given project that could be state supported, if the project were located in an older community. A project could qualify for the higher subsidies if it included redeveloping underutilized, polluted, or vacant properties, locating near new residential construction or renovation, locating on sites positioned near mass transit lines, or locating near and collaborating on research and development with public or nonprofit universities—all conditions that favored older communities.

Connecting Workers with Economic Opportunities throughout the Region

While some governmental and nonprofit development organizations have worked to bring jobs back into older centers in the region, others have focused instead on increasing mobility so workers can gain access to the entire pool of employment across the region. This chapter has shown the region's labor market to be highly decentralized, making mobility strategies crucial, particularly if the goal is to help low-income workers. While low-income populations are concentrated in Philadelphia, Camden, and a number of other older urban centers, the entry-level jobs for which they are qualified are widely scattered across the region. The head of one of Philadelphia's leading development organizations has asserted that effective strategies to help the working poor require "linking the possibilities of the inner city to the regional economy . . .

The most relevant economic category for neighborhood activity is not the neighborhood itself but regional retail, housing, and employment markets."[56]

Mobility from Suburb to Suburb

Substantial numbers of workers now live in one suburb and commute to another. That reality spurred the region's largest highway project of the 1990s, the Blue Route. In the planning stages for decades, that project opened twenty-one new miles of highway through the western suburbs of the region to link Interstate 95 in the south to the Pennsylvania Turnpike in the north. Even if we reject the glib criticism leveled by some critics that the Blue Route's main purpose was to allow residents of the Main Line to drive to the airport in only twenty minutes instead of forty-five, there is no denying that it was built to accommodate suburban travelers. So many motorists flocked to this road that in less than two years after it opened in 1991 the average daily traffic on some sections had reached volumes that transportation planners had not expected until the year 2010.[57]

Although it was built as a transportation project, the Blue Route's most significant impact was its influence on land development in the western suburbs. Near the northern end of the project, where the Blue Route crosses the Schuylkill Expressway, a massive new office complex in West Conshohocken sprang up. Near the southern end, where the Blue Route crosses Baltimore Pike, the seventeen-year-old Springfield Mall shopping center underwent a $100 million expansion. Not surprisingly, all the way along the route, new homes were built at a rapid pace. When the Blue Route opened, the president of the region's largest home builder emphasized the influence of highways on land development when he remarked that the road's completion "made us look in the area more than we would have. When I-95 opened up 20 years ago, we bought our first big piece up in Bucks County . . . That highway opened up Bucks County, and I assume the opening of the Blue Route will do the same for Delaware County."[58]

While it is not uncommon to see suburbanites advocating for more highway miles, it is somewhat surprising to observe the level of suburban interest in building mass transit lines. The region's newest such venture is a light-rail transit line launched in early 2004 extending from the city of Camden north to Trenton, stopping at twenty suburban stations. New Jersey Transit, the statewide public transit authority, spent a decade planning this River Line, the first new mass transit service for South Jersey since 1969. The line ties together many older Delaware River towns. The hope that it would help boost their stagnating economies provided the main justification for investing $1.1 billion in a service whose annual operating costs were estimated to dwarf its fare revenues by ten to one.

Several more proposals for suburban mass transit lines now exist at different stages of exploration. Among them, the most broadly supported (though still far from implementation) is an ambitious proposal to build a sixty-two-mile light-rail line between Philadelphia and Reading, Pennsylvania. Running through Chester and Montgomery counties, the $2 billion line would stop at over thirty suburban towns, including Conshohocken, Norristown, Valley Forge, and King of Prussia. The project has been dubbed the "Schuylkill Valley Metro" because much of its route would parallel the Schuylkill Expressway and, it is hoped, would relieve pressure on that overcrowded roadway. Like the New Jersey light-rail, this line also has the potential to revive some languishing suburban centers whose industrial economies have declined over recent decades. Although its backers have argued the line would help inner-city workers travel to suburban jobs, the Philadelphia city government has been lukewarm in its support of the project. City leaders have seen this as a project that mainly benefits the suburbs.

Reverse Commuting

Without an automobile, many low-income workers are at a serious disadvantage in gaining access to the widely dispersed entry-level jobs in the edgeless metropolis, and public transportation offers limited options to reverse commuters, whose jobs are typically located several miles away from the nearest suburban train station. Those last few miles represent a major obstacle to mass transit planners. It is difficult to build cost-effective and efficient systems for reverse commuting, since they require substantial concentrations of riders at their destinations and points of origin.

The Southeastern Pennsylvania Transportation Authority (SEPTA) is the regional transportation operator controlling bus, subway, and commuter rail services in the city and four suburban counties in Pennsylvania. Since the mid-1990s, SEPTA has attempted to serve reverse commuters by several methods. One is to run its own service lines to some major employment centers in the suburbs like King of Prussia and several Bucks County industrial parks. SEPTA, however, can only operate regular service to destinations where enough riders are available to make the route financially viable. Where SEPTA itself cannot afford to run regular service, it has relied on suburban Transit Management Associations (TMAs) to operate shuttles that carry passengers the last miles from SEPTA stations to their ultimate suburban destinations in office parks or shopping malls. TMAs are nonprofit organizations that get their funds from businesses and the federal government. They bring together employers to plan shuttle services, design routes, coordinate times, and market the shuttles to employees. TMAs send staff members to meet with workers in employee lounges, explain bus routes, and hand out schedules. Each of the suburban counties in the region benefits from the work of a TMA. Typically, the TMAs contract with shuttle services that can furnish transportation at costs far lower than SEPTA's cost, largely because the shuttle companies hire nonunion drivers who earn wages lower than SEPTA employees.

While these partnerships linking SEPTA to TMAs and suburban employers have improved access to suburban job sites, some of their routes have proven unstable. In tight labor markets, companies are eager to help subsidize such services. But when the companies hit hard times, their enthusiasm wanes. For example, a route dubbed the "Commonwealth Breeze" was created by a partnership between SEPTA and several suburban companies to carry workers from a SEPTA stop at Willow Grove Park Mall to nearby job sites. Two of the larger firms that helped fund this service, Advanta Corporation and Prudential Financial, Inc., subsequently withdrew their contributions when they trimmed their workforces along the route.

Reviewing these various transportation projects that have shaped the region, one is struck by how many different agencies play roles. The Delaware Valley Regional Planning Commission disperses federal funds to projects sponsored by two different state departments of transportation, to county governments, to TMAs, to SEPTA, to New Jersey Transit, and to the Port Authority Transit Corporation (PATCO), which is operated by the Delaware River Port Authority. Harmonizing the efforts of all these players is a major challenge for this region. We will have more to say about these coordination challenges in Chapter 6.

Job Training and Workforce Development

Even though their work requires a constant political balancing act, the regional transportation bodies and nonprofit TMAs described above at least manage to function from year to year. Unfortunately, other crucial elements of the region's workforce planning lack a comparable regional framework. This is a serious problem in an era when the availability and quality of the workforce is the most critical requirement for economic growth. Matching the unemployed with available jobs often requires efforts to train or retrain workers as well as place them with employers. Yet the region lacks any coherent system of employment training and placement. Instead, what we observe is a highly fragmented landscape in which multiple agencies pursue their programs with little or no reference to one another.

It was Congress's goal in the federal Workforce Investment Act of 1998 to push regions to create more coherent workforce systems, by mandating coordination for employment services that had previously been funded under 160 separate federal programs (for populations ranging from displaced manufacturing workers to teenagers and military veterans). The federal government instructed states to create workforce investment boards (WIBs) at the local level to ensure that local employers and service providers would collaborate to develop effective workforce plans. These WIBs were to include local business people, educators, government representatives, labor representatives, and community-based and faith-based organizations who would judge whether the local job training programs were meeting the needs of the labor market and customers. Where needed, the WIBs would push for better program coordination.

Pennsylvania's governor initially tried to promote coordination within the greater Philadelphia region, on the theory that the scope of the labor market in this part of the state was regionwide, not limited to the city or individual suburban counties. While rational from a labor market standpoint, the governor's regional approach fell victim to political fragmentation and competition. By the governor's definition, the greater Philadelphia region included the city plus six suburban counties, a scope far more ambitious than the individual counties were willing to accept. After an initial meeting between Philadelphia and the surrounding counties, political officials in the region decided instead to submit separate proposals for each county. Advocates for the city resisted broadening the planning process to include the larger metropolitan area. They feared the city might suffer when competing with its more advantaged neighbors for jobs, funds, and support, particularly since the new model catered primarily to the interests of employers and only secondarily to the needs of the least employable populations. As a result of this political friction, the city and each of the surrounding counties operates its own workforce planning effort. New Jersey counties also operate their own WIBs separately from the Pennsylvania side of the region.

Through a kind of treaty, signed in 2002, the Pennsylvania suburban WIBs and the Philadelphia WIB agreed to collaborate on high-priority workforce challenges. Not surprisingly (given the prominence of the bio-life sciences in the region's economy), their main focus has been the shortage of nurses, technicians, medical assistants, research technologists, and other jobs related to this sector. Under the banner of the Life Science Career Alliance, representatives from the five counties on the Pennsylvania side have sponsored projects to increase public awareness of health careers, especially among young people, including middle and high school students. The governor of Pennsylvania has tried to reinforce this emerging coordination, for example, in 2005 by granting $400,000 in state job training funds for biotech and life science industries in greater Philadelphia and then in 2006 steering a $1.5 million federal grant to the region for similar purposes. The governor explicitly directed that the funds be managed by the *regional alliance,* rather than by any of the county-based WIBs.

Blaming Philadelphia for political timidity is too easy an explanation for the lack of coordination in a complex, highly fragmented system that pulls revenues from federal, state, and local sources to support hundreds of non-profit and for-profit agencies playing their respective roles in developing the local labor force. Compared with this challenge, the more conventional approaches to economic development, like luring a corporation to relocate, seem simple. Even though a financial package to attract companies may involve contributions from federal, state, and local revenue sources, collecting and spending those funds to subsidize corporate relocation requires far less coordination than aligning the ongoing operations of literally hundreds of funders and agencies around a workforce agenda. The fact that political representatives of Philadelphia feared their interests would be overwhelmed by suburban power illustrates the limitations that hem in political actors trying to reach across jurisdictional boundaries.

Conclusion

Our analysis of changes in the regional industrial structure, the increasing dispersal of employment, and an increasingly difficult search for jobs capable of supporting families has led us to examine efforts to bring jobs back to older areas and to improve transportation as ways of improving opportunities for the region's residents. Outside of downtown Philadelphia, most of the prominent examples involve rebuilding the commercial bases of older neighborhoods by reviving retail and service establishments. Even in downtown Philadelphia, much of the effort to generate and sustain employment has focused on tourism and hospitality, again emphasizing service and retail jobs. Unfortunately, many of these jobs are poorly paid compared to the manufacturing jobs that have been lost.

Our findings demonstrate an increasingly tenuous link between work and residence in the region. Fewer and fewer workers expect to live near their workplace, opting instead to live within reasonable commuting distances of a wide geographical area. Nor do firms expect their employees to live close to the company. That is one reason why companies prefer locations that are easily accessible by major highways, giving them access to the widest possible workforce.

Both of these factors—the limited utility of bringing service and retail jobs into older neighborhoods and the diminishing link between work and residence—lead us to question just how much local redevelopment schemes actually improve long-term employment opportunities for those who live nearby. Even when towns succeed in attracting and retaining high-paying jobs with benefits, employers do not necessarily hire local residents. Our findings have demonstrated that high-paying jobs are often located alongside poor populations. Then why do local governments enthusiastically pursue such schemes? The answer is simple. Even if they do not ensure long-term careers for local citizens, redevelopment schemes offer the considerable benefit of bolstering the local tax base. Since the tax base sustains a local government's ability to provide public services, government officials constantly seek to protect and expand it. Among those public services should be programs that give unemployed workers better access to jobs for which they qualify, no matter where those jobs might be located. Some of these efforts must involve transportation improvements, while others should focus on employment training and placement. Here, local governments have been far less active than in rebuilding their local tax bases. Although the labor market may be regional, local government officials see their responsibilities as mainly local. This presents a major challenge to regional planning and coordination, a subject to which we return in Chapter 6.

This chapter has shown that as the link between employment and residence grows more tenuous, the link between employment and education is becoming stronger. In the next two chapters, we will examine in turn the residential and educational opportunities our region provides.

3

HOUSING OPPORTUNITY

⁓

The richly varied character of the region's communities that we described in Chapter 1 provides choices among many different housing markets. Just as suburban employment opportunities and differentials have driven decentralization in the region, housing choices emerging in the suburbs and exurbs have led to a decentralization of residential opportunities far beyond the boundaries of the region as it existed in the 1950s and 1960s.

Housing markets vary significantly across the region, paralleling the patterns of uneven development that differentiate older suburbs and smaller communities from exurban agricultural areas and peripheral industrial towns. Established communities now face disadvantages arising from their older and often smaller homes, as well as limits imposed by aging infrastructure and restricted opportunities for alternative development. At the same time, the townships located at the exurban fringe are experiencing rapid change from small, often rural communities to new suburbs or economic hubs. These transformations are evident in the shifting shape of the regional real estate market, whose advances and declines provide much of the grist for the mill of regional politics.

The uneven quality of housing available in different parts of the region accounts for some of the most important disadvantages suffered by the region's low-income families, because a family's choice of housing represents much more than a choice among dwelling units. Choosing a home means choosing a community environment; the people one will have as neighbors; the public services and amenities one can expect to enjoy, from schools to supermarkets;

and the amount of crime and social disorder that one's family may be subjected to. Where you live may even affect your health, not only because poor neighborhoods tend to provide lesser access to health care, but also because they often constitute harmful physical environments and impose high levels of stress on their residents.[1] Houses in poor neighborhoods often have health and safety violations that cause accidents. Many contain dangerous levels of lead paint. They may be located near environmental hazards like trash transfer stations or brownfields. In short, housing opportunities in large measure determine one's quality of life. Inequalities in housing opportunities are not just caused by socioeconomic differences; they reinforce those differences.

This chapter begins by reviewing the region's housing markets in the context of the history and the demographic and socioeconomic characteristics presented in earlier chapters. It then highlights several key trends that contribute to housing inequality in the Delaware Valley. These include decline and abandonment in older communities, sprawl in the suburbs, housing affordability problems, and the nexus of tax and mortgage delinquencies, foreclosures, sheriff's sales, and predatory lending.

The chapter concludes with a section describing efforts within the region to address housing inequalities, both by making strategic investments that bolster declining markets in older communities and by encouraging the residents living in some of the region's worst housing conditions to move to better neighborhoods. As we will see, the model of housing policy now emerging in the city and the region links governmental initiatives and regulation (constrained by the hard realities of a devolutionary climate of government and a shrinking tax base in the city) with community initiatives on the one hand and for-profit investors on the other. This collaborative model, often described with exaggerated rhetoric, offers some hope of reversing past decades of conflict, stagnation, and decline. As some observers have noted,[2] these efforts are often contentious, as the frictions that have divided communities in the past—indeed, the finger-pointing and demonization common to much of the civic discourse of the past several decades—are apparent immediately below the surface of these efforts.

Housing Variety and the Development of the Region

Taken as a whole, the Philadelphia region's housing market has gained value since 1990. As Table 3.1 indicates, the recent strong performance of the housing sector through 2004 created an improving picture not only for the Philadelphia region but also for other economically challenged regions like Baltimore and Pittsburgh. Among the major northeastern metropolitan areas in Table 3.1, Philadelphia ranked in the middle in terms of price appreciation. While it has enjoyed advancing housing values, it has not experienced the

TABLE 3.1   NORTHEAST REGION PERCENTAGE CHANGE IN
METROPOLITAN AREA HOUSING PRICES, 1990–2004*

Syracuse, New York	−6.5
Rochester, New York	−6.2
Buffalo-Niagara Falls, New York	2.4
Hartford, Connecticut	4.3
Springfield, Massachusetts	7.9
New Haven, Connecticut	10.6
Albany, New York	13.6
Pittsburgh, Pennsylvania	26.1
Philadelphia, Pennsylvania	27.2
Trenton, New Jersey	27.5
Baltimore, Maryland	36.1
Worcester, Massachusetts	38.8
Providence, Rhode Island	41.1
Bergen-Passaic, New Jersey	42.6
Newark, New Jersey	43.0
Atlantic-Cape May, New Jersey	47.4
Monmouth-Ocean, New Jersey	55.4
New York, New York	56.7
Boston, Massachusetts	61.3
Nassau-Suffolk, New York	67.1

*Expressed in 2004 dollars.
Source: "State of the Nation's Housing." Cambridge, MA: Joint Center for
Housing Studies, Harvard University, 2005.

rapid increases and price pressures occurring in Boston and a number of areas
surrounding New York City. Some of Philadelphia's civic boosters have sought
to exploit this middle position by stressing the region's relative affordability as
a selling point to newcomers who may have been priced out of the "hotter"
real estate markets of the eastern seaboard.

Looking at Table 3.1, we are struck by the dramatically divergent fortunes
of housing markets in different locations. At one end of the housing market,
constrained incomes and limited in-migration (e.g., Syracuse and Rochester)
suppress the market and therefore the prices of housing units, while at the
other end of the scale demand expressed by high-income households or other
demands push midrange housing prices and costs beyond affordable ranges for
many (e.g., New York, Boston, and the Long Island communities of Nassau and
Suffolk counties).

When we move below the level of metropolitan areas, the mix of income
levels and differential demand is reflected in housing submarkets that vary significantly in their physical condition, age, price, and style. In parts of greater
Philadelphia, for example, farmlands are giving way to tract developments
and McMansions, while at the same time other communities inhabited by
many older residents are gradually declining as maintenance becomes more
difficult and as homebuyers avoid older properties. Older housing stock is
likely to be located in higher-density communities than many buyers prefer to

live in and is often physically difficult to upgrade, renovate, or modernize. As people "vote with their feet" in favor of larger dwellings in newer styles, they put increasing pressure on older communities to remain competitive within the region. Not only urban neighborhoods, but suburban communities with older housing stock, have also experienced these pressures. In some of the older urban centers of the region (Philadelphia, Camden, Chester, Norristown, Trenton), the conditions of both the housing stock and the public schools have provided powerful disincentives to prospective homebuyers. The rapid depopulation of some of these urban centers has led to crumbling shells and empty, brick- and bottle-strewn fields where houses and businesses once stood.

At the same time, the forces that produced much of the community decline over the past several decades have also created opportunities for new directions in some other areas. Thus, in some older towns, new housing construction is occurring along with significant conversions of nonresidential to residential land uses. Filling specific market niches, some communities have added gentrified neighborhoods, active senior housing developments, gated communities, or upscale subdivisions of one-acre properties (or larger acreages).

The varying styles of the region's housing correspond to the different historical periods during which the region's communities developed and matured. If we recall the discussion in Chapter 1, the strong presence of both row houses and duplexes in the city of Philadelphia and other early manufacturing centers was superseded by the large stone houses of the early upper class and gentry. Chestnut Hill, the Main Line, and smaller but still wealthy communities on both sides of the Delaware River contain many examples of these substantial older homes. In the twentieth century, suburban developments along major arteries extending out from Philadelphia and Camden created subdivisions of detached houses intended for some of the first commuters in the region. While these homes were smaller than contemporary expectations of suburban housing, communities of detached homes with surrounding yards developed within the city of Philadelphia proper, in some of the early suburban communities in Delaware County (e.g., Darby, Upper Darby, Yeadon, and Lansdowne), and in Camden County (e.g., Woodlynne, Brooklawn, and Bellmawr).

As postwar suburbanization accelerated with the emergence of federally insured mortgages and new technologies of home building, the automobile-oriented suburbs expanded beyond the immediately neighboring communities in the inner ring until the Philadelphia metropolitan region took on its now familiar shape. Suburban development pushed beyond the original suburbs to transform a rural and agricultural landscape into one of homes, schools, commercial centers, and, increasingly, new centers of employment. As the region grew, suburban development spilled outward and changed the small towns and farming communities into exurbia, the fringe of the region.

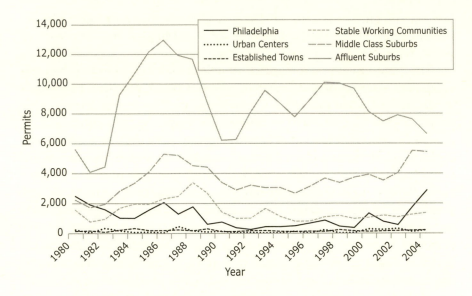

Sources: U.S. Census, Residential Permit Data, 1980-2004.

FIGURE 3.1   Housing permits (by community type), 1980–2004.

In recent decades, the pattern of housing development has followed an unsurprising trend. As can be seen in Figure 3.1, housing permits have shown a robust growth in the more affluent communities of the region since 1980, reflecting overall shifts in the national and regional economies. Both Stable Working Communities and Established Towns—largely older suburban communities—have seen a much lower level of development, as have the Urban Centers of the region. However, the most recent five-year period, from 2000 to 2004, reflects a new level of development activity, especially in the city of Philadelphia, where the combined effects of new housing construction, rehabilitation, and conversion are evident.

The variety of the region's housing stock is immediately apparent in the patterns of housing we see in Table 3.2. Philadelphia's distinct housing stock, with less than 10 percent consisting of single-family detached dwellings, reflects both the legacy of the row houses and the importance of higher-density apartment houses. The relatively low percentages of single-family detached housing in Delaware, Camden, and Montgomery counties indicate their importance as early suburban communities around Philadelphia and, in Camden's case, an important manufacturing center as well. Delaware County's low proportion of detached dwellings demonstrates both the importance of Chester and the manufacturing and refining industries along the lower Delaware River, but it also suggests that the early development of comparatively dense communities limited the options for later development that the more spacious expanses in Camden and Montgomery counties permitted.

The more recently suburbanized counties of Bucks, Chester, Salem, and Gloucester show significantly higher proportions of detached housing. It should also be noted that, with the exception of Philadelphia, there is little variation in the proportion of multifamily dwellings taken as a group.

On the surface, this variety of housing might appear to be an advantage, with diverse choices creating a vibrant market throughout the region. Yet we know this is not necessarily the case. While the city and the metropolitan area represent a significant housing bargain for residents, the underlying reality is that comparatively low housing prices result from the region's modest population growth pattern, and they mask significant city-suburban contrasts in average sales value. Although the decentering of the region has created differential housing demand in different locations, in the aggregate the region has shown sluggish demand for housing when compared with other cities and metropolitan areas.

Table 3.3 looks at differences within the region, comparing the city of Philadelphia not only with newer Middle-Class Suburbs and Affluent Suburbs but also with other types of "suburban" communities that are more urban in their density and history. While Philadelphia's median housing value lags all other communities in the region, the other Urban Centers trail the region as well. Of particular concern to many in the region, housing values in this metropolitan area have not performed well over the decade of the 1990s, as most communities showed losses in real value for their homes during the ten years between 1990 and 2000. Only Affluent Suburbs have seen a marked increase in value, and only Established Towns have kept value, on average.

These data, while showing a decline in housing values that is not reflected in the increases noted in Table 3.1, capture the uneven nature of housing value

TABLE 3.2 HOUSING VARIETY BY COUNTY, 2000 (PERCENT)

	Single Family		Multifamily			
	Detached	Attached	Two to Four Units	Five to Nineteen Units	More than Twenty Units	Mobile, Other
Burlington	64.7	13.7	6.3	9.6	4.2	1.6
Camden	55.2	19.4	7.6	7.8	9.3	0.8
Gloucester	72.8	7.5	6.1	6.8	3.9	2.9
Salem	73.0	4.5	7.9	6.6	3.1	4.9
Bucks	64.1	13.9	5.2	8.0	6.2	2.6
Chester	62.1	16.6	5.3	7.7	5.1	3.1
Delaware	44.1	31.4	9.5	6.4	8.2	0.3
Montgomery	56.0	18.7	7.8	7.1	9.4	0.9
Philadelphia	8.1	60.1	15.0	5.9	10.7	0.2

Source: U.S. Census, Summary File 1, 2000.

TABLE 3.3   MEDIAN HOUSING VALUE* BY COMMUNITY TYPE (DOLLARS)

Community	Median Value, 2000	Median Value, 1990*
Philadelphia	59,700	62,920
Urban Centers	75,692	132,941
Established Towns	185,179	189,921
Stable Working	115,847	159,250
Middle-Class Suburbs	145,391	176,870
Affluent Suburbs	204,931	182,341
Total	150,412	169,934

*Expressed in 1999 dollars.
Sources: U.S. Census, Summary Tape File 3, 1990;, Summary File 3, 2000.

appreciation across the region's communities. Because the last year captured in the census estimates was 1999, these numbers could not capture the effects of the so-called housing bubble that drove up prices rapidly after 2000.[3]

The losses in home values over the decade of the 1990s, especially in the region's older communities, are paralleled by comparatively lower levels of repair and renovation of existing housing. The data in Table 3.4 suggest that the level of home improvement lending in the region's communities is positively related to housing values, with one major exception—the region's Established Towns. (The apparent anomaly of low home improvement loan activity from the Established Towns communities reflects the relatively small number of housing units within them and especially the small percentage of owner-occupied units.) Given the constrained nature of housing values and incomes in the communities we have identified as Urban Centers, it is not surprising to see that the average annual number of loans per 1,000 owner-occupied units is low compared to other community types. Middle-Class Suburbs and Affluent Suburbs have the highest rates of home improvement loans, suggesting that better economic circumstances make it more possible to treat the house as both a residence and an investment.[4]

These numbers put a different face on the argument that affordability is a regional advantage. In 1990, the ratio of housing prices in the Affluent Suburbs to prices in the lowest valued location, Philadelphia, was about 2.9 : 1; by 2000, that ratio had increased to 3.4 : 1. Table 3.3 showed that the other Urban Centers of the region had experienced the greatest drop in housing values of all the community types (in constant 1999 dollars), losing more than 40 percent of their value over the ten-year period. These challenges to the region's older suburban communities are not unique to Philadelphia, as Lucy and Phillips[5] have demonstrated. Their analysis shows that the limited size of older suburban housing stocks and the limited options for further development faced by these older suburbs have combined to create two opposite housing trends—exurban development and revitalized urban centers. Perhaps para-

TABLE 3.4   MEDIAN ANNUAL NUMBER OF HOME IMPROVEMENT
LOANS, 2000–2004

	Loans
Urban Centers	24.0
Established Towns	18.0
Stable Working Communities	27.8
Middle-Class Suburbs	33.6
Affluent Suburbs	57.2

Source: Federal Financial Institutions Examination Council, Home Mortgage Disclosure
Act Data, 2000–2004.

TABLE 3.5   MEDIAN, MINIMUM, AND MAXIMUM MORTGAGE AMOUNTS, 2001–2004
(THOUSANDS OF DOLLARS)

	Median	Minimum	Maximum
Urban Centers	83.1	38.9	152.1
Established Towns	193.0	86.3	365.3
Stable Working Communities	125.7	71.8	248.5
Middle-Class Suburbs	169.0	102.7	477.3
Affluent Suburbs	216.2	132.2	360.8

Source: Federal Financial Institutions Examination Council, Home Mortgage Disclosure Act Data, 2000–2004.

doxically, the dramatically disinvested landscape of some neighborhoods in urban centers has produced opportunities for revitalization at scale, while many older suburbs, having built up to their maximum, have little vacant or abandoned land to use to spur redevelopment.

When we examine home mortgage values from 2001 through 2003, we see mortgage amounts that suggest higher market values than the 2000 census would have led us to expect, with the largest discrepancy occurring in the Urban Centers. Table 3.5 presents information that indicates how housing markets vary across community types, in terms of both averages and the range between the minimum loan and the maximum loan that was written in each of the communities. The median mortgage in the Affluent Suburbs is not only two-and-a-half times larger than the median mortgage for Urban Centers; it is greater than the *highest* mortgage written in *any* community in the Urban Center category. Indeed, the region's Urban Centers lag behind all other community types by a wide margin.

The region's rental housing market is also highly differentiated, as documented in a 2005 report from the National Low Income Housing Coalition (NLIHC).[6] This NLIHC report applied the U.S. Department of Housing and Urban Development's (HUD's) metropolitan area Fair Market Rent, a figure that represents that agency's assessment of prices in the regional rental housing market. HUD determined that Fair Market Rent for this region was $947/month for a two-bedroom apartment. Across the region, it took an annual income of $37,880 to afford the Fair Market Rent for a two-bedroom housing unit, which could be translated into an hourly wage of $18.21, an amount that was three times the minimum wage in New Jersey and three-and-a-half times Pennsylvania's minimum wage.[7] Put another way, if there were one wage earner in the household making minimum wage, she or he would need to work 118 hours per week to afford the Fair Market Rent on a two-bedroom unit in New Jersey; in Pennsylvania, it would take 141 hours per week.

Table 3.6 presents the income and rent disparity at a more fine-grained level, by community type. (Note that the median rents in Table 3.6 fall below HUD's Fair Market Rent because they include apartments with fewer than two bedrooms.) It shows the percentage of renters paying more than the recommended 30 percent of their income in rent. In Table 3.6, Philadelphia is broken out of the category of Urban Centers because its average rent is markedly lower, but the percentage of renters that pay more than 30 percent of their income to cover their rent is very similar to other Urban Centers.

The Paradox of Decline and Gentrification in the Urban Core

The housing markets exhibiting the lowest values are located in the core cities of Philadelphia and Camden, where trends in some neighborhoods have continued their downward slide during the 1990s, running counter to the generally positive regional picture. The starkest evidence of failing markets during that decade was the combined number of vacant houses and lots, seen in Figure 3.2, which climbed in Philadelphia from about 43,000 in the early 1990s to just under 60,000 in 2000. Even though the city government demolished about a thousand homes each year during the 1990s, it could not work fast enough to keep pace with new vacancies constantly occurring. By 2000, almost 300,000 Philadelphians lived on blocks with at least one abandoned house.[8] The va-

TABLE 3.6 RENT LEVELS AND AFFORDABILITY, 2000

	Median Rent* ($)	Renters (%)	Median Rent/Median Metropolitan Area Rent	Paying More than 30 Percent of Income toward Rent (%)
Philadelphia	569	40.7	0.88	46.8
Urban Centers	599	43.1	0.92	46.2
Established Towns	720	45.5	1.11	33.3
Stable Working Communities	655	33.4	1.01	36.7
Middle-Class Suburbs	687	16.8	1.06	34.1
Affluent Suburbs	873	15.1	1.35	34.5

*Median gross rent for metropolitan area = $684/month.
Source: U.S. Census, Summary File 3, 2000.

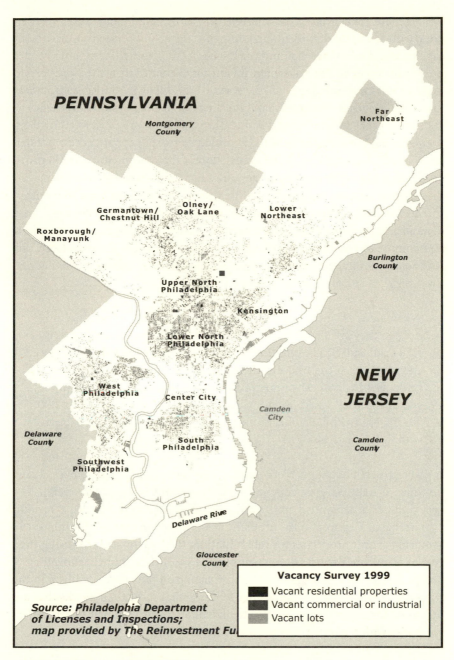

PENNSYLVANIA

Montgomery County

Far Northeast

Germantown/ Chestnut Hill

Olney/ Oak Lane

Lower Northeast

Roxborough/ Manayunk

Burlington County

Upper North Philadelphia

Kensington

Lower North Philadelphia

NEW JERSEY

West Philadelphia

Center City

Camden City

Delaware County

South Philadelphia

Camden County

Southwest Philadelphia

Delaware River

Gloucester County

Vacancy Survey 1999
Vacant residential properties
Vacant commercial or industrial
Vacant lots

Source: Philadelphia Department of Licenses and Inspections; map provided by The Reinvestment Fu...

FIGURE 3.2   Vacant properties, 2000.

cancies were concentrated most heavily in North, South, and West Philadelphia, with signs that they were spreading into the neighborhoods in the northeastern and northwestern sections of the city.

Vacant houses have significant effects on the value of nearby properties, especially in neighborhoods of row homes and duplexes, housing styles that prevail in inner-city Philadelphia. One analysis of over 14,000 home sales in 2000 found that when other variables affecting home prices were controlled, houses located within 150 feet of abandoned properties experienced a net loss in value of $7,627, compared to similar homes that had no abandoned properties nearby.[9] Houses located farther away also experienced losses in value, although of a smaller magnitude—a loss of $6,819 if they were located within 150–299 feet of an abandoned property and $3,542 within 300–499 feet. These dynamics of spreading decay became the subject of a dramatic news report and commentary presented in 2002 on Public Television's "News Hour" by Ray Suarez. As images of Philadelphia's most blighted blocks flashed across the screen, Suarez offered this grim portrait:

> When a city is emptying out, owners stop investing in their buildings because they are assets with declining value. Many neighborhoods enter a death spiral. The buildings can't attract buyers or renters that pay enough to keep the heat on; then finally, the market value crashes to zero; even the real estate taxes cost more than the building is worth; and the owner walks away. Multiply that story by 5,000, 10,000, 20,000. Many Philadelphia homeowners have ended up with property with little or no value.[10]

The growing blight problem has been aggravated by Philadelphia's arcane network of multiple governmental agencies dealing with real property. The very number of separate departments and offices makes it difficult to fashion a coordinated response to the problem. Even when buyers show an interest in acquiring vacant properties for rehabilitation, the lengthy and confusing process of acquiring the title defeats all but the most determined renovators. A prospective buyer can spend months contacting all the offices involved in the transaction. The multitude of agencies means that individual blocks that are identified for renewal may be targeted simultaneously by a half dozen different actors with separate plans. As one observer said,

> A single block can contain homes owned by the Pennsylvania Horticultural Society, slated for demolition by the Department of Licenses and Inspections, included in a Redevelopment Authority urban renewal project, awarded an Office of Housing and Community

Development grant for rehabilitation, and promised for a specific re-development plan by a city council person.[11]

Across the Delaware River, the housing trends of the 1990s were even less kind to the much smaller city of Camden. A 2001 report on Camden concluded that despite "estimates ranging from 3,500 to 6,000, there is no official count of the number of abandoned houses in Camden."[12] The falling demand for the city's housing stock was clearly evident in the prevailing prices. Of all the home sales reported in Camden in 1999, 86 percent were for houses under $50,000.[13] Camden has the smallest tax base (measured in property value per citizen) of any New Jersey town—about half that of other cities and one-quarter of that of Camden County, within which it is located. Many of the blocks containing vacant properties sit directly next to industrial uses. About one-third of the city's land formerly housed manufacturing plants; it is estimated that about half of that old industrial land is environmentally contaminated.

At the same time that some inner-city markets were literally collapsing, other neighborhoods within the urban core saw dramatic price appreciation, as investors rehabilitated them for middle- and upper-middle-class newcomers. Philadelphia's economic shift to white-collar employment has fed gentrification in the city where land and improvements have remained relatively inexpensive (i.e., old and deteriorating industrial lofts, apartment buildings, and abandoned dwellings that stand in the shadows of abandoned factories) and where reinvestment has become a rational response.

A prime example is the rapidly appreciating housing market north of downtown and east of Broad Street known as Northern Liberties. When we wrote our earlier book on Philadelphia, the clear dividing line between Center City and North Philadelphia was Spring Garden Street. Now, that dividing line has moved north to Girard Avenue, with the gentrifying area in between the two demarcations gaining trendy restaurants, loft apartments, rehabilitated row homes, and coffee shops bearing names like "The Latte Lounge." Almost twenty years ago in this heavily blighted area, a community development corporation was established: the Women's Community Revitalization Project (WCRP). The WCRP created community gardens out of trash-strewn lots, developed child care and other community facilities, and built over 100 affordable housing units. Now, WCRP's headquarters sits only one block from rehabilitated row homes with asking prices close to $500,000. The experiences of community-based organizations like WCRP have left some with a concern that dramatically increased private investments will not necessarily benefit the current residents of the community. WCRP's director articulated these concerns: "The city has a strategy to increase the tax base . . . We're not against investment in the community, but the government needs to make sure long-time residents can stay here."[14]

In another instance, an old industrial section slightly north of Northern Liberties contains the neighborhoods of Kensington and Fishtown, whose industrial base predates the 1854 consolidation of Philadelphia with preexisting townships on its early borders. In this worn-out section of the city, dotted with hundreds of vacant lots collecting trash, New Kensington Community Development Corporation has worked to clean and green vacant lots, stimulate individual and community gardens, paint murals, rehabilitate abandoned houses, and promote small business. For the last five years, the group has welcomed artists to congregate on a Frankford Avenue "Arts Corridor," encouraging painters, metal workers, glass-blowers, and sculptors to move their studios into empty spaces. For example, the community development corporation subsidized two stained glass artists to convert the space above their café on Frankford Avenue into a dozen artist studios. Already, some residents fear they may have succeeded too well. Real estate agents have relabeled the southern portion of Kensington "North of Northern Liberties," appealing to people who have been priced out of Northern Liberties.

In this discussion, the conflicts between revitalization and a place-based form of social justice emerge as poles in a policy debate that often appears abstracted from the realities of the communities where the disputes arise. The nature of uneven development is such that one person's hope is another's dread. Neighborhood revitalization has sometimes exacted heavy costs in the past. When rapid gentrification resulted in rapid displacement, individuals were forced to move from their homes; and neighborhoods that formed the social and economic nucleus for many of Philadelphia's low-income families were severely disrupted. Yet for many people seeking strategies for older urban centers to reinvigorate themselves, focusing on the downside of gentrification appears shortsighted. Proponents of redevelopment point instead to the heavy toll that empty buildings and vacant lots exact on the neighborhoods around them. In a decentralized region where cities have limited resources and are hard-pressed to address the current needs of their communities, they welcome any evidence of new investments.

Complex and thorny growth-versus-equity discussions are difficult under the best of circumstances. The desire to redress the legacies of past public policy and housing market disinvestment, while a vital part of community development efforts, runs up against the realities created by limited resources and long-term neglect of many communities. In many parts of the city, the rate of property abandonment, while slowing, has continued to bedevil communities, and the demolition of housing has generated limited new construction. Thus, the complaints against incipient gentrification strike many in the development community as rhetorical excess. The issue is further complicated by the absence of nonanecdotal data, as community activists reiterate their fears of displacement. Interestingly, one of the few systematic analyses of data (looking at the New York City housing market) has suggested that gentrification can actually result in slower housing turnover among the lower-income and less-educated members of communities and result in a more economically diverse community.[15]

Sprawling New Construction in the Suburbs

Since the 1950s, transportation developments in the region have made it possible for households and businesses to live farther and farther from the urban core. A leading example is the explosion of growth around King of Prussia. In midcentury, the Schuylkill Expressway was completed, connecting Philadelphia with the Pennsylvania Turnpike near King of Prussia, then a small crossroads community in the farm land of Chester Valley. Over the next fifty years, the King of Prussia area grew from a rural crossroads to become the largest suburban shopping complex in the eastern United States and the largest concentration of jobs in the Philadelphia suburbs. Although many new housing developments accompanied the job growth in this area, there is no necessary connection between living and working near King of Prussia. In fact, one important reason for choosing to live there is the easy access to highways that allow commuting to jobs in distant parts of the region. As Chapter 2 showed, the geographic pattern of jobs no longer determines the geographic pattern of housing at the metropolitan scale.

The highway network has fueled an expanding suburban housing market which, while not as hot in recent decades as some other East Coast markets, appears to have strengthened significantly in recent years. One way to monitor where new construction is taking place in the region is to track the number of building permits being issued in the region's communities. Table 3.7 shows the differential building activity in the different types of communities, measured by the ratio of the number of building permits compared to the number of existing housing units. Predictably, Middle-Class Suburbs and Affluent Suburbs show far more construction activity than do the other community types, reflecting a pattern of residential construction in higher-valued communities often on the periphery of the region.

All of this new construction has fueled concerns about residential sprawl in the media and public discussion. Newspapers, magazines, and radio talk shows have featured this subject, warning about sprawl's negative impacts, including pollution, traffic congestion, soaring taxes to support suburban services and infrastructure, racial and economic segregation, and even obesity

TABLE 3.7   BUILDING PERMITS PER 1,000 HOUSING UNITS,
2000–2004

Philadelphia	2.2
Urban Centers	4.6
Established Towns	9.9
Stable Working Communities	5.9
Middle-Class Suburbs	21.6
Affluent Suburbs	23.0

Source: U.S. Census, Place Level Residential Building Permit Data, 2001–2004.

associated with low levels of physical activity. And yet, as we showed in Table 1.6, Philadelphia exhibits a regional pattern of *higher* housing density and *lower* residential sprawl than many other metropolitan areas. Why are Philadelphians sensitive to sprawl?

One reason is that major civic organizations have focused attention mainly on *recent*, rather than historical, trends. The principal measure of sprawl used by open space advocates in the region is the comparison between population growth and land consumption during recent decades. By that measure, the recent pace of land consumption has been strikingly high. One widely read study issued by the Metropolitan Philadelphia Policy Center in 2001 called attention to this disproportion: "Between 1982 and 1997, developed land grew by 33%, while our [region's] population grew by only 3%. In the 1970 and 1980s, people in the Philadelphia region consumed land at a rate equivalent to developing one new acre of land every hour of every day for 20 years."[16] The emphasis in this region, which historically developed at relatively high densities, has been on slowing the recent rush toward a more typical U.S. pattern of low-density development.

Fear of sprawl has been heightened because so much expensive, high-profile development has taken place in recent years at the outer edges of the region. Builders have preferred to operate in locations where it is easiest to build, which usually means the exurban fringe. Lucy and Phillips have called this pattern the "tyranny of easy development decisions," observing that lenders, developers, and builders generally favor locations where risks are predictable and manageable. Business calculations favor options that are relatively easy to accomplish, like greenfield residential subdivisions, in preference to more difficult projects like mixed-use residential and commercial developments on infill sites, i.e., properties surrounded or adjacent to existing development.[17] Housing production has been, until very recently, based on high return, least resistance, least risk—a combination of low land assembly costs, low production costs, low regulatory costs, and high market prices. This pattern has been explicitly recognized in civic reports from a variety of sources.[18]

A prime example of the tyranny of easy development decisions is the pro-

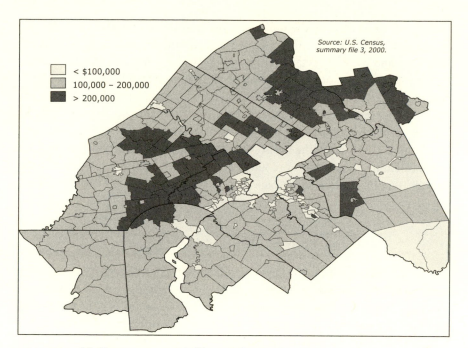

FIGURE 3.3   Median owner-occupied home value, 2000.

duction record of Toll Brothers, a real estate development company based in the Philadelphia suburb of Horsham and actively pursuing multiple projects throughout the region. Toll Brothers, which had been building suburban homes since 1967, began in the 1980s to concentrate on high-end houses that featured cut-glass chandeliers and double-height foyers. Robert Toll came to believe his company "could build any kind of luxury home, in any style, in any place where there was opportunity."[19] Known for his blunt style, Toll once asked a reporter, "Remember the idea that smaller is better? . . . It was B.S. then and it's B.S. now. People want size. It's the capitalist system and it has its own logic. People want more."[20] What drives Toll and other developers to build luxury homes on large lots is the extraordinary profitability of this suburban style. Compared to 1999, when Toll Brothers earned a profit of $28,570 on each house, by 2005 the company's strategy of focusing on luxury homes had driven up its profit to an amazing $91,914 per home, a 322 percent increase.[21]

The regional map of home values (Figure 3.3) highlights the elevated housing values in three main parts of the region: one area in upper Bucks County, a second area that spans Montgomery and Chester counties along U.S. Route 202, and a third area in southern Delaware and Chester counties. A glance at the map shows that the first of these areas sits on the northern edge of the region, stimulated by the rapid development of the Princeton corridor in New Jersey. Many homes in this area have been bought by New Yorkers as investments and weekend getaways. The other two high-priced areas are located on the southern edge of the region, along the Pennsylvania border with Maryland and Delaware. If we expand the geographic definition of the region to include the Princeton corridor in the north (Mercer County, New Jersey) and the southern border counties of New Castle (Delaware) and Cecil (Maryland), we find that a number of the twenty-five suburbs with the highest home values are located in those border counties. The centrifugal forces exerted on Philadelphia by the New York–New Jersey region in the north and the Wilmington region in the south are evident.

Housing Affordability and Mortgage Credit

The fundamental issues for the region's households seeking to purchase a home are the relationship of the price of housing to incomes and access to mortgage financing. Figure 3.4 presents a graphic depiction of the limits that household income places on housing choices by examining each community's median-priced house (based on a pooled average of mortgages from 2000 through 2004) against the region's income distribution. If a homebuyer earns an income that is at or below the median for the region (approximately $52,000 in 2004), affordable home ownership (as estimated from Fannie Mae's Housing Calculator) is available in most neighborhoods in Philadelphia and Camden, and in many of the older, inner-ring suburbs.[22] Moreover, there are home ownership opportunities in more distant suburban communities, some of which have some of the oldest housing stock in the region.[23] It should be noted that for households at the lowest income quartile (incomes up to $25,000), the median-priced house is affordable in only a restricted number of communities. In contrast, the vast majority of suburbs on the Pennsylvania side of the region require incomes well above $52,000.

Mortgage access plays a part in determining selective access to home ownership. We examined the degree to which loan applications achieved differential rates of approval, depending upon the racial or ethnic background of the applicants over a five-year period, 2000 to 2004. Figure 3.5 presents the approval percentages for each of the years 2000 through 2004, broken out by the major racial groups in the region, and suggests that the racial and ethnic identities of mortgage applicants are systematically related to approval rates.[24] African American and Latino mortgage applicants are less likely to receive approval of their applications than Whites or Asian-American applicants, regardless of the overall approval rates for any given year.

Paradoxically, while home borrowers in older urban communities have

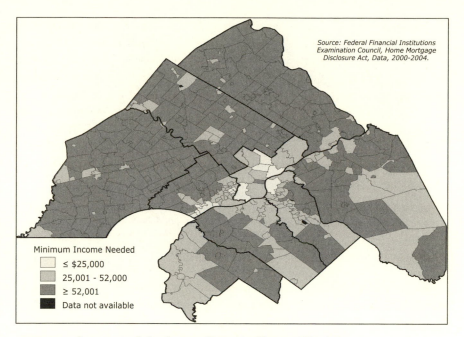

Source: Federal Financial Institutions Examination Council, Home Mortgage Disclosure Act, Data, 2000-2004.

Minimum Income Needed
≤ $25,000
25,001 - 52,000
≥ 52,001
Data not available

FIGURE 3.4   Income needed to buy median-priced house, 2000–2004.

faced difficulty gaining access to conventional mortgages, they have simultaneously been plagued by too much credit of the wrong kind. The past decade has
seen the rapid growth of a series of mortgage products that depend upon passing along to borrowers the costs of increased risks through additional interest,
fees, or insurance policies accompanying what are known as "sub-prime" mortgage loans. In many ways this approach to broadening access to mortgage credit
has encouraged the development of lending practices that negatively affect the
region's poor communities. While they have opened up home ownership opportunities, they have also created issues of sustainability and foreclosure.
Credit that is too readily available—oftentimes in amounts greater than the
sums people are seeking—or available to people who are not seeking credit at all
creates the possibility that the terms of the loan will become financially ruinous.

In the city of Philadelphia, mortgage lenders have historically invested heavily in certain communities, while leaving other communities to rely upon smaller
banking institutions and other sources for housing capital.[25] Patterns of lending
that skipped over areas of minority concentration many decades ago contributed
to racial segregation that remained entrenched for many years.[26] Were it not for
the federal Community Reinvestment Act and local programs like the Philadelphia Mortgage Plan (and its successor, the Delaware Valley Mortgage Plan),
many of Philadelphia's lower-income and minority communities would have
been without reasonable access to the city's mainstream financial institutions.

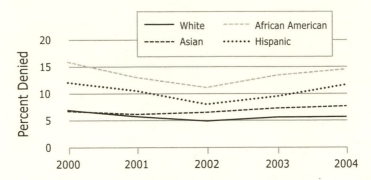

Sources: Federal Financial Institutions Examination Council, Home Mortgage Disclosure Act Loan Application Registry Data, 2000–2004.

FIGURE 3.5   Mortgage denial rates by race, 2000–2004.

Founded in 1975 in response to community-based charges of redlining and disinvestment, the Delaware Valley Mortgage Plan provided nearly 28,000 loans totaling $763 million before it ceased operation in 2000. The vast majority of the money was invested in the city of Philadelphia. As large as that sum sounds, it is important to recognize that in a typical year, more than 15,000 loans are made for the purchase of homes or to refinance mortgages in Philadelphia. So while the Delaware Valley Mortgage Plan clearly helped many borrowers, it did not fundamentally alter access to credit for the majority of Philadelphia's low-income people and places.

However, the pressures placed on the mortgage industry for wider access to credit, combined with overwhelming emphasis on home ownership as the primary federal housing policy (while public housing was effectively downsized), created a second mortgage market characterized by risk-based pricing: the sub-prime market.[27] By pricing loans so that the costs associated with high-risk lending could be recaptured in the loans themselves (and by making these loans available to a secondary mortgage market) lenders provided credit to formerly excluded applicants and communities. One observer[28] has estimated that during a recent ten-year period, the sub-prime market increased by a factor of fifteen times, from $35 billion in 1994 to $530 billion in 2004, and from a 5 percent share in 1994 to a 19 percent share in 2004.

In general, sub-prime borrowers suffer from either (1) impaired credit; incomplete or unverifiable documentation of income, savings, down payment sources, or employment; or housing and other debt that exceeds 45 percent of monthly gross income or (2) difficulties based on the property being mortgaged, with high loan-to-value ratios (i.e., exceeding 95 percent)[29] or collateral property that fails to meet one or more critical appraisal standards (e.g., detrimental conditions that adversely affect a property's marketability, hazardous conditions, etc.). While prime mortgage borrowers usually repay on a regular schedule, sub-prime borrowers exhibit a greater likelihood of late payments, default, and foreclosures. Because there is a positive relationship between the risk associated with a transaction and the interest charged to the borrower, prime borrowers tend to pay less than sub-prime borrowers.[30] Some research suggests that many sub-prime borrowers could have qualified for prime loans, and that the cost difference between the two loan products exceeds the increased risk profile. In the city of Philadelphia in 2000, 12 percent of all purchase money mortgages (i.e., mortgages used for the purchase of a property) recorded in the Home Mortgage Disclosure Act (HMDA) dataset were sub-prime and 18 percent of mortgage refinance loans were sub-prime.[31]

When we performed a similar analysis for the metropolitan area, we found that for the region as a whole, the percentage of mortgages that were sub-prime was much lower—just under 5 percent. The average loan amount for all loans was between $146,000 and $147,000, while for sub-prime loans it was under $107,000. When we took a closer look at the type of communities in which sub-prime loans were given (Table 3.8), we saw that the lower average incomes in Urban Centers and Stable Working Communities (discussed in Chapter 2), combined with lower average housing values, were associated with higher percentages of sub-prime loans found in these areas. These community types comprise significant lending areas within the region, as over 90,000 of the roughly 220,000 home purchase mortgages were written on properties in these two types of communities. In analyses that have focused on census tracts, rather than municipalities, the share of mortgages classified as sub-prime has been reported as high as 50 percent, indicating that active sub-prime markets are often embedded within larger communities that have access to more favorable forms of credit.

One of the major risks associated with sub-prime loans and other approaches to increased credit access is the increased exposure to foreclosure. While the high costs of sub-prime loans may shield the lender from losses, the foreclosure process inflicts losses on many communities that have experienced such foreclosures and resulting sheriff's sales. A recent study of foreclosures in Pennsylvania reported that if the total number of foreclosed properties in the state from 2001 to 2003 (estimated at over 55,000) were assembled in one location, they would constitute a collection of households outnumbering the households living in any city in Pennsylvania except Philadelphia and Pittsburgh.[32] That analysis strongly suggested that homes bought using sub-prime mortgage instruments were a significant contributing factor to the increased foreclosure rates in both the Philadelphia region and the state as a whole.

TABLE 3.8   DISTRIBUTION OF SUB-PRIME MORTGAGES, 2002–2004

	Sub-prime	Prime	Total
Urban Centers			
Average Mortgage	$80,962	$91,681	$90,869
Percent of Loans	7.6	92.4	
Established Towns			
Average Mortgage	$184,192	$236,607	$234,753
Percent of Loans	3.5	96.5	
Stable Working Communities			
Average Mortgage	$109,477	$125,653	$124,589
Percent of Loans	6.6	93.4	
Middle-Class Suburbs			
Average Mortgage	$147,473	$163,968	$163,091
Percent of Loans	5.3	94.7	
Affluent Suburbs			
Average Mortgage	$188,210	$215,563	$214,632
Percent of Loans	3.4	96.6	

Source: Federal Financial Institutions Examination Council, Home Mortgage Disclosure Act Data, 2002–2004.

TABLE 3.9   KEY FORECLOSURE INDICES BY COUNTY, 2000–2004

	Bucks	Chester	Delaware	Montgomery	Philadelphia
Sheriff's Sales, 2000–2003	4,018	2,481	6,002	4,950	23,742
Sales per 1,000 (2000)	5.2	4.3	8.4	5.4	14.6
Sales per 1,000 (2003)	5.7	5.2	11.3	6	18.1
Sub-Prime Loans	9%	n/a	10%	8%	16%
Foreclosures, Sub-Prime	73%	n/a	64%	61%	72%

Source: The Reinvestment Fund, "Mortgage Foreclosure Filings in Pennsylvania," 2005.

Of course, the relationship between economic hardships, mortgage fore-closures, and sub-prime mortgages is complex and varies significantly from one household to another. Households with limited assets (and hence limited financial reserves) who have resorted to sub-prime loans face significant hard-ships if their mortgage repayments increase faster than their incomes, if they face job layoffs, or if a sudden financial emergency arises. Table 3.9 points to both a rising incidence of foreclosures across this region and a link between foreclosures and the type of mortgage loans obtained.

As measured by sheriff's sales, foreclosures have increased in both raw numbers and as a percent of owner-occupied housing units. Delaware and Philadelphia counties show higher rates (Philadelphia much higher) than the remaining three Pennsylvania counties in the region. The implications for the communities experiencing increased foreclosures are several. First, the most immediate pain is felt by the households who must seek alternative housing and whose future access to mortgage credit is jeopardized. Second, communities must forego tax revenues (even though some may be recouped at the point of the sheriff's sale) and suffer from the negative market signal that increased foreclosures send to buyers and lenders alike, potentially reducing both sale prices and assessment levels. Finally, the resale of foreclosed homes has been found to bring lower prices than the market would be expected to produce.[33] Recent events within the sub-prime lending industry and the mortgage-backed securities industry have heightened concerns that foreclosures will increase in communities with concentrations of sub-prime loans.

Sub-prime lending has provided an opportunity for an especially problematic set of practices known as "predatory lending" to emerge in cities and communities across the country. Predatory lenders and their loan instruments erode the gains in housing assets made possible by increased credit access. "Predatory lending" has been defined as making loans using a variety of practices, including targeted marketing based on a characteristic that is unrelated to credit worthiness (e.g., race, age, limited English language skills), unreasonable or unjustifiable loan terms and outright fraud, a lack of transparency not rising to the level of legal fraud, a waiving of some borrowers' rights to redress (e.g., mandatory arbitration clauses), or a loan structure that results in serious and disproportionate harm to borrowers.[34] Predatory loans generally carry interest rates and fees that cannot be justified by the credit characteristics of the borrower or collateral.[35] Fees that have no reasonable justification are added into these transactions, *over and above fees to cover that risk that would have otherwise been presented by the borrower.*

In interviews conducted as part of a focused study of predatory lending in the region, Goldstein[36] found a series of practices used to identify likely customers. One broker, for example, reported going to a Web site that allows a broker to enter any number of characteristics, from age, sex, and income, to the likelihood of home ownership or likelihood of living alone. Then, for pennies per name, the broker can obtain a listing from which to target potential customers by mail or telephone. Another broker reported searching the public records for people who held mortgages with a previously active finance company; he reasoned that anyone who had a loan with that particular company could easily be talked into a loan with another similar entity. Other brokers reported working from leads provided by lenders with whom they work.

Not all questionable targeting and marketing comes exclusively from brokers. Housing counselors report that one prominent sub-prime lender is known to mail actual checks to a variety of consumers (many of whom are already delinquent). These mailings tell the customer that this "live check," which is in effect a home equity loan, can be immediately deposited in his or her bank account; in the case of delinquent borrowers, the "live check" can be used to bring the loan up-to-date. Once borrowers deposit these checks, the same mortgage company contacts the consumers, reports that their new home equity line is for a very high rate, and attempts to sell them a full mortgage refinance with the home equity loan folded in.

In a study of predatory lending in Philadelphia, a review of documents for loans considered predatory, as well as interviews with attorneys, suggested that many transactions make no economic sense. If borrowers had full and accurate information, they would never have entered into the transactions.[37] This lack of information is perhaps *the* defining characteristic of the transactions. There are critical gaps in information across the population as a whole, but acutely so among minority adults.[38] These gaps contribute to the success of predatory lenders. Evidence suggests that those borrowers who end up with some of the more expensive (and oftentimes complicated) loan products are least able to understand and appreciate them, with sub-prime borrowers being less knowledgeable and less prepared. They are less likely to have searched for the best loans available and more likely to respond to telephone calls or other advertisements.[39] Unlike the prime mortgage market, sub-prime lenders generally operate under a veil of secrecy when it comes to pricing, thus intentionally placing the borrowers at a disadvantage. As White states:

> sub-prime mortgage rates at the retail level are secret. No newspaper's real estate section will list current sub-prime mortgage rates. The rate tables used by wholesale sub-prime lenders are made available only to brokers and are sometimes regarded as trade secrets.[40]

Interviews with both brokers and borrowers affirm a historical pattern in which residents in minority and low-priced areas typically have not had complete access to mainstream financial institutions. The absence of mainstream mortgage money has left a void in these communities that was initially filled by consumer discount and finance companies charging very high interest rates for small loans. One interviewee, a former owner of a finance company active in the Philadelphia market, reported that his institution was more lenient than mainstream banks, which refused to lend money in those communities where his finance company operated. Another interviewee, an attorney who conducts closings primarily for sub-prime lenders, noted that there are few traditional bank branches found in many low- and moderate-income African American communities of Philadelphia.[41] However, with changes in the legal environment and the concomitant evolution of the lending industry, the consumer discount and finance companies have largely been replaced by bigger sub-prime lenders willing to make loans in areas of more modest means.[42] However, their loans are typically in amounts far in excess of what people need—or want.

People have often been talked into paying off debts that simply made no financial sense to retire.

The Philadelphia predatory lending study is instructive in what it describes as the behavior of a group of lenders who operate within the sub-prime mortgage market. It is important to note that not all sub-prime loans are predatory, but predatory lending depends upon both the vulnerabilities of consumers and the absence of effective regulatory oversight. The ultimate consequence of a predatory loan, should some form of relief not be obtained by the borrower, is to strip most of the value from the house. Sub-prime lending practices and foreclosures combine to create negative outcomes that neither the market nor regulatory mechanisms are likely to address effectively, although there is some evidence that local, state, and national bodies are increasingly aware of the need to address this issue.

Investing to Revitalize Housing in Older Places

Strategies to address these disparate housing outcomes must recognize that housing is a marker of the economic and social viability of a neighborhood or a community. The social well-being of a community, along with the viability of its tax base, depends upon its ability to attract investors to fund new construction, maintenance, and improvements. Because housing both embodies household preferences and affects the viability of the community, there are always personal and political dimensions to discussions of housing—especially to discussions about how communities deal with change through planning, zoning, taxes, and municipal services like streets, water and sewer provisions, and education. And because housing is an asset that can appreciate or depreciate over time, householders and community governments share the goal of at least maintaining, or preferably increasing, its value.

Recent debates surrounding housing developments in exurban communities suggest that what were previously *implicit* limits to growth imposed by physical and transportation geographies are now becoming *explicit* concerns expressed by communities resisting sprawl.[43] The added costs of a decentered region (e.g., high energy expenditures, increased maintenance of public roads, limited public transit options, and environmental impacts) have combined to increase tensions at the periphery of the region's development map. These growing concerns have helped fuel revitalization efforts in older urban centers and inner-ring suburbs.[44] And they have heightened the need for regional awareness and increased collaboration across municipal boundaries—although there has been more evidence of state-level policy than regional collaboration, as we shall see.

Our previous book portrayed redevelopment politics in the city of Philadelphia as overwhelmingly favoring downtown development rather than neighborhood renewal because redevelopment programs over the decades since the 1950s have consistently used government dollars to leverage private investments. In the years prior to the election of John Street as Mayor, when significant public sector funds have been spent in North Philadelphia and other inner-city neighborhoods, private investors have rarely been attracted to follow government builders into declining residential areas. They have preferred to spend their money elsewhere, either in downtown Philadelphia or the suburbs.

Philadelphia's most recent attempt to revitalize the city's many troubled residential areas was the Neighborhood Transformation Initiative (NTI), launched in 2001 by Mayor John Street. To persuade the Philadelphia City Council to support a bond issue borrowing $275 million for NTI, the mayor's presentation proposed a menu of different housing strategies for different neighborhoods, depending on how far blight had advanced. In the worst areas, NTI would use demolition to clear large parcels for rebuilding. In the strongest housing markets, the plan recommended nuisance abatement, removing dead trees, and other actions to maintain market appeal. Between those two extremes, NTI identified four other types of neighborhoods classified by different levels of distress, with appropriate actions specified for each—from acquiring and rehabilitating vacant properties, to stepping up code enforcements, removing abandoned cars, and making streetscape improvements. In formulating this strategy, the mayor recognized the political rule that benefits must be promised to enough councilmanic districts to secure majority support. Thus, NTI mentioned every single councilmanic district, specifying the steps appropriate to improving all ten housing submarkets.

Despite the wide array of strategies described in the NTI blueprint, in practice its implementation focused heavily on demolition, particularly in a few neighborhoods with high rates of abandonment. The plan aimed to demolish about 5,000 properties, more than the city had condemned during the entire decade of the 1990s. One target area was Mantua, a section of West Philadelphia not far from the campuses of the University of Pennsylvania and Drexel University. Since 1960, Mantua had lost nearly 60 percent of its population, an exodus that produced over a thousand vacant structures and lots. A newspaper columnist in 2001 referred to Mantua as "a coma neighborhood—barely viable, on the civic equivalent of life support."[45]

Another target was Brewerytown, a section of North Philadelphia that had once been the center of the city's beer-making industry but had begun to decline following prohibition. There, the city planned to transform twelve acres into a combination of 400 new housing units, including market-rate town homes, condominiums, loft apartments, and affordable housing.[46] Some of the land was turned over to Westrum Development Company, a suburban firm that pledged to build several hundred market-rate town houses to sell for $200,000 or more. Another private developer, Pennrose, secured title to convert a former grocery warehouse and bring 200 more housing units, including affordable lofts.

In demolition areas around the city, several thousand homes were slated to be torn down, sometimes on blocks where only a small number of homes remained occupied. When whole blocks were razed, the remaining residents were to be relocated, some of them vigorously protesting against losing their homes. The city Redevelopment Authority (RDA) has estimated that out of 5,500 properties condemned up to 2005, only 250 homes were occupied by residents who had to be relocated. The rest were vacant. Despite these small numbers, at city council hearings advocates for the dispossessed homeowners along with other protesters expressed outrage and opposition, carrying signs like "Build, don't kill our community" and "Vote to save our houses." Even facing this kind of opposition, the mayor and city council proceeded with condemnation of large tracts of land in a few neighborhoods with high rates of vacancy and abandonment, as a first step toward luring private developers to invest in large-scale projects. Like all previous redevelopment efforts, this five-year plan was based on the assumption that reversing widespread neglect and blight in housing markets requires persuading private developers to invest their money in building and rehabilitating units. Government funds act as a catalyst but are insufficient to do the entire job, so private capital must be lured into the city. When builders can construct hundreds of units at a time, their cost per-unit is low enough to make projects in the city financially attractive.

City officials deliberately selected neighborhoods whose locations make them attractive to developers. Mantua, for example, sits only minutes from downtown Philadelphia. Brewerytown has easy access to Fairmount Park and downtown Philadelphia (fifteen minutes by the river drive along the Schuylkill River). Yet another target area is located west of the campus of Temple University, where the city hopes that developers would be lured to build housing and commercial projects to serve the campus and community. City officials based their support on the hope that low mortgage rates combined with the city's automatic ten-year tax abatement for all new construction would bring developers who previously avoided building in the city. It is an indication of the sense of urgency—even desperation—about Philadelphia's deteriorating housing picture that NTI's targeting of specific neighborhoods did not draw the same level of broad opposition seen in earlier redevelopment eras, but it instead provoked resistance only from specific blocks slated for demolition.

If we turn from market-rate housing to affordable housing, we see that the single largest developer of affordable housing during the last decade has been the Philadelphia Housing Authority (PHA), the agency that has for decades operated public housing projects. PHA manages more than 12,000 of its own housing units and issues more than 15,000 Section 8 vouchers for clients to secure privately managed housing. (A Section 8 voucher is a financial commitment from PHA to pay landlords the difference between the market rate for a rental unit and the amount that low income households can afford under a HUD-determined formula). Since the mid-1990s, PHA has demolished over 7,500 apartments in massive projects, while constructing in their place 3,000 units for rent and sale, responding to federal inducements to create a new style of public housing. Philadelphia's housing programs of recent years reflect a major shift in national housing policy. The federal Department of Housing and Urban Development is encouraging cities to demolish large projects that concentrate poverty, relocate the previous residents—preferably to better neighborhoods—and convert the areas to mixed-use, mixed-income developments that typically employ neotraditional designs and reduce the number of units per acre. Across the nation and in Philadelphia, many of these projects combine rental and owner-occupied housing within the same development.

The twin drivers of this change in federal policy are (1) a determination to change public housing developments from isolated enclaves for the poorest community residents and (2) a desire to move low-income people out of areas of concentrated poverty and into better neighborhoods. These twin goals have led federal housing officials to encourage local housing authorities to allocate more public housing assistance units to working families, particularly those in federal welfare-to-work programs, in an effort to foster mixed-income projects. Rather than reserving public housing units for the most distressed families, housing authorities across the country have been allowed to exclude problem tenants from public housing developments. Some of the lowest-income tenants are given vouchers to help them find housing in the private rental market. At least since 1998, Philadelphia's approach to housing has closely tracked that federal shift.

As has happened in other U.S. cities, PHA has secured multiple federal grants to build Hope VI projects for mixed-income residents, with the aim of luring working- and middle-class families into public housing developments. Nearly 20 percent of the homes in each Hope VI development are sold at subsidized rates, usually for $95,000 to $120,000. (Note that it usually costs PHA around $190,000 to build the units they sell for much less.[47]) After demolishing the previous structures, many of them high-rise buildings, PHA has replaced them with low-rise buildings and reintroduced the traditional street patterns that had previously been closed off. Each new home has a yard and driveway. The preferred architectural designs are neotraditional—mainly Tudor, Arts and Crafts, or, in the words of a local architectural columnist, "vaguely Victorian."[48]

Most of these new projects have been partially financed by for-profit investors who expect a return on their money. These private investors have been motivated to put their money into affordable housing because the Low Income Housing Tax Credit (LIHTC) program gives them credits against their federal tax obligation for investing in projects that serve low-income renters. This tax break for investors in affordable housing projects, adopted by Congress in 1986, has become a standard component of the financing package for most low-income housing projects, whether sponsored by nonprofit or for-profit developers. Participation by private investors in PHA's projects has contributed to the authority's decisions to exclude tenants with bad credit records and behavior problems, who are regarded as problems that discourage private investors.

There are even instances where affordable housing developments include privately built housing for sale at market rates. For example, PHA sold the Westrum Development Company a portion of a site in the northwest section of Philadelphia that formerly contained a decayed high-rise public housing project known as Schuylkill Falls. Those high-rise buildings had sat vacant for twenty years before PHA had demolished them in 1996. Residents in a nearby middle- and upper-middle-class neighborhood had pressed PHA for years to fulfill its promise to replace the demolished structures with new construction, going so far as to sue the local and national agencies in court. In 2003 PHA finally built 135 units of subsidized rental housing and two years later sold the unused part of the site to the suburban developer for market-rate town houses and condominiums.

In the city of Camden, housing redevelopment is underway on an even broader scale. Camden officials have planned major housing developments that are expected to produce over 9,000 new housing units over the five-year recovery plan—a number greater than one-third of all the city's occupied units in 2003. The Municipal Rehabilitation and Economic Recovery Act enacted by the state of New Jersey in 2003 provided $175 million for a five-year plan to revitalize Camden. The state's money would be invested to expand colleges and hospitals, improve roads and other infrastructure, demolish abandoned buildings, and rehabilitate some housing. However, the funds needed to construct new housing were expected to come from private investors. Following the prevailing model of redevelopment, the state's money was intended to leverage private funds. Hence, most recovery funds were to be invested in areas considered viable by private developers.

The largest of Camden's redevelopment projects was to take place in Cramer Hill, a predominantly Latino community located along the Camden waterfront. About one-third of the residents of Cramer Hill live in poverty. Cramer Hill by no means contains the city's most blighted housing. In fact, its one square mile of row houses and semidetached houses qualifies as one of the city's more stable housing markets. Many residents own their homes. However, its location along the waterfront makes it attractive to private developers. So the City of Camden planned to replace the private homes and public housing with a waterfront marina, retail outlets, and new housing. Cherokee Investment Partners, a North Carolina development firm, offered to invest $1 billion over ten years in the Cramer Hill section, to be matched by about $150 million in federal, state, and city dollars, in order to transform 450 acres into the mixed-use waterfront community. The development included 6,000 new houses, of which 1,000 units were affordable housing and 5,000 market-rate homes, to be located on the waterfront and sell for $200,000 and more. Perhaps the most startling feature of the developer's plan for this gritty waterfront neighborhood was the transformation of a ninety-acre landfill into an eighteen-hole golf course.

Two other neighborhoods slated for renewal were located next to one another just south of downtown Camden—Bergen Square and Lanning Square—both hard-hit areas marred by rundown properties, abandoned buildings, and trash-filled lots. Their appeal to developers was their proximity to downtown and also to Cooper Hospital, a major medical institution. The Bergen Square plan would replace the area's current structures with 2,500 new or rehabilitated units of housing. In Lanning Square, planners said that 800 new homes would rise, 600 of them at market rate, and $4 million would be invested in restoring the Carnegie Library, a major community institution that had been allowed to crumble.

Even more than Philadelphia's NTI, Camden's massive rebuilding plan required relocating existing residents. In Cramer Hill alone, the initial plan would have displaced nearly 1,000 households and two dozen businesses. The Bergen Square project foresaw displacing another 480 households and dozens more businesses. Residents and business owners protested strenuously as the Camden City Council moved forward with sweeping plans. Protestors wanted the city and state to fix up existing homes and businesses, and a number of them challenged the redevelopment plans through lawsuits.

South Jersey Legal Services (SJLS) represented more than thirty low-income homeowners who did not wish to sell their property to the city. SJLS filed lawsuits challenging the redevelopment proposals on a variety of federal and state grounds, sometimes under antidiscrimination and environmental protection laws. In an effort to help some of the dispossessed Camden householders, the same legal services agency even filed an amicus curiae brief with the U.S. Supreme Court on behalf of three clients in the case of *Kelo v. New London*, a 2005 case arising in London, Connecticut, that challenged the constitutionality of using eminent domain powers for urban renewal and redevelopment purposes. Residents' lawsuits ultimately stopped the Cramer Hill project, although smaller housing projects have proceeded elsewhere.

In other Urban Centers of the region beyond Philadelphia and Camden, we can find partnerships between government, for-profit developers, and nonprofits to revive older housing markets. Older communities have been receiving help since 2000 from the state government of Pennsylvania, which has been subsidizing affordable home ownership through the Pennsylvania Housing Finance Agency (PHFA). It encourages partnerships between nonprofit community development corporations and for-profit developers to build low-income units, using funds secured from federal and local governments, foundations, corporations, and other sources. State money covers the difference between the construction cost and the sale price. Like most affordable housing developments in Philadelphia and Camden, these deals secure private investments mainly through the vehicle of Low Income Housing Tax Credits. The state program was established in response to the basic reality that in stagnant real estate markets in declining areas, it often costs more to build a new home than the finished house can be sold for on the market. For example, a Home Ownership Choice development in Pottstown (Montgomery County) included houses that cost $180,000 to build but sold for only $110,000. PHFA has subsidized similar developments in Coatesville (Chester County) and in the city of Chester (Delaware County), both older Urban Centers that have seen no new home construction in decades.

Reviving these older towns and boroughs has become a priority for anti-sprawl forces in the region, who point out the irony that many of these older main street communities are declining even as suburban developers promote neotraditional places: "The small cities and boroughs are the true traditional neighborhoods that developers are now building from scratch on farmland all over the country. They are the places in which people say they want to live where kids can walk or bike to school or the library and a quart of milk is not a car ride away."[49]

In addition to the Urban Centers of the region, other communities facing severe decline are many first-generation bedroom suburbs whose aging housing stocks are serving increasing numbers of low-income and working-class immigrants and families of color. Although the perception is often that these older suburbs have declined *because* of the arrival of new populations with more modest resources, studies have shown that the housing markets in these first-generation suburbs began to deteriorate *before* the population transition. Examining financial lenders' practices in Camden County, New Jersey, Neil Smith and his coauthors found that lenders have long denied home loans in suburban communities near the city of Camden, which has led to declining property values and made the housing accessible to lower-income households and families of color: "The pattern cannot be explained simply as the product of racial transition that leads to white flight but instead suggests that disinvestment *precedes* transition."[50]

Housing advocates in the region have championed revitalization in these older suburbs in a way that includes affordable housing. Moorestown Ecumenical Neighborhood Development, Inc. (MEND) is an affordable housing developer formed by nine churches in suburban Burlington County in 1969. Over thirty years, this organization has built more than 300 units of low- and moderate-income housing in infill developments. In recent years, MEND has chosen to develop properties in some of the older suburbs along the Delaware River situated near stations that serve the new light rail line, financing their work with a combination of funds from banks, Burlington County government, and a local developer.

Encouraging Housing Mobility

As we have seen, programs to improve housing in older disadvantaged neighborhoods have often led to the displacement of former residents. Where do they go? The Philadelphia Housing Authority's building campaign has shifted some of the displaced households away from its newly redeveloped units by giving them housing vouchers to look for rental housing from private landlords. These vouchers are funded through Section 8, the federal housing policy that promotes mobility for low-income households. It provides a rental voucher to families who qualify, giving them the ability to rent a housing unit wherever they can find a landlord who is willing to accept the Section 8 allowance as partial payment of the monthly rent. The program's creators aimed at deconcentrating poverty by allowing recipients to move into a neighborhood of their own choice rather than being assigned to a unit in a public housing project.

The Moving to Opportunity (MTO) experiment, begun in 1994 in five U.S. cities (not including Philadelphia), was undertaken to study differences between regular Section 8 tenants (who may use their vouchers anywhere and who often end up in high-poverty areas) versus an experimental group of Section 8 recipients who were *required* to use their housing vouchers to move to low-poverty neighborhoods and who received extra counseling that is not normally given to Section 8 tenants. A number of evaluations have been conducted in the five cities, several of them showing positive effects for the movers, at least in the short term. The MTO households that relocated to low-poverty neighborhoods appear to be safer from crime and drugs, their children are less likely to exhibit behavioral problems or be arrested, and they experience fewer injuries and fewer episodes of asthma.[51]

Starting in 1998, federal housing policy began encouraging local housing authorities to shift their poorest clients to Section 8 vouchers, moving them into the private market instead of housing them in the new generation of government-built projects that were intended for working poor families, sometimes, mixed with middle-class householders paying market prices.[52] PHA, following the federal lead, has been dispersing low-income residents away from massive housing projects as they have been demolished. Tenants have been given Section 8 vouchers that they have taken into other parts of the city, while PHA builds new projects for mixed- income tenants. Dispersing the poorest public housing tenants into residential neighborhoods has provoked opposition from neighborhood associations and even from politicians running for office. In Philadelphia, as in other cities, Section 8 is politically controversial because of its perceived negative impact on properties located near Section 8 housing units. At packed community meetings, residents have made clear that they want the mayor and the federal government to keep the program from hurting their neighborhoods. In several recent congressional campaigns, both Republican and Democrat candidates have singled out the Section 8 program as a neighborhood problem they would address if elected. One such candidate, who lost in two successive campaigns for the 13th Congressional District seat in the largely White northeast section of Philadelphia, was publicly labeled a racist for using racially charged rhetoric to imply that Section 8's minority tenants were the source of neighborhood problems. Her campaign was intended to appeal to long-time White residents who had seen growing numbers of African American, Latinos, Asian-American, and Eastern European immigrants moving into their area (by no means all of them with Section 8 vouchers).

Trying to test the common perception of Section 8's negative impacts, researchers in Baltimore showed that although Section 8 units had no damaging effect on surrounding property values in stable neighborhoods, concentrations of Section 8 units in declining neighborhoods did have an adverse effect on home sale prices. They could not be certain whether to attribute that finding to uncivil behavior of Section 8 tenants, poor property maintenance by Section 8 landlords, or race and class prejudice on the part of prospective buyers who ruled out purchasing homes in the neighborhood.[53]

Not all of Section 8's critics can be dismissed as racially biased. Philadelphia's African American mayor John Street criticized the program and pledged that "irresponsible tenants and landlords will not be allowed to disrupt neighborhoods by failing to maintain their properties or monitor the conduct of their tenants to the detriment of hardworking, taxpaying homeowners."[54] Responding to criticism from political leaders and community groups, PHA has increasingly focused the Section 8 program on the working poor by reserving half of all vouchers for low-income working families (the authority defines this favored group as families engaged in work at least twenty hours per week, families who have been trained and certified as "work ready" by local workforce development agencies, or those who are elderly, disabled, or veterans). Further, PHA now invests more resources in checking the criminal records of new tenants, inspecting properties where Section 8 tenants are renting, and deploying community relations staff to defuse neighborhood conflict.

PHA now proclaims that the goal of its Section 8 program is "to help low-income tenants toward home ownership . . . at PHA, we know that increasing the number of homeowners is key to revitalizing the city's neighborhoods"[55] In 2003 PHA announced plans to limit an individual's eligibility for Section 8 to only seven years (except the elderly and disabled), becoming only the second housing authority in the United States to place a limit on the tenure of its tenants. PHA has organized home ownership training programs to move tenants toward ownership, a move contested by low-income housing advocates who say that the time limit on rental assistance is based on unrealistic assumptions. When housing costs are compared with workers' earnings from low-wage jobs, there is a huge gap that no amount of home-ownership training can bridge: "The time limit is used to appease critics of the program but doesn't address the real concerns of people who can't compete in the marketplace."[56]

In theory, the Section 8 system should make it possible for at least some inner-city residents to rent housing in the suburbs. Such moves would not necessarily increase their job opportunities. (In Chapter 2 we acknowledged that proximity to good jobs does not translate automatically into better jobs for low-income workers.) However, the move would probably afford access to better schools, additional social networks, and many other advantages tied to place. But low-income households, even if they secure Section 8 vouchers, can exercise this option only if they can find rental units that are affordable when they combine the voucher with what they can afford to pay each month. Uncooperative landlords or high rents exclude voucher holders from many parts of the region, especially the fast-growing suburban job centers, where market demand for rental housing is strong enough that landlords are not motivated to accept Section 8 vouchers (and they are not required by law to accept them). And even if there are suburban landlords willing to accept Section 8 vouchers, a suburban housing authority that accepts the transfer of tenants from the central city must assign one of its scarce units of affordable housing to an outsider instead of a family on the local waiting list. Many suburban housing agencies have long waiting lists of local families who qualify for Section 8, and they give preference to people on their own waiting list over families who want to transfer. This friction between local housing authorities has led some commentators to argue that in metropolitan regions, the Section 8 program should no longer be administered by localities, but rather by a single, regional housing authority whose scope would match the geography of regional housing and labor markets.[57]

The picture for prospective *buyers* seeking affordable housing is no brighter than for prospective *renters* in the faster-growing, more affluent suburbs. Nonprofit developers have a difficult time finding sites to develop for affordable home building. Townships have adopted zoning ordinances that discourage low-end construction, and builders favor building expensive housing. Although a number of suburban county governments have been operating programs to help first-time buyers get into the private market to purchase a home, the number of homes bought under these programs from 2000 to 2005 actually declined by 60 percent.[58] Typically, these programs provide low- and moderate-income buyers with loans and grants to address down payments and closing costs. However, house prices have shot up so far in recent years that even with loans and grants (that in some counties can reach $17,000), prospective buyers with modest incomes cannot find affordable homes.

Compared to Pennsylvania, New Jersey has a more aggressive affordable housing policy that goes beyond offering help to homebuyers, to pressuring private developers to build a specific number of affordable units at the same time they are building market-rate housing in the suburbs. New Jersey's "inclusionary housing" policy was instigated by the court, forcing "largely unwilling localities—and a less-than enthusiastic state—to tackle social and racial integration."[59] In a 1983 judicial decision named for the suburb outside of Philadelphia where plaintiffs brought the initial lawsuit ("Mt. Laurel II"), the New Jersey Supreme Court directed suburban townships to grant development permission to builders who agreed to include within proposed projects an appropriate proportion of low- and moderate-income housing units. It was thus developers who drove the creation of affordable units in New Jersey towns, as part of the obligation they had to meet if they were to build market-priced units.

An example from Cherry Hill, an older suburban community that is almost entirely built out, shows how the Mt. Laurel court cases have been used by housing advocates to include affordable housing in redevelopment plans. When the Garden State Racetrack closed, a large parcel of land became available for redevelopment. The developer, who proposed a mix of 1,650 condominiums, retail space, offices, and open and civic space, initially wanted to satisfy the Mt. Laurel obligation by paying a fee instead of building affordable units, but the New Jersey Supreme Court insisted that the condominium development include 13 percent affordable units. In addition, the developer funded twenty-five more affordable units elsewhere in the township and donated $1.8 million to the town's affordable housing trust fund.

Although the Mt. Laurel court decision led to construction of thousands of affordable units in New Jersey suburban communities during the 1980s, researchers have noted that many of the state's wealthier suburbs have fulfilled their obligation by donating money to other municipalities to assume their assigned "fair share" responsibility. (This is legal under the Mt. Laurel framework.) Not surprisingly, the receiving jurisdictions in these "regional contribution agreements" tend to be poorer communities with more people of color. Even when wealthier White suburbs have built affordable units within their own boundaries, most of the units have been occupied by people who had previously lived in the suburbs rather than newcomers from central cities: "If the underlying social goals of the Mt. Laurel decision are held to be reducing urban-suburban disparities and fostering racial and economic integration within metropolitan regions, it has not substantially succeeded."[60]

Conclusion

Both of the policy approaches discussed above (i.e., redeveloping housing markets in older neighborhoods and moving disadvantaged residents to new neighborhoods) carry significant risks and disadvantages. Critics of the revitalization efforts in both Philadelphia and Camden point out that their avowed goal is to lure higher-income households into rebuilt areas, changing the population mix in those areas. Even when population change is not the explicit goal of redevelopment efforts, pumping major new investments into the housing markets in older neighborhoods often leads to increasing rents, house prices, and real estate taxes that make the area less affordable to long-time residents. Not since the 1970s has gentrification been viewed as a serious problem in Philadelphia's inner city, but in recent years some community organizations that spent the last decade or more struggling to improve their neighborhoods have begun to fear that the "positive" real estate trends they helped spawn are now threatening to displace established residents. In Camden, similar fears have fueled lawsuits against the state's ambitious redevelopment plan.

Policies that promote mobility also have drawbacks. The harshest critics of mobility strategies see these programs as having the harmful effect of "redirecting community development efforts away from the declining housing stock of poor neighborhoods and/or away from the poorer residents."[61] They associate mobility programs with neoconservative views of urban policy that "reduce efforts to improve the lives of poor people in place, and encourage (or force) their relocation."[62] Even advocates of housing mobility caution against overestimating its promise.

One reason not to overestimate the benefits of mobility, based on the federal experiments, is that volunteers who choose to move from disadvantaged neighborhoods to locations with greater resources are likely to be systematically different from people who do not choose to move. The fact that numerous evaluations have identified positive effects for members of the families that moved may reflect that the volunteers were more skilled, more ambitious, and more committed to improving life for their children, than the families who remained in place. These traits make them more likely to benefit from moving than other inner-city residents. In any case, taking mobility strategies to a larger scale has inherent limitations. The larger the scale of mobility programs, the more likely they are to excite political opposition. This has been amply demonstrated by efforts to increase the number of people using Section 8 vouchers to move into "non-impacted" neighborhoods.

Moreover, moving to a new housing unit, even one located in a low-poverty neighborhood, does not necessarily solve all the problems faced by disadvantaged families, and it may even create some new ones. Being able to afford to rent in a better-off neighborhood does not assure that public transit, day care, medical care, or a host of other services will be affordable, nor does it mean a network of family and friends can be as easily reached for personal and financial support. The main advantage it usually *does* grant is that children can attend better funded schools. In the next chapter, we turn to this crucial issue of improving educational opportunities.

4

EDUCATIONAL OPPORTUNITY

S chooling is key to acquiring the skills and credentials needed to take advantage of opportunities, from obtaining consumer goods and services at reasonable prices to participating in the larger culture and finding gainful employment. Increasingly, success in our information-based society depends on our ability to manage the avalanche of information confronting us in every domain of life, particularly in our jobs. Admittedly, not all occupational categories require increasing levels of education. In fact, some forms of technology are being used by employers to automate processes in ways that reduce the need to invest in human capital. However, there is little doubt that higher-paying occupations are demanding more and more education. Technological changes in the world of work confer increasing advantages on workers with higher educational attainment and disadvantages on those with lower education levels. The most direct measure of the advantages of education involves income differences: more educated people earn higher wages.

Researchers disagree somewhat on why this is true, some believing that the knowledge and skills obtained in school enhance the ability to perform valuable work, while others think that diplomas and degrees signal to employers that the graduate has demonstrated an ability to meet the challenges posed by teachers and tests and that this ability to "navigate in the system"—more than the knowledge obtained—is valued by employers. Whatever the explanation, there is no doubt that having more education increases a worker's chances for earnings.

Educational attainment, however, creates benefits beyond the level of individuals. In a knowledge economy, productivity growth within metropolitan areas is largely driven by shifts toward more skilled employment. Hence, the economic well-being of the region's population as a whole depends on broadly increasing the skill levels and productivity of the citizenry. As Chapter 2 showed, the economy operates regionally, with people commuting in many directions across local borders. In effect, every resident of the region, no matter where she or he lives, has a stake in the quality of the regional labor force, because that labor force is a commonly shared asset that affects the productivity of all of the region's employers. Yet the educational experiences and achievements of students in different communities are dramatically uneven.

How Do Educational Opportunities Differ across the Region?

To portray the differing levels of educational opportunity available in different parts of the region, we must first decide how to measure the quality of educational opportunity. Some studies have used measures of the resources applied to education, like expenditures per student or the student-teacher ratio. While these are important pieces of information about school districts, we believe a better measure of the quality of education in different communities is *student achievement,* which most consumers of public education see as the important consideration in choosing a school. When we surveyed households in the greater Philadelphia region about how they judged the quality of schools in their area, less than 4 percent of respondents cited the dollars spent per student as an indicator of school quality, but the most important indicator of quality was the percent of students graduating from area schools who go on to college—cited by 24 percent of respondents.[1] (Other important indicators of quality cited by our survey respondents included class size, up-to-date resources like computers and textbooks, and the proportion of students obtaining jobs after graduation.)

At least since the Coleman Report,[2] educators have known that an individual student's chances of succeeding are significantly higher when she or he is surrounded by high-performing students. The aspirations and achievements of a child's schoolmates represent an important component of the opportunity to learn and succeed. Following this logic, we chose to measure the quality of opportunity in different school districts according to a standardized measure of student achievement—namely, the average combined Scholastic Assessment Test (SAT) scores earned by high school students in the district.

Although SAT scores have well-known drawbacks as measures of individual student abilities, their virtue for our purpose is their standardization across schools and districts. Since the control of schools is local, most measures of school or student performance vary widely across places. Even where there are attempts to impose wider standards, as in the federal No Child Left Behind (NCLB) program, evaluation methods vary by state. As is typical in different states, New Jersey and Pennsylvania assess student performance differently. Thus we must look to the scant data that describe schools in standard terms. SAT scores do just that.

The SAT produces highly varied results in the different high schools of the region, even within a single county. Table 4.1 shows the average combined verbal and math SAT scores achieved by students enrolled in the highest-scoring and lowest-scoring high schools within counties. (It omits only Salem County, for which we do not have comparable data.) Each county contains over a dozen high schools serving communities with different student bodies. The widest gaps are seen in Philadelphia (which is both a city and a county in Pennsylvania's intergovernmental system), and in two other counties containing older urban places, Camden and Delaware counties. Philadelphia is especially marked by extremes, since it has the high school with the highest SAT average of any school in the region (1255) along with a high school producing the lowest average score (610).

Figure 4.1 shows the school districts in which students have been achieving combined SAT scores at or above the national average for suburban test takers (which was a combined math and verbal score of 1066); they are the darker shaded areas.[3] The lighter shaded areas are the school districts whose students scored below 1066.

Figure 4.1 shows a sizeable number of suburban communities whose students have not been attaining the national suburban average of 1066, a pattern that worries civic leaders in the region who focus on the quality of the regional workforce as the chief ingredient for economic growth. To be fair, a good number of the school districts scoring below the national suburban average are not "suburbs" in the conventional sense, but rather older towns with a

TABLE 4.1   AVERAGE COMBINED SAT SCORE (VERBAL AND MATH) REPORTED BY HIGH- AND LOW-SCORING HIGH SCHOOLS WITHIN EACH COUNTY, 2004

	Point		
	Highest	Lowest	Difference
Bucks County	1134	820	314
Chester County	1152	915	237
Delaware County	1181	705	476
Montgomery County	1199	914	285
Philadelphia	1255	610	645
Burlington County	1151	848	303
Camden County	1162	705	457
Gloucester County	1070	871	199

Source: "Report Card on the Schools," *Philadelphia Inquirer,* March 6, 2005.

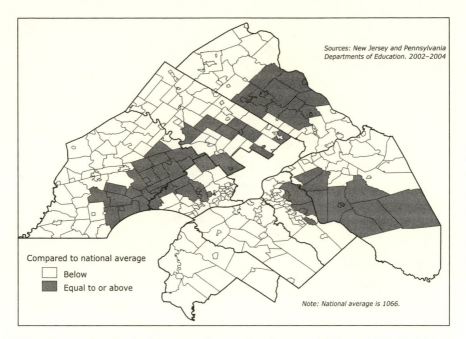

FIGURE 4.1   Districts with SAT scores above national average, 2002–2004.

more urban than suburban character. That is the case for a number of the communities lining the Delaware River on both sides. It would perhaps be fairer to compare their SAT scores with the national average that the College Board reports for small cities or towns. Yet on that basis, the region's older towns, many of which produce scores below 1000, fall short of the national average of 1010 for small cities or towns. Average scores in the two major urban centers of the region, Philadelphia and Camden, are only 828 and 763, respectively, compared with a national average of 1000 for large cities. In sum, we see wide variations in student achievement across different communities and a significant number of school districts lagging behind national averages.

One explanation for lagging scores in public schools may be the region's unusually large number of students attending private high schools, which typically report higher SAT scores than do public high schools. When *Philadelphia Magazine* listed the region's fifty highest-scoring private high schools alongside the fifty highest-scoring public schools, the average score for the private schools (1168) was 86 points higher than for the public schools (1082).[4] The popularity of private education may be removing enough high-scoring students from public high schools to depress the public schools' scores. We will examine private schooling later in the chapter.

Perhaps the most direct predictor of any school district's SAT performance

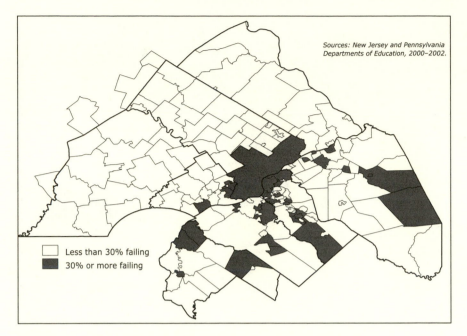

FIGURE 4.2   Districts with high failure rates on reading tests, 2000–2002.

is the achievement level of that same district's students in prior grades. We investigated the performance of 8th grade students across the region on standardized reading tests. Although the states of Pennsylvania and New Jersey administer different tests, both try to determine whether students are performing at appropriate grade levels. Figure 4.2 displays the school districts in which 30 percent or more of 8th grade students received test scores below expectations for their grade.[5] It is almost a mirror image of the previous map. Where 8th grade failure rates are highest, high school seniors score below the national average on the SAT. The districts with high failure rates either serve inner suburbs like those of eastern Delaware County or the towns adjacent to Camden, or they serve outlying older towns with working class or poor populations like Coatesville, Chester, and Norristown on the Pennsylvania side and Glassboro, Burlington City, and Mt. Holly on the New Jersey side.

Race and Class and Differential Access to High-Performing Schools

Many researchers have documented the profound influence that a child's family background has on her or his school performance. However, since our focus is on how *communities* affect opportunity, we will examine how the so-cioeconomic composition of communities is related to student performance. For this part of the analysis, we will use two measures of a high performing school: (1) districts with average SAT scores above the 80th percentile of all districts in the region and (2) districts with average SAT scores above the 90th percentile of all districts in the region. The first measure identifies districts that scored at or above 1068 and the second taps districts that scored above 1100.[6]

To assess the effects of socioeconomic status, we measure two community characteristics: (1) educational attainment of a district's population and (2) median household income. Although these characteristics are highly correlated with each other at the level of school districts, they measure different aspects of socioeconomic status and are differentially predictive. Table 4.2 shows that the effects exerted on our SAT measures by high incomes and college-educated adult populations could hardly be more dramatic: all of the eleven districts that rank at the 90th percentile are districts with highly educated, high-earning populations, and all but one of those in the 80th percentile have similar educational and income characteristics.

The effects of a community's educational and income profile remain significant predictors of SAT scores even when we control for other factors presumed to affect SAT scores. Table 4.3 reports an analysis that took into account several alternative explanations or confounding factors. Those variables that could affect SAT scores include district population size, the percentage of district students taking the SATs, the percentage of students in private schools,

TABLE 4.2   NUMBER OF DISTRICTS WITH SAT SCORES IN
THE 80TH AND 90TH PERCENTILES BY EDUCATION AND
HOUSEHOLD INCOME, PHILADELPHIA METROPOLITAN
AREA, 2002*

	80th Percentile	90th Percentile
Percent of Adults Aged 25 or older with BA+		
32%+	22	11
17.1%–31.9%	1	0
15.1%–17%	0	0
≤15%	0	0
Percent of Households with Incomes of $75,000+		
40%+	21	10
30.1%–39.9%	1	0
20.1%–30%	1	1
≤20%	0	0

*SAT scores are the averages for the years 2001–2003.
Sources: New Jersey and Pennsylvania Departments of Education, 2001–2003;
National Center for Educational Statistics, *Common Core of Data*, 2003.

TABLE 4.3   EFFECT ON SAT SCORE OF A ONE-UNIT CHANGE
OF VARIABLE, CONTROLLING FOR THE OTHER VARIABLES

Percent BA+	2.78*
Percent of Households $75,000+	1.11**
Percent taking SAT	.10
Percent in Private School	−1.64*
School Expenditures per Student	.00
Property Taxes per Student	.00
Population	.00
Percent African American Households	−2.28*
R^2	.86
(N)	(111)

*Statistically significant at the .01 level.
**Statistically significant at the .05 level.
Sources: U.S. Census, Summary File 3, 2000; National Center for Educational
Statistics, *Common Core of Data,* 2005.

school expenditures per student, and property taxes per student. We included the population size of the district on the grounds that districts' capabilities vary with size. The percentage of a district's students who took the SAT reflects the fact that districts with a lower percentage of test takers tend to have troubled school systems. The percentage of students in private schools is included because private schools tend to draw away the better students and thus lower average SAT scores in local public schools. We also controlled for school expenditures per student. And finally, we controlled for property taxes per students. Here the measure reflects the resources potentially available for spending on students' education.

To highlight the effects of these variables, Table 4.3 reports the gain or loss of SAT points associated with a one-unit change of any particular variable, controlling for all the other variables. Thus, we see that if the percentage of persons with a bachelor's degree or graduate degree in a school district were to increase from 29 (which is the average for all school districts) to 30, the combined SAT score achieved by its high school students would improve on average by 2.78 points. By comparison, if the percentage of households with incomes above $75,000 were to increase by one point, the average SAT score would only go up by 1.11 points. In other words, the effect of the educational level of the school district is 2.5 times more powerful than the effect of the household income level in the district.

It is often asserted that those school districts that spend more money achieve better educational outcomes. Yet the information in Table 4.3 does not confirm that assumption. When we take the other factors into account, spending per student does not have a statistically significant impact on SAT scores. Some higher-spending districts are the ones that pay higher salaries to attract better teachers, offer a wide variety of programs, and provide their students with richer resources. However, other high-spending districts are those with lesser- quality schools; their spending rates are high because of their higher costs for security, school maintenance, multiple language classes, special education, and compensatory programs. Thus high expenditures are not necessarily associated with high test scores. Similarly, Table 4.3 reveals that the effect of property taxes per student is statistically insignificant. The kinds of costs that districts confront vary widely depending upon their mix of students, the age of their buildings, and their locations. Those factors appear to diminish the expected correlation between dollar resources and SAT scores. (We examine the factors affecting school spending later in the chapter.)

In addition, Table 4.3 reveals that a school district's racial composition has a statistically significant negative effect on SAT scores that is independent of our measures of socioeconomic status and the control variables. In other words, the effect of the racial composition of the district is notable and cannot be explained by the educational and income levels of the district, its population size, the percentage of students taking the SAT, the percentage of students in private school, the expenditures per student, or the property taxes per student. After all these factors are taken into account, a 1 percent increase in the percentage of African American households is associated with a decrease of 2.28 points in average SAT score.

Within districts, the average test scores of African American and Latino youths tend to be lower than the scores of their White school mates. Consider, for example, the results of a 2004 standardized 11th grade reading test administered in all Pennsylvania high schools. In order to capture those communities with substantial African American school populations, we limit our review to the dozen school districts in the Philadelphia suburbs that were serving at least fifty African American 11th graders in 2004. In those dozen school districts, the proportion of students scoring "Below Basic" proficiency level in reading (essentially, reading below their grade level) was consistently 20 points larger for African American youths than for White youths in the same district. The percent of White students scoring Below Basic hovered between 16 and 28 percent, whereas the percent of African American students scoring Below Basic ranged between 36 and 48 percent.[7]

One explanation for these racial gaps in test performance in the 11th grade may be that African American and White high school students often enter high school with very different educational experiences at lower grade levels. Even within the same school district, elementary schools may contain racially different student bodies. An analysis in 2004 of elementary schools in the Philadelphia suburbs examined these school-by-school differences. It calculated the proportion of elementary school pupils who would have to be moved to a different school in order to make the racial balance within each elementary school the same as the racial balance across the school district to which that particular school belonged. The analysis identified *twenty* suburban districts where more than one-quarter of all the elementary students would have to enroll in a different school in order to create the same racial balance within each school as prevailed across the district.[8] Other researchers have discovered that racial segregation of *neighborhoods* may be more important in explaining gaps in African American–White test scores than the composition of the *school's* student body. A national study showed that while both school segregation by race and neighborhood segregation by race have negative effects on the test scores of African American students, in the end "neighborhood composition matters more than school composition."[9]

The Relationship of Housing Markets to Schools

Numerous researchers have observed that educational quality and housing values are mutually reinforcing: the quality of housing affects schools and a school district's reputation affects housing values. We have already seen in this chapter that household income and the educational attainment of adult populations strongly predict children's school performance. So we would expect in communities with higher-priced housing, affordable only to households with above-average incomes, to see children performing at higher-than-average levels. We know from the previous chapter that housing submarkets in the region are highly stratified. Chapter 3 described the dramatic differences in housing density, housing types, and prices in different communities. Different school districts serve feeder areas that house very different populations of residents, and we would expect student performance to vary accordingly in these communities.

To examine the relationships between housing markets and educational quality, we identified the twenty communities in the region with the highest and lowest house prices. If educational quality is strongly associated with housing markets, then these different submarkets should exhibit different educational profiles, as measured by SAT scores, expenditures per student, and pupil-teacher ratios. Table 4.4 provides a glimpse of how this relationship operates. We measured housing prices using the average value of mortgage loans made in these communities over a five-year period (2000–2004). After determining the twenty highest- and lowest-ranking mortgage values, we examined several housing and educational characteristics of those same communities. Not surprisingly, the table shows that higher value and better quality housing markets (i.e., those with the lowest proportion of sub-prime loans, newer housing, and highest mortgage values) are associated with higher SAT scores (almost 240 points higher) and a differential of nearly $4,000 per pupil in educational expenditures. One surprise in Table 4.4 is that communities with more expensive housing have a *less* favorable pupil-teacher ratio than do communities with lower-priced housing. We interpret those high pupil-teacher ratios to be the result of much higher educational demand in high-priced housing markets. Other characteristics of the housing market as well, such as the age of the housing stock and the proportion of mortgages that are subprime loans, are also related to differences in educational performance.

These data suggest that house prices are associated with school performance, but they do not explain exactly how. For one thing, communities with higher house prices have socioeconomic profiles that alone account for some of the difference in SAT scores. Research examining the choices made by high-status families suggests that they often choose the neighborhoods and schools they prefer largely on the basis of informal judgments about "good schools" that they hear expressed by other parents of similar socioeconomic status (see also Chapter 5). Many parents assume that when other parents of their own social status have chosen a particular school district (and perhaps even a particular school feeder area), it signals a "good school" for their own children. In effect they are relying on the social status of the district's (or the individual school's) student body to signal the quality of the program.[10]

Another reason for the association of housing values and educational performance is that homebuyers are willing to pay more for a house where they see favorable indicators of educational success, such as high test scores and college admission rates. There is considerable research suggesting that high-performing schools attract home buyers.[11] The resulting competition for housing in these communities drives the housing market, with at least one outcome being higher housing values. Affluent communities can, and do, invest more in the community's educational system. At the other end of the spectrum, in housing submarkets where communities have lost population in the last five decades, housing markets have suffered. In a downward cycle, educational support typically shrinks and educational quality in turn erodes.

To investigate the effects of school performance on housing markets, we ranked school districts according to their three-year average SAT score and

TABLE 4.4   HOUSING AND EDUCATIONAL CHARACTERISTICS OF HIGHEST AND LOWEST TWENTY RANKED (BY AVERAGE MORTGAGE AMOUNT) COMMUNITIES, 2000–2004

	Average Mortgage ($)	Sub-Prime (%)	Average Age	Five-Year SAT	Education Expenditure per Pupil ($)	Pupil-Teacher Ratio
Lowest	67,608	16.1	1946	868	6,763	14.7
Highest	296,375	2.8	1973	1106	10,629	15.1

Sources: New Jersey and Pennsylvania Departments of Education, 2001–2004; National Center for Educational Statistics, *Common Core of Data*, 2001–2004; U.S. Census, Summary File 3, 2000; Federal Financial Institutions Examination Council, Home Mortgage Disclosure Act Data, 2000–2004.

examined housing patterns associated with them, again comparing the top and bottom twenty ranked communities (see Table 4.5). (This reverses the view we previously took in Table 4.4., which looked at how housing values may drive school performance.) As expected, there continues to be a wide disparity between the average mortgage amounts found in school districts with the top SAT scores compared with communities with the lowest scores, but the gap is somewhat smaller. Educational quality appears from this to produce higher-value housing markets but not as unequivocally as might be expected.

Note that residential mobility—measured by the proportion of households in a community that had moved into their current home within the previous five years (according to 2000 census data) —is about the same in both types of communities. The key distinction between high-ranked and low-ranked districts is the proportion of households that had moved into the communities during the previous five years *from outside*. Only 5 percent of the newcomers in high-ranked communities had moved from other homes inside the same town, whereas in lower-ranked communities, almost 30 percent of movers had come from locations within the same town.

Some of this migration pattern is driven by the realities of regional housing markets. Compared to the lower-performing districts, the highest-performing districts have newer housing stocks; more than twice the proportion of all housing units are new. This is true for both owner-occupied units and rental units. It suggests that communities still in the process of developing, whose land area contains options for building new housing, are more likely to exhibit high housing prices and higher educational performance.

These are only aggregate patterns. If we look at the specific educational, housing, and mobility characteristics of those school districts that rank among the highest twenty or the lowest twenty by SAT scores (see Appendix 3), we can find exceptions to these generalizations. For instance, among the low SAT group, the Coatesville Regional District shows strikingly higher housing prices than other school districts with low SAT scores (a mean mortgage amount of

TABLE 4.5   EDUCATIONAL, HOUSING, AND MOBILITY CHARACTERISTICS OF HIGHEST-AND LOWEST-RANKED SCHOOL DISTRICTS (AVERAGE SAT SCORES, 2001–2004)

	Average SAT Score	Pupil-Teacher Ratio	Education Expenditure per Pupil ($)	Average Purchase Mortgage ($)	Moved since 1995 (%)	Moved: Same Town (%)	New Units, Owner (%)	New Units, Renter (%)*
Lowest	886	13.9	11,282	104,685	37.4	29.9	3	2
Highest	1,118	14.7	11,439	204,530	40.8	5.2	7	5

Sources: New Jersey and Pennsylvania Departments of Education, 2001–2004; National Center for Educational Statistics, *Common Core of Data,* 2001–2004; U.S. Census, Summary Tape File 3, 2000; U.S. Census, Summary File 3, 2000; Federal Financial Institutions Examination Council, Home Mortgage Disclosure Act Data, 2002–2004.

$137,196 compared to the average of $104,685). That is because the Coatesville Regional District contains many communities that have shown recent housing growth (8 percent of owner-occupied housing is new, compared to an average of 3 percent). Among the higher SAT scoring districts, the range in average mortgage amounts is wide, ranging from only $148,520 in Jenkintown to over $365,000 in Radnor. Also, it is apparent that newer housing stock is found in only *some* of the communities with high SAT scores; other high-performing districts like Cheltenham, Jenkintown, and Haddonfield contain little open land for new construction.

These anomalies draw our attention to a generally unrecognized aspect of the relationship between school quality and housing markets. School quality has an inertial dimension that is rarely acknowledged when researchers examine the association between schools and housing prices. Both the school districts that show low test performance and those that score higher have long histories of educational investment that continue to influence educational quality over the long term (positively and negatively), regardless of the current vicissitudes of local housing markets. Some established communities with a long tradition of good schools show little property appreciation because there is little housing turnover. Such communities with extremely stable housing markets confound the general assumption that high test scores drive property appreciation.

What then are we to conclude about the argument that good schools drive housing markets? The data we have examined suggest that there is a persistent association between higher value housing and school quality. However, an important qualifier needs to be considered—it is that households that can afford to live in the high-priced housing markets are the same households whose children are likely to experience academic success. The corollary is that households with only limited residential choices are more likely to be households whose children struggle in school. The relative importance of these two factors in drawing new families to move into communities is a subject to which we will return in Chapter 5.

Decoupling School Choice from Housing Choice

The discussion so far assumes that families exercise educational choices via their housing choices. But what about families whose incomes are too modest to allow them to secure better schooling by moving to high-priced neighborhoods? Such families are often confined to urban neighborhoods that offer the advantage of affordable housing, coupled with the disadvantage of weak public schools. Their plight has prompted reformers to seek options beyond the neighborhood school to which families are automatically assigned—in other words, to break the geographic framework of conventional public education. Proponents of school choice believe that widening educational options will ensure that parents are not forced to keep their children in failing neighborhood schools, but instead they can seek schools that better serve their needs. Educational choice, they point out, is an advantage that well-to-do families have long enjoyed, gaining entry for their children into good schools by moving to suburban housing markets or by paying private school tuitions. There is growing sentiment in many parts of the country in favor of granting lower-income parents more choices as a matter of equity.[12]

These ideas of choice and mobility are built into the federal No Child Left Behind (NCLB) law, under which children in schools that are underperforming are supposed to be given the option of transferring to higher-performing schools. NCLB requires that school districts spend up to 20 percent of their allotment of federal Title I money to pay for extra tutoring or transportation to take pupils to schools other than their neighborhood schools. Up to now, the small number of such transfers that have taken place in Philadelphia all have occurred within the city school district. The federal law permits, but does not require, suburban districts to accept transfers from underperforming schools within the city. Most suburban districts are reluctant to accept transfers. In 2004 the Philadelphia district reported that 142,000 pupils were eligible to be transferred from underperforming schools within the city, but only 135 students actually transferred, partly because the district simply could not find enough open places at higher-performing schools. Fully two-thirds of Philadelphia schools had failed to meet their targets for yearly improvement for at least two years in a row and therefore had to offer students the transfer option, leaving only one-third of the city's schools eligible to accept transfers. We should perhaps not be surprised that in many "failing" schools, only a small number of eligible families have actually requested transfers. Parents may well recognize there are no viable alternatives for students to choose. For example, students who attend the only high school in the troubled Chester-Upland district have the right to transfer, but there is no eligible school within the district to which they could transfer.[13] This is a significant point for most of the 183 school districts that serve the 353 municipalities of the region: all but about a dozen districts have only one high school; consequently, there is scant possibility for transferring. There are only two alternatives currently: (1) enrollment in a private school or (2) organizing a charter school.

For several decades, school officials have promoted various forms of choice within the public system—for example, by opening magnet schools organized around instructional themes such as technology, the performing arts, science and mathematics. Originally intended in the 1970s to help desegregate schools, magnet schools are now promoted to retain middle-class children in urban districts. More recently, a growing array of choices within the public school system is provided by the charter school movement. Charter schools are new public schools created by groups of interested parents, teachers, college professors, and others who commit themselves to certain educational goals and results in exchange for a waiver from most state and local regulations. Free of many union and regulatory limits, charters are intended to promote more flexible curriculum and practices.

Local districts pay the cost of establishing new charter schools out of the regular district budget, diverting funds that would otherwise support existing public schools. For example, from 2004 to 2005 the Philadelphia School District disbursed about $6,500 to charter schools for every Philadelphia student enrolled in the charters. While this diversion of public funds might seem reasonable—after all, the charters are taking responsibility for students who would otherwise be served by the existing schools—it is nevertheless resented by many teachers, administrators, and parents.

Despite that diversion of funds, the Philadelphia district embraced charter schools more enthusiastically than might have been expected. By the 2005–2006 school year, fifty-five charter schools served 26,000 pupils. This number, reflecting the decisions made by parents of tens of thousands of school children, shows evidence of the level of dissatisfaction with the performance of neighborhood schools. One reason for the district's cooperation in such a massive shift of resources may be that school administrators believe offering more choices to parents will help keep students in the public school system.

In both Pennsylvania and New Jersey, the largest number of charter schools can be found in older school districts with lower student performance. Like private schools, charter schools are more numerous in the older, financially strapped districts than in more affluent communities. Philadelphia, which has far more charters than anyplace else in Pennsylvania, enrolls over 10 percent of its public school students in these alternative schools. The school district with the single highest proportion of its student population in charter schools serves the distressed city of Chester, where parents have sought an alternative to public schools that are failing their children.

Our analysis of charter school patterns in the city of Philadelphia suggests that families that have opted for charter schools have improved the educational environments for their youngsters. To arrive at this conclusion, we used pupil address data to identify the neighborhood public school that every charter student would otherwise be attending if that family had not opted for a charter school. We collected data on several important performance indicators that describe the learning environments prevailing within schools: reading and math scores on standardized tests at 5th, 8th, and 11th grades, school crime rates, and school suspension rates. We then applied those indicators to both the charter schools and the neighborhood public schools that students would otherwise be attending. The results are compared in Figure 4.3, which shows that charter school students, on average, are in higher-performing schools and safer learning environments than the schools they would otherwise be attending in their neighborhoods.

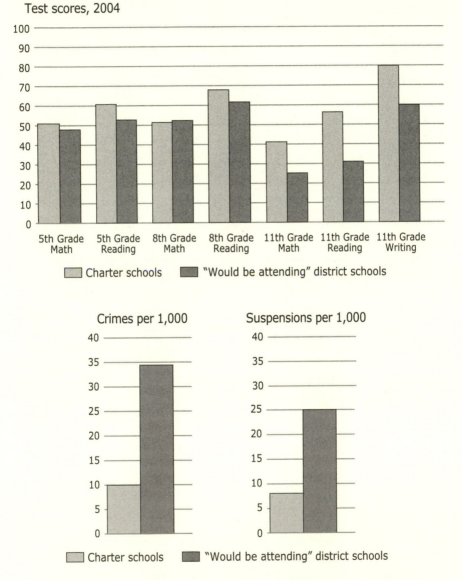

Ira Goldstein, "Charter Schools," Philadelphia: The Reinvestment Fund, 2004.

FIGURE 4.3   Charter schools versus "would be attending" schools, 2004.

National research on charter schools shows strong evidence of parental satisfaction with charter schools,[14] but what about the academic performance of individual students enrolled in charters? Have charter schools been shown to improve academic performance? The available research paints a complex picture. Numerous charter schools have been judged as failing to meet their targets for yearly improvement, yet their record is somewhat better than traditional public schools. About half of Philadelphia's charter schools (compared with two-thirds of the city's traditional schools) were classified as failing to make Adequate Yearly Progress in 2004.[15] A statewide evaluation in Pennsylvania showed that while charter schools appear to have a "modestly positive influence" on student achievement, they routinely report lower test scores than public schools. The explanation may be that "charter schools appear to be attracting students with lower-than-average achievement levels," and therefore the gains that charter students are making still do not place them at average performance levels.[16]

In theory, school choice should push school administrators to create innovative, effective programs in order to attract enrollments. However, one national researcher has observed that charter schools seek to improve their market position mainly by recruiting particular kinds of students rather than by producing innovative curriculum.[17] Since there is evidence that parents often make school choices based on the character and composition of the student body (i.e., who else attends the school) rather than on systematic information about the curriculum, it is not surprising to learn that in a competitive educational marketplace, schools are marketing themselves based on student body characteristics as much as program quality. We would expect such marketing practices to contribute to sorting of students by class, race, ethnicity, and other characteristics that parents use as signals when choosing schools for their children. And in fact, a study that examined student transfers in Philadelphia found that White families tend to avoid transferring their children to schools that serve a large number of African American students, no matter what the school's class composition is.[18]

While critics of charters argue that charter schools may actually harm public schools—not only by siphoning money from the public school district but also by removing the best-performing students—some researchers studying open enrollment within the Chicago Public Schools found that when high-ability students transfer out of neighborhood schools, the remaining students *do not* appear to have been hurt by the loss of their peers. They concluded that "open enrollment apparently benefits those students who take advantage of having access to vocational programs without harming those who do not."[19] The Chicago study is one of only a few that systematically evaluate the results of charter schools. Although increasing numbers of urban students are enrolling in charter schools, there is relatively little evidence about the positive or negative effects that charter schools may have on either the students who choose them or the students who remain in traditional neighborhood schools. With respect to improving both the *quality* and *equality* of education, researchers have had insufficient time to measure the success of charter schools. Based on our findings reported earlier in this chapter that school performance appears to track school demographics, we would predict that the charter experiment will not assure higher test scores for pupils unless school choice leads to mixing income groups in the schools.

Private Schools: Choices beyond Public Schools

Long before charter schools were established to provide school choice, Philadelphia families were exercising options through private schools. Compared to other metropolitan areas, a substantially larger proportion of families living in greater Philadelphia have traditionally opted to send children to private schools (Table 4.6). The numbers are largest within the city of Philadelphia, where as many as 30 percent of school-age children attend private schools. However, a surprisingly large proportion of suburban school children as well are enrolled in private schools. In more than sixty suburban districts surrounding Philadelphia, over 20 percent of youngsters have chosen private education. In the New Jersey suburbs, private schools are less popular; few districts have private schools serving as many as 10 percent of children, and none reaches as high as 20 percent.[20]

Philadelphia has a long history of providing private schools going back to 1689 when a group of the city's Quakers hired their first schoolmaster. They secured a school charter from William Penn in 1701 to operate a system of schools throughout the city that charged tuition but also provided for families who could not afford to pay tuition. Shortly after the American Revolution,

TABLE 4.6   PERCENTAGE OF SCHOOL-AGE STUDENTS ATTENDING PRIVATE SCHOOLS IN SELECTED METROPOLITAN AREAS, 2000

Baltimore	16
Boston	13
Chicago	14
Cleveland	17
Detroit	11
Minneapolis	11
Philadelphia	20
Phoenix	6
Pittsburgh	12

Source: U.S. Census, Summary File 3, 2000.

local Anglicans founded the first Episcopal academy.[21] By the opening years of the nineteenth century, private schools were still the only option for Philadelphia families, but by that time an early voucher plan existed by which private schools could admit poor children for free and then apply to the city commissioners for reimbursements. Not until 1818 did Philadelphia's city government establish free public schools, and then only as a way of educating the poor. Pauperism was actually an entrance qualification for these early public schools.

These days, of course, public schools are mandated to serve children from all classes. So it is interesting to see which socioeconomic groups choose to send their children to private schools. In the Philadelphia region, families in many different social circumstances opt for private schools. Serving some of the most affluent families of the region, exclusive private schools and established Quaker and Catholic schools have enrolled several generations of the same family. It may surprise readers to know that in some of the region's most affluent suburbs, which generously fund their public schools, more than one-third of all school-age children bypass the public schools to attend private schools. However, it would be a mistake to think of private schools as serving only wealthy families. In the region's two core cities, Catholic schools comprise the largest number of private schools, operated by the Philadelphia Archdiocese and Camden Diocese on the New Jersey side. As Table 4.7 shows, the Philadelphia Archdiocese ranks behind only Chicago in the number of children its schools serve.

The sheer numbers of children enrolled in the urban Catholic school systems in Table 4.7 make clear that the interest in private schools extends beyond the well-to-do. We can confirm this with findings from our household survey, which asked parents of children currently enrolled in public schools whether they would like to send their daughters and sons to private schools (see Table 4.8). As expected, the number expressing that view was highest—55 percent—in the Urban Centers of the region. Yet even in the region's Affluent

TABLE 4.7   STUDENT ENROLLMENT BY URBAN ARCHDIOCESE, 1994–1995 AND 2004–2005

	1994–1995	2004–2005	Change (%)
Chicago	140,209	106,738	−24
Philadelphia	122,982	104,128	−15
Cleveland	65,433	57,272	−12
Boston	53,745	51,067	−5
Detroit	58,346	43,645	−25
St. Paul/Minneapolis	33,283	37,910	+14
Baltimore	33,821	36,030	+7
Pittsburgh	37,154	26,146	−30
Phoenix	n/a	14,258	n/a

Source: D. McDonald, *U.S. Catholic Elementary and Secondary Schools, 2004–2005: The Annual Statistical Report.* Washington, D.C.: National Catholic Educational Association, 2005.

Suburbs, 20 percent of respondents said they would like to send their children to private schools if they could.

Why do so many families choose private schools? This is a subject of debate in the literature, with some observers contending that racial and religious factors are the primary influences on parents' decisions,[22] while others have correlated private school enrollment with parents' judgments about the comparative quality of education in public versus private schools.[23] This is a debate we cannot resolve. Those who see the choice for private education as a choice in favor of higher-performing schools can point to research showing that private school enrollments tend to be higher in school districts plagued by low test scores and graduation rates, but it is not always clear which way causation is operating. Do more families enroll their children in private school because of lower test scores in public schools? Or are public school test scores lower because private schools have "creamed" off the higher-performing students? The question is unsettled. Additional questions can be raised about research showing that on standardized tests, students in private schools typically score above their peers in public schools. In one case, the very study that identified this performance difference also showed that the difference disappeared once the researchers had taken account of the students' socioeconomic status, race, and disability status.[24] This suggests that it is the composition of the student body rather than the instructional quality that accounts for higher performance measures in private schools.

Those who see the choice in favor of private schools resulting from parents' effort to distance their children from minority or lower-income children can demonstrate that private school enrollments are highest in urban districts with large minority populations. However, those districts also typically contain many underperforming schools, schools with which parents of all races are dissatisfied. This raises the possibility that it is the schools' instructional failures that have prompted families to opt for private education. That motivation could explain why so many African American families have chosen to enroll their children in private schools. There is in fact some evidence that African American students gain more benefits from private school enrollments than other groups of students gain.[25]

TABLE 4.8   PERCENTAGE OF HOUSEHOLDS NOT SENDING
CHILDREN TO PRIVATE SCHOOLS BUT WOULD LIKE TO, 2004

Urban Centers	55
Established Towns	insufficient responses
Stable Working Communities	20
Middle-Class Suburbs	22
Affluent Suburbs	20

Source: Philadelphia Metropolitan Area Survey. Philadelphia: Temple University, 2004.

It has even been suggested that the city's many private schools might become options under NCLB. Although the U.S. Supreme Court's 2002 decision in *Zelman v. Simmons-Harris* opened up the possibility that public school district funds could be channeled to families choosing to enroll their children in private religious schools, neither Pennsylvania nor New Jersey has adopted voucher programs to do so. (In that decision, the Supreme Court upheld the ability of Ohio to furnish Cleveland families with vouchers they could use at private schools of the parent's choosing, including religious schools, as a way of implementing a school desegregation decree.) Several school voucher proposals introduced into the Pennsylvania legislature during the 1990s failed to gain enough support to become law. So there is currently no government subsidy for parents to send their children to private schools in the region. It is worth noting, however, that one Philadelphia superintendent has considered the possibility that the city's Catholic schools might provide an option for families whose children are enrolled in schools labeled as low-performing under the federal NCLB Act. That superintendent observed, "The mandate from the federal government was to seek out and expand school choice options by approaching other districts, both public and private. The Archdiocese (of Philadelphia) is another school system in the city."[26]

Clearly, the debates about what fuels private school attendance cannot be resolved here. What seems incontestable, however, is that private schools cream the school population within districts, systematically attracting the higher-income students whose families can afford to pay tuition.[27] The fact that the Philadelphia region has such a large private school sector, we suspect, contributes to the disappointing test scores in many public schools.

Inequalities in School Spending

Spending levels differ dramatically among school districts in this region, as shown in Figure 4.4. From 2003 to 2004, spending per student ranged from less than $7,000 to a high of $20,059. A cluster of affluent communities at the intersection of Montgomery, Delaware, and Chester counties supported the largest concentration of high-spending schools in the region. In New Jersey, spending levels were generally lower. However, it is worthwhile noting that among the higher-spending communities in the region were five that have been designated as "Abbott" districts by the state of New Jersey; they are among several dozen districts across the state whose tax bases have been deemed insufficient to finance local schools. By allocating disproportionate aid to these districts, the state government has been supporting a higher rate of spending for their schools than for other districts on the New Jersey side of the river. (We will return to the Abbott districts later in this chapter.)

What accounts for these dramatic variations in school spending? We would expect that a district's population size, racial composition, educational attainment, income, private school attendance, and tax levels all would affect expenditure levels. There is ample evidence that the largest districts are often troubled and have inadequate tax bases. For example, comparisons are often made between central city and suburban districts to show that affluent suburban districts typically spend far more per student than central city districts. The racial composition of a district also plays a role inasmuch as African Americans live with a legacy of racial segregation that has left them concentrated in older, deteriorated former manufacturing centers that have yet to recover from decades of economic decline and abandonment by middle- and upper-middle- class Whites. Educational attainment is a factor since the higher a district's educational level, the more likely its residents will press for quality in its schools and be willing to pay for it. Similarly, the higher the income of households, the more they want quality schools and have the means to pay for them. (However, we remind readers that the relationship between incomes and expenditures is not simple: school districts with a substantial population in poverty often incur significant expenditures because the poor require remedial programs that are costly.) Private school enrollments may affect public school expenditures because the higher the percentage of stu-

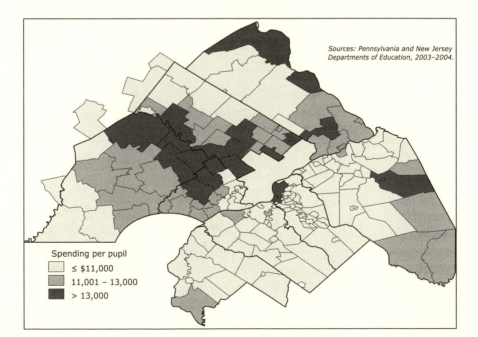

FIGURE 4.4   School spending per student, 2003–2004.

dents in private schools, the more the public school boards are likely to see themselves competing with them; consequently, they are likely to be willing to spend money to meet the competition. Since expenditures require tax levels to support them, higher *taxes* per student permit higher *expenditures* per student. Finally, expenditures are likely to be higher in newly developing areas because rapidly growing populations need new and expanded schools to serve them.

We examine the validity of these expectations in Table 4.9, which reveals a mixed and complex picture. The strongest influence on expenditures per student is the educational level of the district's adults; every additional percent of those with a bachelor's degree or graduate degree increases expenditures by $63.01 per student. In contrast, the percentage of households with incomes of $75,000 or more has no statistically significant impact on expenditures. But at the opposite end of the income distribution, a 1 percent gain in the share of households with incomes under 150 percent of the poverty line pushes up expenditures by almost $54 per student. Considered in connection with the analysis of SAT scores earlier in this chapter, it appears that school district performance and expenditures are, in socioeconomic terms, largely a function of the educational attainment of a district's adult population. The impact of the community's income is substantially more modest and more complex. Perhaps unexpectedly, the racial composition of the district has no statistically significant effect on expenditures, once the other variables are taken into account. Given the relatively high correlation between the percentage of households that are African American and the percentage whose incomes are less than 150 percent of the poverty line (.711), these results suggest that a "race effect" is often the result of inadequate controls for socioeconomic status.

What differences for children result from the substantial inequality in spending that we have described? Earlier in this chapter we found that once we

TABLE 4.9   EFFECT ON EXPENDITURES PER STUDENT OF
A ONE-UNIT CHANGE IN VARIABLE, CONTROLLING
FOR OTHER VARIABLES

Percent BA+	$63.01*
Percent of Households $75,000+	−$24.21
Percent of Families < 150% of Poverty Line	$53.87**
Percent in Private School	$49.03*
Percent New Residents since 1995	−$6.35
Property Taxes per Student (in hundreds)	$21.20*
Population (in thousands)	−$1.00*
Percent African American Households	$9.78
R^2	.47
(N)	(111)

*Statistically significant at the .01 level.
**Statistically significant at the .05 level.
Sources: U.S. Census, Summary File 3, 2000; National Center for Educational Statistics, *Common Core of Data*, 2005.

controlled for the educational and income levels prevailing in different communities, their expenditures per pupil did not correlate with SAT scores. Our analysis within greater Philadelphia fits into a substantial research literature that provides a decidedly mixed interpretation of the relationship between money and school performance. While some scholars have contended that money has little bearing on school performance,[28] others have pointed out that money has significant effects if it is spent on the right things, like well-qualified teachers, small class size, and proven instructional programs.[29] The message coming out of the research appears complicated—namely, that simply spending a higher dollar amount per pupil does not invariably improve performance, yet spending in effective ways is necessary to improve performance. As our numbers for the Philadelphia region show, communities that are affluent enough to exercise choices often choose to spend generously on schools precisely because they believe spending is necessary to produce quality schools.

Investing to Improve Education in New Jersey's Disadvantaged School Districts

Efforts to boost funding for disadvantaged districts invariably involve state governments since insuring the quality of public education is ultimately the responsibility of states, whose constitutional obligations include providing an education for all the state's children. Yet in Pennsylvania and New Jersey, more responsibility falls on local governments than on the state government for funding public schools. Compared to many other states, Pennsylvania and New Jersey provide a smaller percentage of K–12 expenditures.[30] The school districts of Pennsylvania and New Jersey rely on property taxes to pay school costs, a practice that gives rise to sharp inequalities, as the tax base supporting schools can differ dramatically between property-rich and property-poor districts. Although both states are marked by serious disparities in this regard, the two state governments have acted quite differently to help disadvantaged districts.

In New Jersey a quarter century of litigation, known as the Abbott cases, has significantly changed the pattern of school finance. The state court first ruled in 1973 that the state was failing to meet its constitutional requirement to provide "a thorough and efficient" education in urban schools. In 1990 the New Jersey Supreme Court ruled that the state's educational finance system was "unconstitutional as applied to poorer urban school districts" and in 1997 the court ordered the state to reduce spending inequalities between rich and poor communities. New Jersey's court ordered the legislature to make sure that thirty poor urban districts involved in the lawsuits started spending at least as much on average as the state's property-rich suburban districts. Subsequent rulings paid particular attention to the concentration of social needs in

TABLE 4.10   SCHOOL SPENDING AND STATE REVENUES IN ABBOTT SCHOOL
DISTRICTS, 2004

	Spending per Student ($)	Revenue from State (%)
Abbott Communities		
Burlington City	11,859	54
Camden	14,632	87
Gloucester City	13,007	77
Pemberton	14,467	76
Salem City	9,034	63
Wealthier New Jersey Communities		
Cherry Hill	9,834	13
Haddonfield	10,069	7
Moorestown	9,558	9

Source: New Jersey Department of Education, 2004.

inner-city schools, recognizing that addressing the needs of poorer students imposes additional costs on the schools and therefore ordering the state to spend disproportionate amounts in order to guarantee equal educational opportunities. In 2000, New Jersey's court extended this principle to preschoolers, telling the state to offer additional support to poor youngsters to counteract the ill effects of poverty on readiness to learn.

The political pattern throughout several decades of Abbott litigation has been for the court to announce its decision, the legislature to craft a bill responding to the ruling, and then the court to hear challenges from advocacy groups arguing that legislative remedies were inadequate and calling for more vigorous state action.[31] Prompted by a series of Abbott decisions, a sometimes-reluctant legislature fashioned an approach to equalizing school spending that attracted national interest because it stipulated not only the dollar amounts directed to poor districts but also what services were needed to address the effects of poverty. (This strategy acknowledged the principle that dollars alone cannot guarantee educational gains unless the money is spent on effective strategies.)

What are the results of these disproportionate state allocations to poorer districts? In 2004 New Jersey spent over half of its annual budget for public education on the Abbott districts, which served just 22 percent of the state's school population. The most direct result is that the burden of paying for local services in the Abbott districts fell less heavily on local taxpayers and more on higher levels of government. Table 4.10 compares the proportion of education costs provided by the state in the Abbott districts compared with other New Jersey districts in the greater Philadelphia area.

There were educational gains to report as well. Preschool enrollments in

Abbott districts more than doubled from 1999 to 2004, to the point of serving over 80 percent of three- and four-year-olds in those districts. From 2001 to 2004, the passing rate on 4th grade standardized tests improved in Abbott districts from 62 percent to 75 percent, compared with average statewide gains of only 5 percent. It must be acknowledged that even after achieving this improved passing average, Abbott districts still lagged significantly behind the statewide average of 90 percent. Still, the gains were significant.[32]

Pennsylvania's Approach to Funding Urban Schools

Pennsylvania officials might have taken actions similar to New Jersey's to equalize resources, since the inequalities among districts in Pennsylvania are dramatic. The state's highest spending districts are investing more than twice as much per pupil as the lowest spending districts. National rankings have repeatedly placed Pennsylvania near the bottom of the fifty states in equitably distributing school funding. However, Pennsylvania state courts have *not* taken actions comparable to New Jersey's Abbott decisions.

Possibly inspired by New Jersey's example, the City of Philadelphia struggled throughout the 1990s to litigate its way to more equitable funding from the state government. The lawsuit of the 1990s with the longest history was a case that had begun in 1968 when the Pennsylvania Human Relations Commission had told the Philadelphia School District to devise a desegregation plan. That case dragged on for decades with a succession of judges. Over the years, the case's focus shifted from traditional desegregation involving busing to providing quality education in racially isolated schools. As Whites fled the city, racial integration of the city schools became impossible in a district where the White enrollment steadily shrank to only 15 percent by the 2003–2004 school year. Not racial balance, but assuring equal educational opportunity through school quality and effectiveness, became the goal of reformers. In 1994 a panel of education experts delivered a costly proposal for achieving quality education for all Philadelphia students, including those in racially isolated schools. It was a dramatic plan, including full-day kindergarten for all children and a reduction of class size to twenty in grades K–3. Philadelphia needed an extra $1.3 billion to underwrite the prescribed reforms. How to pay for them? To the city's disappointment, state officials did not see it as their obligation to help Philadelphia comply with the judicial order and refused to pay, so the plan dissolved.

In *Marerro v. Commonwealth*, Philadelphia sued the state in state court in 1997, claiming the state had failed to meet its constitutional funding obligation to Philadelphia public schools. Noting that most of its pupils were poor and had greater-than-average educational needs, the city asked for $53 million more dollars initially and more equitable funding after that. The Pennsylvania Supreme Court dismissed the suit in 1999, saying the state constitution did not confer on every student the right to a particular level or quality of education. Throughout this litigation process, Pennsylvania's Supreme Court took the position that school funding should be decided by the legislative and executive branches of state government, not by the courts.

Having no luck litigating in the state courts, in 1998 Philadelphia filed suit in federal court, charging that Pennsylvania's system of funding city schools violated Title VI of the Civil Rights Act of 1964, which prohibits any recipient of federal funds from discriminating on the basis of race, color, or national origin. The lawsuit was believed to be the first in the nation to charge that a state funding system that underfunds heavily minority districts violates federal civil rights law. The lawsuit emphasized that Philadelphia received less in state aid than predominantly White districts with similar levels of poverty. The same was true of eleven other districts in the state with student bodies that were more than 50 percent minority; they also received less state support than districts with comparable poverty levels but largely White student bodies. This suit, *Powell v. Commonwealth*, brought no more budget relief than earlier litigation.

Not everyone subscribes to the view that the state of Pennsylvania is underfunding education in poor districts. Differences of opinion arise because funding the schools is the *joint* responsibility of state and local governments. There is no agreement about how much of the burden each side should bear. Thus there is no simple yes-or-no answer to the question of whether the state is underfunding education in disadvantaged communities. State officials typically point out that the state gives affluent districts a much *smaller* proportion of their annual educational budgets than it gives disadvantaged districts. Table 4.11 shows four affluent suburban districts near Philadelphia that receive only 9 percent to18 percent of their annual budgets from the state, whereas in Philadelphia and other less affluent districts, the state supports as much as 30 percent to 59 percent of the school budget.

Looking at percentages like those in Table 4.11, some state politicians have criticized Philadelphia officials for not devoting enough of the tax revenue they raise locally to pay for schools. The city, they have asserted, spends too many of its own tax dollars to fund other functions. What they rarely mention is that Philadelphia serves simultaneously as both a county and city government and therefore faces an extraordinary burden of paying for county services as well as city services—all in a jurisdiction with a large population of poor citizens. County services include child welfare, juvenile justice, public health, judicial, and corrections programs. Because the combined cost of city-county services is so high, Philadelphia residents carry a heavier tax burden

TABLE 4.11 SCHOOL SPENDING AND STATE REVENUES IN PHILADELPHIA AND SELECTED
SUBURBAN JURISDICTIONS

	Spending per Student ($)	Revenue from State (%)
Poorer Districts		
Upper Darby	10,496	30
Philadelphia	8,748	44
Chester-Upland	9,945	59
Wealthier Districts		
New Hope–Solebury	14,098	9
Lower Merion	16,174	10
Jenkintown	14,337	12
Phoenixville area	11,336	18

Source: "Report Card on the Schools," *Philadelphia Inquirer,* March 7, 2004.

than is carried by their suburban neighbors. City officials maintain that with
disproportionately large costs for social services, police, welfare, and such
regional responsibilities as the airport and art museum, Philadelphia cannot
afford to spend any more of its locally generated revenue on schools.

For decades Pennsylvania state politicians have believed the fiscal problems of Philadelphia and other financially strapped school districts result
mainly from poor management rather than insufficient state allocations: if
those school districts would only run their programs in a businesslike fashion,
they probably would not need large increases from the state. Surprisingly, this
is a view shared even by some state-level politicians who have been elected by
Philadelphia voters. Indeed, numerous state legislators representing the city
have pressed the school board to adopt balanced budgets rather than helping
find ways to channel new money to the Philadelphia schools.

What new management strategies have state officials favored? Since the
late 1990s, Republican leaders in Pennsylvania have pressed troubled urban
districts to contract with private school management companies to supervise
significant portions of their systems. Edison Schools, Inc., a for-profit firm
that operates public schools in more than twenty states, has received particularly strong backing from the state capital. In response to the fiscal crisis facing
the Philadelphia School District starting in the late 1990s, a Republican governor and legislative leaders wanted local school officials to hire Edison Schools
to act as central manager of the entire district. Philadelphia resisted handing
over that much control to a single for-profit company. The city and state com-
promised by putting central management under a superintendent while assigning Edison Schools and several other for-profit and nonprofit managers to
manage individual schools. In effect, this represented an experiment with outsourcing the operation of the worst-performing schools to different "school
managers," to test whether they could produce better educational results us-

ing the same dollars and the same unionized teaching staff that have tradition-ally been available to the district managers. These school managers write their own curriculum and operate their schools according to their own policies.

By the 2004–2005 school year, the Philadelphia District had contracted out a substantial portion of its work:

- Two for-profit companies and four nonprofit organizations (includ-ing two universities) were managing forty-five schools in the district.
- Six of the district's seven disciplinary schools were being managed by for-profit companies.
- One for-profit and two nonprofits were running schools for 9th graders who were older than their student peers.
- A for-profit company, Kaplan Inc., had been hired to write a stan-dardized curriculum for core subjects in fifty-five high schools.
- Four profit-making companies were hired to improve academic per-formance in twelve high schools.

The Philadelphia superintendent summed up his approach this way: "We're a public school system that has learned to play the market."[33] As the urban school district with the largest ongoing experiment in privatization in the country, Philadelphia's experience has national implications. NCLB stipu-lated that when a school fails to show improved test scores for three consecu-tive years, the school district may take "corrective actions," which could include being turned over to private management.

Several independent researchers have completed studies that are not opti-mistic about the effects of privatization. A team of Johns Hopkins researchers examined student performance on standardized mathematics tests in the 5th and 8th grades and concluded that "privatization has been an expensive ex-periment in Philadelphia. So far (through Spring 2004) this experiment has not paid off by producing better math achievement in the privatized schools."[34] Another interim evaluation done by a nonprofit research group concluded that the private contracting to operate many Philadelphia schools has failed to produce competition among providers or higher test scores.[35] In fact, the greatest improvements in tests scores have been occurring in schools run by the district, not by outside managers. During the elementary grades, most families send their children to the neighborhood school, no matter who is managing that school. So the introduction of multiple managers has not fostered competition for enrollments.

A 2007 study done by the Rand Corporation with funds from local foun-dations concluded that Philadelphia's privately managed schools produced no higher test scores than schools managed by the district, despite receiving extra funding above the dollars granted to regular district schools. Although many of the privately managed schools improved test scores over five years, their gains proved no better than the gains scored by regularly operated schools.[36] Defenders of privatization argued that private managers should not be expected to exceed the results in the rest of the district because they have been assigned to manage some of the district's worst performing schools. The interim reports have failed to detect the improvements expected from privatization.

A completely different conclusion was reached by a 2007 study by Harvard's Paul Peterson (partly funded by Edison Schools, Inc.). Peterson concluded that 8th graders in Philadelphia's privately managed schools had made more progress than the city's other school children, measured by the proportion of 8th graders who had scored in the lowest test category as 5th graders, but who had subsequently improved their test performance in the intervening three years.[37] No matter what conclusions dueling evaluators may reach, it would be difficult for the Philadelphia School District to abandon the experiment with privatization, because it continues to receive strong support from state government officials, including some powerful Philadelphia legislators.

Conclusion

In this chapter, we have placed some of the important national debates about educational inequality in the context of one metropolitan region. Those debates focus on inequality in educational spending and on the important effects of the socioeconomic context that surrounds a neighborhood school. We have seen that in greater Philadelphia, the highest-spending school districts do not necessarily produce the best results on standardized tests. In fact, when other factors are taken into account, we detected no significant influence of spending on standardized test scores.

One reason stressed by many educators is that more dollars applied to education cannot improve results unless they are spent for proven approaches—in other words, programs that have been demonstrated to enhance student achievement. However, a more important reason why higher spending does not necessarily produce better results is that schools in poor communities must spend considerably *more* money per student in so many budget categories (e.g., instruction, transportation, health, and safety) compared to schools serving more affluent students. Disadvantaged communities need not just equal allocations for their educational programs. They need more money per capita than most other communities. Differences in education, skills, and experience, combined with other human challenges to overcome, make low-income pupils more expensive to serve effectively. Even New Jersey's landmark decision creating Abbott school districts sought simply to reduce the gaps between wealthy and poor districts, bringing spending in the Abbott districts closer to spending levels in more affluent suburban schools. It did not require that disadvantaged districts spend *more* per pupil than wealthy districts.

Perhaps the most important message in this chapter is the dominant influence on school performance exerted by educational attainment levels among adults in the communities surrounding the schools. More powerfully than any other variable, the proportion of a community's adult population holding bachelor's degrees predicts student performance on the SAT test. This finding suggests a "virtuous cycle" in which communities that increase their college-educated adult population can anticipate improvements in high school test performance, which in turn can lead to more youths securing a college education and thus a higher proportion of college-educated adults.

Solving the problem of low student performance in some public schools of the region may require addressing the low levels of college degree holders among adult populations. That is precisely the goal of an initiative established in Philadelphia in 2005. Known as "Graduate Philadelphia," the project was jointly initiated by the Economy League of Greater Philadelphia, a nonprofit think tank, and Philadelphia's Workforce Investment Board. Although greater Philadelphia compares favorably with other similar metropolitan areas in the proportion of the *regional* population holding a bachelor's degree or higher,[38] the city of Philadelphia ranks only 92nd among the 100 largest U.S. cities in the percent of college graduates in its workforce.[39] As Table 4.12 shows, the trend of the last decade has placed Philadelphia and other Urban Centers within this region at an increasing disadvantage, as the degree-holding population in older communities has not kept pace with other parts of the region.

Since the mission pursued by the two partner organizations in Graduate Philadelphia is to spur economic development, their emphasis is on a college-educated workforce as a necessity for a vibrant urban economy in the twenty-first century. They note the irony that despite Philadelphia's strong presence of higher education institutions, the number of Philadelphians who at some point started college but failed to finish actually exceeds the number of persons holding completed bachelor's degrees.[40] They have proposed a number of ways to increase the rate of degree completion among adults who once started

TABLE 4.12   PERCENTAGE OF COMMUNITIES WHERE PERSONS
WITH BA OR BETTER GREW 10 OR MORE, 1990–2000

Urban Centers	0
Established Towns	27
Stable Working Communities	8
Middle-Class Suburbs	3
Affluent Suburbs	27

Source: U.S. Census, Summary Tape File 3, 1990; U.S. Census, Summary File 3, 2000.

college but never completed a degree. Many of their strategies link college education to employment, asking state government to create programs that recognize the needs of working adult students, asking businesses to provide incentives for employees to complete degrees, and asking colleges to make it easier for working adults to return to school, for example by scheduling instruction in intensive weekend formats.

If they succeed in improving the share of adults holding degrees, the partners in this initiative will have served a double purpose: both improving the quality of the city's workforce and increasing the prospects that the performance of public school students in Philadelphia on standardized tests will improve, helping the city's youth to enroll in college and earn their own degrees.

5

THE REGION'S COMMUNITIES
AND THE VALUE PROPOSITION

⌒

Thus far, we have described the many ways in which the geographic distribution of employment, housing, and education—built on a base of class, race, and spatial disparities—reinforces these very same disparities, as the region expands and decentralizes. Residents of the region are keenly aware of these differences when they make decisions about where to locate. This chapter looks at how their choices are affected by jobs, housing markets, and schools. It explores this question: to what extent are households using a "value proposition" that includes assessments of both the opportunities available within particular locations and the costs in taxes and commuting times?

The concept of a value proposition originated in the business world, but it need not be limited to that context. It began as a business diagnostic—assessing the contribution of a product or service line to a business by examining the value it added to the business. As a tool in assessing business locations, the term denoted the process of evaluating the mix of land costs, a labor pool, wages, taxes, and transportation costs when expanding or relocating. We will use the term to examine how households evaluate a community's mix of schools, public safety, proximity to jobs, and access to recreational amenities when they make housing choices. Both the flight from declining value markets and the demand for new housing appear to be influenced by such factors as educational access and public safety.

Thus, we suggest that individual homeowners engage in their own assessments of the value proposition, comparing residential locations by access to jobs (where the travel times affect potential choices), traditional community status concerns (community reputation), and the resale or appreciation (investment value) of a house. Housing thus acquires value from its community context. In a recent analysis of the greater Philadelphia housing market, incorporating twenty-one counties in Pennsylvania, New Jersey, Delaware, and Maryland, Sirmans and Macpherson[1] found that the highest prices for homes were found, regardless of county, where housing approached a suburban model: newer, larger homes in good repair, with a greater number of beds and baths, and with environmental amenities. In a subsequent meta-analysis of multiple studies of metropolitan housing markets,[2] Sirmans, MacDonald, and Macpherson reported that the perceived quality of school districts had a positive effect on house price, while public safety concerns (crime) depressed prices.

By contrast, the perception of a home purchase as an investment decision may discourage buyers from considering areas where they perceive that values are declining. Especially in older communities, factors like proximity to parks or employment centers may not be sufficient to sustain the value of the housing market if lenders and buyers regard the area as declining. Even proximity to good jobs does not guarantee high market demand for houses; as we saw in Chapter 2, some neighborhoods located close to good jobs may have housing markets priced low enough for low-income renters and buyers. Outward signs like vacancy and abandonment can quickly undermine the perception of outsiders as to the investment value of nearby properties. In Chapter 3, we reported that an abandoned house in Philadelphia has been estimated to diminish the market value of nearby properties by as much as $7,627.

This chapter examines the contextual factors that affect the value of a house. What is the value proposition that buyers engage in as they assess a home? And by extension, on what factors do elected officials focus when they seek to support residential values and maintain their tax base?

Why Do People Move?

Research tells us people move largely because of housing and neighborhood conditions. Two main streams of research have sought to explain the choices movers make. The first is a line of sociological research following a classic work about Philadelphia published by Peter Rossi in 1955, *Why Families Move*,[3] which reported survey findings from four neighborhoods in Philadelphia (Oak Lane, West Philadelphia, Kensington, and Center City). The survey asked both why respondents left a previous location and what attracted them to their new homes. The most important factor prompting people to move was dissatisfaction with the amount of space in their homes, followed by complaints about their neighbors and the costs of either renting or main-taining their current homes. As attractions toward their new locations, the respondents focused on features of the housing unit, for example, the space in their new dwelling, particular design features, the home's location or cost.[4] These latter reasons for picking a new home seemed to be based heavily on family circumstances like the presence of new children in households or, conversely, children leaving home, divorce, or the death of a partner. We should note, however, that this study from the mid-1950s was written before several decades of metropolitan change had exacerbated the differences in-herent in different locations throughout the region—differences in access to employment opportunities or educational opportunities. Having seen in ear-lier chapters how widely these opportunities have diverged in different parts of the region, we can speculate that people's residential choices these days may be far more influenced by employment and educational opportunities than in the 1950s.

A second line of scholarship has put greater emphasis on services, amenities, and taxes as reasons for moving. This second line of research also started in the mid-1950s, with economists using theories drawn from microeconomics to explain how households decide where to live. Charles Tiebout[5] and others tested the proposition that people choose where to live based on a cost-benefit analysis of the services and amenities that different communities offer them, balanced against the taxes that communities im-pose in order to pay for services.[6] Put simply, communities are seen as com-peting with one another in the combination of public services, amenities, and returns-on-investment that they offer to householders, compared with the costs they impose on residents. Seeing the metropolitan area as a mar-ketplace in which different communities offer different packages of services and taxes, some rational choice theorists have argued that it is better to have large numbers of local governments in the region because they provide a wide range of choices, increasing the probability that households can find the types and amounts of services they prefer. Tiebout and his followers have seen movers acting as consumers in a marketplace of different community options. In this view, deciding to relocate is equivalent to deciding that the costs of the new location (in terms of taxes and commute times) are worth paying in order to secure the package of services offered there. It is impor-tant to note that Tiebout's theory has a slightly different focus than Peter Rossi's: Tiebout focused on movements from one community to another while Rossi dealt with movements from one home to another. It is also worth noting that the theoretical ideas driving these two lines of research are not mutually exclusive. Both may be valid, and the empirical question con-cerns their relative importance. In addition, we note that both focused on voluntary movements, but a significant number of relocations arise involuntarily from such factors as marriage, divorce, separations, death, evictions, dwelling unit conversions and destruction, job changes requiring relocation, and loss of income.

This region should provide an ideal context in which to examine Rossi's and Tiebout's models, because it provides a highly fragmented marketplace of options for movers. In previous chapters, we have described wide variations in proximity to jobs, in the age, style, and price of housing, and in the quality of education. Beyond these differences, another important factor that often influences household moves—crime rates—displays dramatic variation in different parts of the region. The number of violent crimes per capita is about ten times higher in Philadelphia and Camden than in the group of communities we have labeled the Affluent Suburbs. The difference in property crime rates (mainly burglary and car theft) between the core cities and the Affluent Suburbs is fourfold—a smaller, yet still substantial, difference in the average resident's exposure to crime depending on where one lives.[7]

Although one research tradition tells us people decide to move mainly based on housing characteristics and another research tradition emphasizes the value people place on community environments, services, and costs, greater Philadelphia offers such dramatic variation in *both* of these conditions that we can test both perspectives in this region.

How People Explain Their Residential Choices

We have already shown in Chapter 1 that many moves people make are within the same city or community. Data from the *American Housing Survey*[8] indicate that, in fact, most movers are renters, and that when they make moves almost three-quarters of renters remain in rental housing rather than entering the ownership market. Perhaps surprisingly, almost half (45.7 percent) of owners who move become renters in the process (see Table 5.1).

This suggests that we need to be cautious about how we identify the features that different households value in their choice of community. Moves may result from demographic as well as economic circumstances. We can see this in the results of the *American Housing Survey* reported in Table 5.2. Asked

TABLE 5.1   MOVES MADE BY OWNERS AND RENTERS, 2004 (PERCENT)

	Owning	Renting
Respondents' prior residence (if in U.S.) ($n = 189,500$)	36.1	63.9
Residential destination of previous owners ($n = 69,000$)	54.3	45.7
Residential destination of previous renters ($n = 120,500$)	25.7	74.4

Source: U.S. Census, *American Housing Survey for the Philadelphia Metropolitan Area: 2003,* 2004

TABLE 5.2   MAIN REASON FOR LEAVING PREVIOUS HOUSING
UNIT (PERCENT)*

	Owners	Renters
Private displacement	0.0	2.6
Government displacement	0.0	0.0
Disaster loss (fire, flood, etc.)	0.0	1.8
New job or job transfer	1.6	7.4
To be closer to work/school/other	9.9	7.2
Other, financial/employment related	2.7	4.2
To establish own household	16.1	9.4
Needed larger house or apartment	20.9	6.6
Married widowed, divorced, or separated	4.1	5.5
Other, family/person related	9.9	9.6
Wanted better home	4.0	12.2
Change from owner to renter or renter to owner	6.8	0.0
Wanted lower rent or maintenance	1.3	5.5
Other housing related reasons	6.8	6.2
Other	11.3	16.3
Not reported	1.7	5.5

*All respondents had previously lived in the United States.
Source: U.S. Census, American Housing Survey for the Philadelphia Metropolitan
Area: 2003, 2004.

to identify the main reason for leaving their previous housing unit, significant proportions of both owners and renters said they moved from their previous home in order to get a more desirable housing unit.

Admittedly, the two groups of respondents expressed the desire differently: while owners were more likely than renters to say they needed a *larger* house or apartment, renters were more likely than owners to say they wanted a *better* home. Yet for both groups of respondents, the top reason they gave for leaving their homes suggests that their economic circumstances had improved, giving them a chance to secure a larger or better unit. A second important reason for both groups of respondents was "to establish their own household," often occasioned by changing family circumstances, while a third important reason given by both groups was "other, family/person related." This pattern of responses shows that both economics and household configurations enter into decisions to move.

When we shift away from the reasons why people left their previous homes to examine their reasons for choosing their new neighborhoods, we see some differences between owners and renters, portrayed in Table 5.3. Significant proportions of both groups of respondents chose new neighborhoods that were convenient to friends or relatives. However, renter households were more likely than homeowners to cite the convenience of the neighborhood to their job and to public transportation. Owners, on the other hand, were far more likely than renters to emphasize the looks or design of the new neighborhood, somewhat more likely to cite the neighborhood's good schools, and

TABLE 5.3   MAIN REASON FOR CHOICE OF NEIGHBORHOOD (PERCENT)*

	Owners	Renters
Convenient to job	12.7	16.0
Convenient to friends or relatives	23.8	21.2
Convenient to leisure activities	0.0	0.0
Convenient to public transportation	0.0	5.4
Good schools	9.0	8.2
Other public services	0.0	1.0
Looks/design of neighborhood	24.9	15.4
House was most important consideration	8.8	7.6
Other	7.8	16.6
Not reported	3.0	7.5

*No owners and 1% of renters reported all reasons about the same.
Source: U.S. Census, *American Housing Survey for the Philadelphia Metropolitan Area: 2003*, 2004.

much more likely to say that the housing unit itself was the most important consideration. Given that people's homes constitute a major financial asset, it is not surprising that owners report they have chosen their locations based on the house itself and the curb appeal of houses in well designed neighborhoods, along with the quality of schools.

The clearest indication of the different perspectives held by owners and renters is in Table 5.4. When recent movers were queried about the extent of the search they engaged in to find their new housing, the results sharply differentiated owners from renters. About two-thirds of homeowners looked at multiple neighborhoods. Less than half of renters did. A far larger proportion of renters limited their search to just the neighborhood they moved to. Since renters appear far less inclined than homeowners to engage in comparison shopping among different neighborhoods or communities, this chapter focuses mainly on the value proposition from the vantage point of homebuyers. We seek to understand what drives homeowners toward certain communities and how the cost-benefit balance affects their choices.

While these data provide a national context for the decision to move, we gain additional insights from the *Philadelphia Metropolitan Area Survey*,[9] a random digit dialing survey of 1,000 households conducted annually between 2003 and 2005. Although the time frame and questions differ between

TABLE 5.4   NEIGHBORHOOD SEARCH (PERCENT)

	Owner	Renter
Looked at just this neighborhood	33.0	48.8
Looked at other neighborhood(s)	65.2	45.6
Not reported	1.7	5.5

Source: U.S. Census, *American Housing Survey for the Philadelphia Metropolitan Area: 2003*, 2004.

the national and regional surveys, they are broadly consistent. However, in contrast to the national data, our regional survey permits us to distinguish between households that moved from one municipality to another and households that moved within the same municipality, a distinction that is not possible with the national data. This distinction is critical to evaluating the Tiebout theory, given its focus on community choice. Since most public services and tax rates vary little or not at all within municipal boundaries, households that move within the same community may differ in their reasons for moving from people who move from one place to another. The *Philadelphia Metropolitan Area Survey* asked householders who had moved to their present home within the past decade about the relative importance of thirteen factors influencing their moves. Respondents reported whether a factor was very important, somewhat important, not very important, or not at all important. Table 5.5 reveals the percentage who said a reason was very important classified by whether the householder owned or rented and whether the householder moved within the same municipality or from a different one.

The results indicate some differences from the national pattern, in that closeness to work is substantially less important and good schools are more significant than in the national data. There is a broad similarity in the reasons respondents give for their moves, regardless of whether they moved from one municipality to another or within the same community. Housing costs are clearly the most important factor in housing choice for all groups. No other factor draws as large or consistent support, but good schools and closeness to shopping and schools, friends and relatives, and work follow in significance. In

TABLE 5.5   PERCENTAGE CHOOSING REASON FOR MOVING TO PRESENT HOME AS "VERY IMPORTANT" BY WHETHER OWN OR RENT AND WHETHER MOVED FROM DIFFERENT MUNICIPALITY, PHILADELPHIA METROPOLITAN AREA, 2003–2004

	Moved from Different Municipality		Moved within Same Municipality	
	Own	Rent	Own	Rent
Housing costs	64.1	60.7	68.0	62.7
Good schools	59.7	41.1	54.4	50.3
Convenient to shops/schools	40.1	49.4	49.4	62.6
Openness of area	39.1	29.3	33.7	34.7
Close to family/friends	38.2	47.3	46.0	49.7
Close to work	31.2	46.3	36.9	41.8
Near natural areas	31.2	33.2	30.2	29.1
Familiar with area	30.0	33.2	41.7	53.6
Lower taxes	25.9	24.4	35.7	36.1
"People like you"	21.3	29.5	31.7	32.2
Recreational opportunities	21.3	20.2	28.6	36.3
Community size	18.8	16.8	23.5	30.5
Close to church	17.0	21.8	28.2	36.5

Source: Metropolitan Philadelphia Indicators Project, *Philadelphia Metropolitan Area Survey,* 2003–2004 combined file.

the lower part of Table 5.5, we see the factors that distinguish households that moved to a new municipality from those that did not. Familiarity with the new area, lower taxes, recreational opportunities, community size, and closeness to church—almost all of which reflect the significance of local knowledge—appear more important to households that moved within their municipality than to those who changed communities.

The results for lower taxes provide a surprising twist to the assessment of the Tiebout argument; in these data, contrary to the theory, householders who moved within the same municipality are more likely to find taxes important than those who moved to a new place. Since tax rates are presumably the same within a municipality, it is likely that these respondents are reacting to differences in assessed values rather than tax rates per se.[10]

In a few cases, we see differences between owners and renters. Good schools appear less important to renters than to owners when we look at those who moved from another municipality (but not those who moved within the same place). But among those who changed municipalities, renters value proximity to work more than owners—a difference absent among those who moved within the same place. Access to shopping and schools and familiarity with the area are more important to renters than owners among those who moved within the same place, but there is no meaningful difference for those who moved from elsewhere.

Our survey also asked respondents which reason for their move was most important.[11] The same five reasons were cited most often by all four groups (Table 5.6), although their rank within the five varied. Four of the five are substantive—good schools, closeness to family and friends, proximity to work, and housing costs—but the fifth is a catchall for all of the other reasons that were not on the list of reasons we provided to respondents. The results from these analyses provide support for both the life cycle and Tiebout or value proposition theories. The life cycle theory receives support from our

TABLE 5.6   TOP FIVE "MOST IMPORTANT REASON" CITED FOR CHOICE OF PRESENT COMMUNITY BY WHETHER OWN OR RENT AND WHETHER MOVED FROM DIFFERENT MUNICIPALITY, 2003–2004 (PERCENT)

	Moved from Different Municipality		Moved within Same Municipality	
	Own	Rent	Own	Rent
Good schools	27.1	12.2	20.6	19.0
Close to family/friends	14.2	18.9	13.5	24.3
Close to work	13.5	24.3	11.8	16.1
Housing costs	10.6	15.3	15.4	10.7
Other	7.7	7.2	13.6	8.9

*$p < .01$, two-tailed test.
Source: Metropolitan Philadelphia Indicators Project, *Philadelphia Metropolitan Area Survey*, 2003–2004 combined file.

findings that housing characteristics such as costs, space, and proximity to work, friends, and relatives are important to community choice. But the emphasis on good schools supports the value proposition. Lower taxes—so central to value proposition arguments—were mentioned as most important by only 1.3 percent of homeowners who moved from a different municipality, ranking eleventh in the list. This low ranking is surprising, especially if we take into account how dramatically different are the tax bills facing residents in different parts of the region.

Tax Patterns in the Region

Local and state governments in the region impose two main types of taxes: taxes on real estate and taxes on earned income. While the tax laws of the two states give local governments in Pennsylvania a wider range of local revenue sources to tax, compared with fewer options in New Jersey, real estate taxes comprise the single largest source of revenues for municipalities in both states (with the notable exception of Philadelphia, whose wage tax generates larger revenues than its property tax generates).

To compare the tax burdens in different communities, we have imagined that a hypothetical household might have chosen to live in each of the 353 municipalities in the region. No matter which municipality this hypothetical household lived in, it is assumed to have earned the median household income for the region ($51,980) and to have owned a house priced at the average market value for the region ($174,044). We calculated what this household would have been paying in combined state and local taxes, depending on whether the earner(s) worked inside Philadelphia or outside Philadelphia. The results of this exercise are displayed in Figures 5.1 and 5.2.

The reason for dividing our findings into two separate maps is that any suburbanite who works in Philadelphia must pay a wage tax to the city government. Although the 3.7 percent tax that the city imposes on wages earned by nonresidents is lower than the 4.3 percent tax on wages paid by Philadelphia residents, it is still higher than the earned income tax rates levied by suburban communities, which rarely exceed 1 percent. It therefore makes sense to look separately at the taxes paid by suburban residents who work within Philadelphia versus suburban residents who work outside the city. (Recall from Figure 2.1 that in only a few suburbs does more than one-quarter of the workforce hold jobs in Philadelphia. Therefore Figure 5.1, rather than Figure 5.2, depicts the tax burdens levied on the majority of suburban workers in the region.)

Figure 5.1 shows that in the majority of suburbs, our hypothetical household would have been paying under $6,500 in combined state and local taxes, compared with the same household paying over $6,500 if they lived in

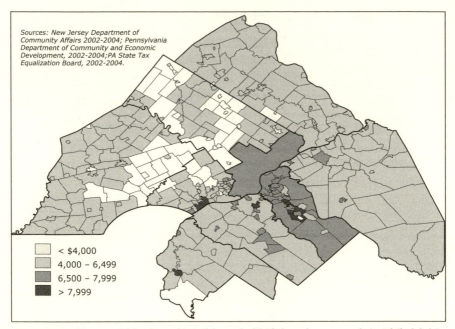

Sources: New Jersey Department of Community Affairs 2002-2004; Pennsylvania Department of Community and Economic Development, 2002-2004;PA State Tax Equalization Board, 2002-2004.

☐	< $4,000
▨	4,000 – 6,499
▨	6,500 – 7,999
■	> 7,999

FIGURE 5.1   Taxes paid by hypothetical household if they do not work in Philadelphia, 2002–2004.

Philadelphia and over $8,000 if they lived in the distressed city of Chester. Figure 5.2. shows that for the suburban workers commuting from New Jersey to Philadelphia, the generally high property taxes combined with the Philadelphia wage tax would result in higher burdens on them than on most other suburban taxpayers in the region. However, in some of the more distant Pennsylvania suburbs, the city's wage tax would have boosted the tax bill for our hypothetical household from the second-lowest into the second-highest category. The same boost would be felt by some higher tax municipalities in eastern Delaware County and lower Bucks County.

Regarding federal taxes, a recent analysis of this region concluded that suburban taxpayers in some of the most affluent communities in the region enjoy disproportionate advantages flowing from the tax benefits that the federal government affords to homeowners. That study estimated the value of federal tax concessions to homeowners in different parts of the region, showing that in the middle-ring suburbs on the Pennsylvania side of the region (mostly classified as Affluent Suburbs in our community typology), the average homeowner was reaping over $6,000 annually in federal tax benefits, while for the average Philadelphia owner, the annual benefit was only $1,166.[12] That disparity occurs, of course, because the value of the tax benefit is tied to the value of the home, and Philadelphia properties have systematically lower

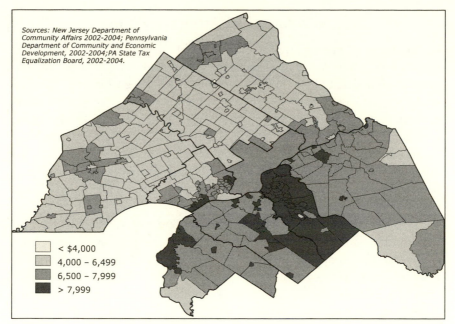

FIGURE 5.2   Taxes paid by hypothetical household if they work in Philadelphia, 2002–04.

values. Rather than redressing the imbalance between owners of high-value and low-value properties, federal tax laws reward those with greater resources.

Despite their higher tax burden, residents of the core cities and other urban centers of the region do not get higher levels of benefits than suburbanites, or even equivalent benefits to those enjoyed in more affluent suburban communities. Or put another way, suburbanites do not necessarily pay costs aligned with the benefits they enjoy. Why? The main reason is that the value of the tax base (i.e., the combined property and wages supporting local services) diverges dramatically from one community to another. In municipalities where high-value real estate is concentrated, the local government can generate large amounts of revenue even from a tax rate that is comparatively lower than the rates levied in less property-rich places. The result of the region's intense fragmentation into hundreds of small jurisdictions is that by exercising choices among communities, people can opt out of paying the full cost of their location choices. In the words of Myron Orfield, "The increase of property wealth in outer suburbs and the stagnation or decline of central city and inner-suburban values represents, in part, an interregional transfer of tax base."[13]

Which Communities Attract Newcomers?

Up to this point, our exploration of how people choose their community has relied on what people say in response to survey interviewers. Now, we bring other kinds of data to bear on the subject, in order to see whether people's responses to surveys are borne out by the migration patterns we observe on the ground. We focus attention on households whose last move was to a new community. The question we ask is what types of communities have attracted high shares of incoming migrants over the last decade (i.e., since 1995). This part of our analysis is entirely based on the objective characteristics of the communities, and thus any conclusion about households' reasons for their choice of community is entirely inferential.

Rossi found that people's housing choices were most affected by their position in the family life cycle and by certain features of housing units, especially cost. In this analysis, we use the percentage of families with children under eighteen and the percentage of nonfamily households to indicate different stages in the family life cycle. We measure housing characteristics through a single variable: housing cost. We measure the socioeconomic status of communities through the percentage of the community's residents who hold a bachelor's degree or better and the change in this percentage between 1990 and 2000. Households of differing socioeconomic status have differing ranges of community and housing choice. People of higher status typically prefer to live among those of similar status and, other things being equal, have the means to do so. Higher status may also be a proxy in movers' minds for other community characteristics such as low crime levels, good schools, and good public services. We also measure each community's job potential (i.e., its access to the region's job centers).[14] The job potential measure provides an objective indicator of the prominent place given to closeness to work seen in Tables 5.5 and 5.6 and prior research.

To measure the municipal attributes that reflect the value proposition, we use the average household real estate tax, the school expenditures per student, and a three-year average of SAT scores.[15] Tax levels have been central to the Tiebout literature since its inception—the argument being that movers will choose communities that offer that best combination of low taxes and good services. School expenditures per student reflect the community's willingness to invest in its children, and SAT scores are one indicator of the success of the school system.

Finally, we add two variables as controls: municipal population size and percentage African American.[16] We control for population because the region's municipalities differ markedly in size. We control for the percentage African American because there is ample evidence from prior research that movers take the racial composition of their destination into account,[17] although neither the life cycle nor the value proposition literatures have considered race as a factor.

Table 5.7 compares the effects exerted by two different factors on a community's appeal to newcomers during the past decade. (The beta weights reveal the relative sizes of the effects of the variables on the percentage of persons in 2000 who lived in a different municipality in 1995.) Our results suggest that the life cycle factors play a larger role than value proposition factors in influencing people to move into particular communities. A community's share of families with children under eighteen has the largest effect, with percentage of persons in nonfamily households also having a sizable effect. However, these two variables have led to growth in quite different types of communities. Communities with many children tend to be places on the urban fringe, which are often what we have termed Middle-Class Suburbs. Nonfamily households are especially prevalent in more settled places such as the city of Philadelphia and our category of Established Towns. Higher socioeconomic status and improvements in a community's status have also attracted movers into communities. These socioeconomic characteristics have drawn households into what we have termed Affluent Suburbs as well as the Middle-Class Suburbs. Interestingly, the positive effect of home cost indicates that communities with more expensive housing attract more newcomers. This pattern of growth helps to explain the negative effect of job potential. Growth has occurred disproportionately in the more expensive residential markets, which tend to be located at considerable distance from job locations.

Turning to the Tiebout hypothesis, the importance that movers attributed to good schools in our survey (see Tables 5.5 and 5.6) is *not* reflected in the aggregate data on municipalities presented in Table 5.7. Neither average SAT scores nor school expenditures per student had any significant effect on the percentage who moved into a community. Although property taxes had the expected negative effect, it was only a modest one. Readers may find this at odds with our finding in Chapter 4 that communities with high SAT scores have been attracting more newcomers than those with lower SAT scores. We also observed in Chapter 4 that those communities attracting large numbers of newcomers tend to exhibit high housing prices. Our findings here in Table 5.7 suggest that when both these factors (housing market and schools) are considered side by side in a single analysis, the housing market exerts a stronger appeal to newcomers than the schools. Once the housing variable is taken into account, the education variable lends little additional explanatory power to help us predict which communities will draw more newcomers.

We are faced with some important differences between what people *say* about choosing a community and what they actually *do*. When they respond to surveys, people indicate that housing costs, good schools, and low taxes influ-

TABLE 5.7   EFFECTS OF COMMUNITY CHARACTERISTICS
ON THE SHARE OF RESIDENTS WHO HAVE ARRIVED IN
THE COMMUNITY IN THE PAST FIVE YEARS, 2000

	ß[a]
Population	−.265
	(−5.753)
Percent African American	.087
	(1.628)
Percent BA+	.188
	(2.472)
Difference in percent BA+, 1990–2000	.126
	(2.614)
Percent married families with children under 18	.331
	(7.296)
Percent nonfamily households	.260
	(5.510)
Home cost (log)	.279
	(3.534)
Average SAT scores[b]	−.063
	(−.941)
Expenditures per student	(−.016)
	(−.309)
Property tax per household	−.119
	(−2.546)
Job potential[c]	−.147
	(−2.828)
Adjusted R^2	.46
(N)	353

[a]With *t* values in parentheses.
[b]Average over three years.
[c]Measures accessibility of municipality to jobs elsewhere in metropolitan area
(see text).

ence their choice. Yet the pattern of choices that households have actually
made in recent years appears somewhat at odds with those survey responses.
In fact, the communities gaining large shares of newcomers are those with
higher, not more affordable, housing costs, and they are not necessarily the
communities with high SAT scores or school expenditures.

To explore this apparent contradiction, we chose to look not only at what
our regional survey respondents have said, but what they have done. That is,
we separated out those respondents who reported they had moved into their
present community within the past decade and then examined the types of
communities they have chosen.[18] We excluded renters and limited the analysis
to homeowners—the group that most demands good schools. We examined
whether they have systematically chosen to live in communities with high SAT

TABLE 5.8   CORRELATIONS AMONG MEASURES OF MIGRATION TO NEW COMMUNITIES
AND SELECTED EDUCATIONAL AND FISCAL ATTRIBUTES, 2003–2004

	Moved in Past Ten Years	Moved in Past Five Years	SAT Scores	School Expenditure per Student	Property Taxes per Household
Moved in past ten years	.725*	.214*	.040	−.140*
Moved in past five years		.139*	.005	−.081*
SAT scores			.467*	−.418*
School expenditure per student				−.429*

* Statistically significant at the .01 level.

scores, high school spending, and low property taxes. Once again, Table 5.8
shows only very modest correlations between household moves and our three
community characteristics: SAT scores, school expenditures per student, and
property taxes per household. So the very households that responded to our
survey appear to have made choices bearing little relationship to their stated
priorities.

Thus the problem that remains is why school attributes appear so weakly
related to actual movement, given the emphasis that movers have reported they
placed upon good schools. We have no easy answers, but one possibility is that
homebuyers do not accurately assess the quality of local schools in the communities to which they are considering moving. In Chapter 4, we reported that
people attempting to evaluate the quality of schools in unfamiliar circumstances often rely on judgments expressed by friends and acquaintances rather
than relying on objective indicators. We can further speculate that respondents
are drawing an implicit contrast between their schools and those of the most
impoverished communities of the region: Philadelphia, Camden, and Chester.
As long as their children are outside of these districts, they may believe they are
in adequate schools. Unfortunately, our data do not permit investigation of this
hypothesis. Recall that in Chapter 4, we showed that since 1995, many people
have chosen to move into housing units in low-performing school districts.
Table 4.5 showed that a large proportion (61 percent) of people occupying
housing in low-performing districts have come from another home within the
same town. In contrast, among the people who moved into housing units in the
higher-performing school districts, only 5 percent had come from the same
town, whereas fully 95 percent had come from elsewhere. In part, that dramatic
difference is probably explained by the fact that the higher-performing districts
are ones where many more new housing units have been built since 1995. However, another implication of the difference is that only *some* of the region's residents are using housing choices to gain educational advantages.

This observation reminds us of the important role that race and class play in circumscribing mobility and opportunity. Even when minority families and White families dispose of equivalent incomes, they do not enjoy a similar range of housing choices. This is true for suburbs as well as cities. Much has been made of the movement of increasing numbers of minority households to the suburbs. During the 1990s, the percentage of the region's African American population that lived in the suburbs increased from 27 to 32 percent—an increase of about 70,000 people. Media attention has focused mainly on the growing African American middle class. Our research identified more than seventy-five suburban municipalities in 2000 whose median African American household earned an annual income *exceeding* the incomes of the Whites living in the same community.[19] Typically these municipalities have only small populations of color, composed of affluent householders who can make choices across a wide range of communities.

Most suburban African Americans do not live in these more affluent subdivisions in isolation from other African Americans. Instead, suburban minority residents tend to cluster in suburbs where their average incomes are no higher than their White neighbors. Out of more than 350 suburban municipalities in this region, only thirty contain what we would characterize as substantial populations of African Americans. (We define "substantial" as at least 3,000 African American residents comprising 10 percent or more of the community's total population.) As might be expected, a good number of such communities are located on Philadelphia's border, although a small number can also be found farther out in the suburbs, in towns where African American communities have been long established—for example, Willingboro in New Jersey and Chester, Norristown, and Coatesville in Pennsylvania. (To see the locations of towns with substantial African American populations, refer back to Figure 1.15). The towns containing substantial African American populations tend to be older and poorer than other suburbs. Although both White and non-White residents have modest incomes, minority households face particular challenges. For example, we showed in Chapter 2 that 64 percent of African Americans and 70 percent of Latinos living in the region's suburbs lack access to an automobile. For them, moving to the suburbs has not necessarily translated into greater employment opportunity. Nor has living in the suburbs automatically conferred educational advantages. Chapter 4 showed that suburban minority students tend to be enrolled in schools that produce lower test scores than White schools.

State government expenditures do not help much to reduce the disparities between communities in the region with respect to the resources needed to serve their citizens' needs. One study that examined this question concluded "that the poorest jurisdictions tend to have the highest local tax effort, and that state and federal flows do not redistribute effectively to offset the extra costs of delivering public services to the poor."[20] Rather than improving the position of older, poorer communities relative to those that are better off, some types of state expenditures disproportionately benefit the communities that are experiencing the most growth and thereby gaining more ability to fund their own services. The message this gives to local government officials is that they must find ways to support local services with local taxes. The system breeds competition rather than coordination.

Competition among Communities

The legal and administrative framework prevailing in the region does not encourage regional coordination. On the contrary, the most important characteristic of the region's political arrangements is the extreme degree of governmental and administrative fragmentation that has resulted from 300 years of municipal development. Each of its 353 separate local governments jealously guards its autonomy. Greater Philadelphia has been characterized as among the most diffuse regions in the United States by Miller, a researcher who has created a "Metropolitan Power Diffusion Index" to measure the degree to which local government power is diffused versus unified.[21]

This region's fragmentation is not purely a matter of the large number of separate jurisdictions. Table 5.9 ranks the number of local governments in greater Philadelphia against our selected comparison metropolitan areas. It shows that while the number is high in Philadelphia, it is not beyond the level of some other metropolitan regions. Among the peer regions, Cleveland, Minneapolis, and Pittsburgh actually exceed Philadelphia's ratio of seven local governments for every 100,000 citizens.

Although the numerical comparison in Table 5.9 does not single out Philadelphia as especially fragmented, other factors exacerbate the effects of the region's balkanization. One is the nature of Pennsylvania state law, which gives local governments an extraordinarily high degree of responsibility for

TABLE 5.9 LOCAL GOVERNMENTS PER 100,000 RESIDENTS	
Baltimore	1
Boston	5
Chicago	6
Cleveland	9
Detroit	5
Minneapolis	11
Philadelphia	7
Phoenix	1
Pittsburgh	17

Source: U.S. Census, 2002 Census of Governments.

planning, zoning, and taxes. One might assume that controlling these important decisions would guarantee local governments substantial leverage over the character of their communities. But in fact, the experience of the past several decades has created patterns of development often at odds with the interests expressed by local government leaders. Particularly in the Pennsylvania suburbs, state land use laws have exposed township governments to costly lawsuits from developers who want to build unwanted developments. Pennsylvania state law has required all communities to adopt zoning ordinances that make provision for *all* types of land uses. Because of that requirement, town governments that have tried to prevent developers from introducing certain types of unwanted development within their borders have often been sued by developers seeking "curative amendments" to municipal zoning ordinances. In many such cases, municipal plans and preferences have been overturned simply because some developer wanted to build something on a site zoned for a different use.

Rather than working cooperatively with adjoining communities, townships have often located troublesome projects on the border with adjoining jurisdictions, pushing some of the unwanted impacts onto neighboring towns. In 1987, residents of affluent Lower Merion Township unsuccessfully tried to stop construction of a large corporate center in neighboring West Conshohocken, whose overflowing congestion they feared. More recently, a group of citizens in Whitpain Township managed to defeat a developer's proposal to build a seventeen-story condominium on the border between their town and neighboring Ambler. In another recent example, residents in the Montgomery County suburb of Towamencin were surprised to see a giant cell phone tower rising behind their homes, just over a hundred feet across the boundary in neighboring Hatfield. Such unwelcome surprises occur fairly often in a planning context where each local government operates independently.

Another factor aggravating the region's fragmentation is the disproportionate responsibility that local governments carry for funding local services, especially schools. We saw in Chapter 4 that the state governments in both Pennsylvania and New Jersey pay lower shares of public school costs than other mid-Atlantic states, placing greater burdens on local taxpayers. Dependence on locally generated taxes forces some municipalities to seek constant growth within their borders, even when it may be undesirable on environmental or other grounds—for example, when it siphons economic activity out of already-established centers and imposes heavy burdens on new infrastructure and on the environment. Localities compete against one other in hard-fought campaigns to lure developers into one community or another in order to bolster the tax base.

This region is marked by fierce competition among neighboring municipalities for new development that generates tax revenues for local government. In our previous edition, we focused mainly on competition between Philadelphia and its suburbs. Now, however, suburbs compete with each other for development. Sometimes, a firm can gain substantial subsidies by moving only a few miles to a neighboring suburb. In late 2004, for example, the consulting firm of Towers Perrin benefited from over $14 million in promised state and local government incentives to move 1,100 employees one mile from Voorhees, New Jersey, to Cherry Hill, New Jersey. The deal included tax rebates that over ten years would be worth $7.6 million, plus an additional $7 million worth of state expenditures for a parking deck, a pedestrian tunnel connecting the company's building to a public transit station, and training programs.[22] The director of economic development activities for a suburban Philadelphia county described the competition this way: "Companies now show up with site selection consultants and incentive consultants for meetings with economic development officials. They say, 'Here's what New Jersey is doing for us, what Maryland is doing for us. Match it!' "[23]

In a metropolitan region that spans two states, the stakes are especially high when state governments get involved in offering competing subsidies. In 1999, one of the large suburban pharmaceutical companies, AstraZeneca, was persuaded to move its headquarters from Pennsylvania across the state line by an irresistible package of incentives from the Delaware state government. In 2004, when CIGNA Corporation was being actively courted by New Jersey to move its 1,500 jobs from Philadelphia, New Jersey offered a package of subsidies totaling around $100 million. Pennsylvania and Philadelphia had to bid against that offer with an equally attractive counter offer, consisting of at least $10 million in cash and loans plus some tax breaks. This interstate struggle over CIGNA's location looked so costly and irrational even to members of the business community that it prompted the Greater Philadelphia Chamber of Commerce to start working with the governors of New Jersey, Pennsylvania, and Delaware to dampen what the chamber termed "intra-regional poaching."

Do Local Governments Compete to Hold Down Tax Rates?

The defenders of the existing pattern of governmental fragmentation in metropolitan regions argue that the proliferation of jurisdictions helps to keep the costs of public services down, as local officials work to keep taxes low. Within the marketplace of local governments, they assert, competition serves to keep local spending down. But does competition between local governments necessarily lead a community to hold down costs and hold down taxes? If it did, then we would have expected that the increasing competition faced by

Philadelphia over recent decades would have led city officials and citizens to call for spending cuts and tax reductions. Yet the reality has been far more complicated than that.

Interestingly, even though they complain about taxes as bitterly as taxpayers anywhere in the United States, Philadelphia citizens have expressed less enthusiasm for tax cuts than might be expected. For example, the chief criticisms against the property tax made by a recent citizens' Tax Reform Commission concerned the unfairness of assessments rather than the tax rate. Largely because of time lags in reassessing properties in changing neighborhoods, the areas where housing prices are increasing enjoy low taxes, while the areas where prices are declining are over taxed. The system is regressive, requiring that homeowners in low-income neighborhoods pay more than their share, while more affluent residents in gentrifying areas pay less than their share. Although the city government is currently undertaking an overhaul of property tax assessments, it is expected to be revenue neutral rather than reducing taxes.

In contrast to the property tax, Philadelphia has taken some steps to reduce its wage tax rate. Since the mid-1990s, the city government has made small annual reductions in the wage tax rate. From a high in 1990 of 4.9 percent per year for residents, the wage tax rate had declined by 2007 to 4.3 percent for residents (3.7 percent for nonresidents). Mayor John Street proved to be unenthusiastic about cutting taxes, emphasizing that paying for public services is more critical to the city's viability than cutting taxes. Faced with difficulty in paying for public services in 2002, the mayor even suggested the city should suspend its plan to continue small annual reductions. Possibly sensing that wage taxes were not a hot button issue for very many Philadelphia voters, the mayor's greater fear was that the city would have to cut public services. In the end, the city council overruled the mayor and continued the small year-to-year cuts. The mayor's position was not merely that he preferred to avoid painful budget cuts, but that cutting public services could make the city less attractive to prospective residents and businesses. He argued that the quality of the urban environment, much of which depends on public services, influences location decisions more than tax rates. Furthermore, in an era when many U.S. regions are trying to persuade suburbanites to share the costs of central city services and facilities, Philadelphia should not be giving away its most important form of tax base sharing—the nonresident wage tax.

Our survey data tend to support the mayor's view, at least with respect to how *residents* see these choices. A majority of Philadelphia households responding to our surveys said they would even pay *higher* local taxes if they knew the proceeds would go to improve their schools, arts and culture, and some other amenities. However, we cannot extend these observations to the *business owners* operating in Philadelphia (who may or may not live within the city). In contrast to residents, business groups in Philadelphia have become increasingly vocal in favor of tax cuts. Businesses depend less directly than residents on the schools, libraries, health and welfare, and many other public services that local taxes pay for, so they have a smaller stake in maintaining those service levels. Moreover, they see both business taxes and wage taxes as directly adding to their operating costs. Even though wage taxes are levied on workers' earnings rather than company earnings, many employers report they must pay their employees a higher salary to work in the city than they would have to pay workers in a suburban location, merely to compensate employees for losing 3.7 percent of earnings to the city wage tax. Most of the civic energy supporting wage and business tax cuts has therefore come from the business community and from civic and media groups supporting them.

Considerable civic debate in Philadelphia in recent years has been generated by another element, the relative effectiveness of tax breaks given to individual firms versus across-the-board tax cuts that benefit all businesses. Since 2000, we have witnessed growing opposition to offering tax breaks and other concessions to individual firms and growing support for across-the-board tax cuts. This is especially true in Philadelphia, where existing businesses have expressed resentment about special deals accorded to individual firms. For example, in 2004 the Center City Owners' Association, representing the landlords of many downtown buildings, protested loudly against granting subsidies to two new skyscrapers that would draw corporate offices out of existing buildings. The Center City District, representing downtown businesses more generally, criticized these same projects, noting that they would generate greater tax revenues for Philadelphia only if the new space were leased by tenants moving into the city—and no such stipulation had been attached to the subsidies.[24] However, even if business groups could demonstrate that broad tax cuts—as opposed to special deals struck with individual firms—are the most effective way for Philadelphia to attract businesses, it is not clear that the city's residents would support broad tax cuts. As mentioned earlier, the citizens who elect Philadelphia's mayor and city council may resist cutting public services in order to reduce tax rates.

Turning to the suburbs, let us consider the same question: does competition between jurisdictions serve to keep local spending and taxing down? It would be difficult to detect such a pattern in recent years. In the four suburban counties on the Pennsylvania side of the region, school tax levies (which typically comprise three- quarters of all local taxes) rose by an average of 30 percent from 2000 to 2005.[25] Despite those steep increases, a majority of suburban school boards in 2005 rejected the state government's offer to use state allocations to reduce local property tax burdens, provided the locals would commit to holding voter referendums on any future budget increases that would exceed the annual rate of inflation. The local school boards sacrificed the extra state help because they feared that the requirement for future public referendums would inhibit them from raising taxes in the future to pay for school improvements. There was little sign of the commitment to holding down spending and taxing that is theoretically supposed to result from competition among communities. Consider, for example, the findings of a 2004 opinion survey taken in the highest-spending school district in the entire region—Lower Merion Township. When residents were asked how they preferred to see the community's budget balanced, fully two-thirds favored increasing taxes "moderately" in order to maintain township services rather than reducing services in order to get lower taxes.[26] One antitax activist in suburban Pennridge recently expressed frustration that the influx of more affluent families in her community makes it increasingly difficult to build opposition to local tax increases: "The new generation is yuppies making good money, and if their kids want something, they'll pay anything for it . . . Soccer moms are running the district now."[27]

On the New Jersey side as well, property taxes have risen 29 percent since 2001.[28] In fact, the pattern in this region looks like the pattern predicted by Fischel,[29] who argued that communities compete with each other to provide the best quality services, especially schools, rather than competing to offer the lowest tax rates. According to Fischel's view, the homeowners' drive to bolster property values is the main motivator of local government actions. In a fragmented system, local governments choose to raise taxes to improve schools, knowing that the benefit to residents will be higher property values resulting from the community's improving schools. And in fact, research done in New Jersey has shown that for every one percent increase in per-pupil spending, there was an increase of 1.6 to 3.1 percent in the odds of someone wanting to move into that community.[30]

Promoting Smart Growth

The combination of governmental fragmentation and disproportionate reliance on property taxes fuels sprawl. In earlier chapters, we have reported that job sprawl is more pronounced than housing sprawl in this region. Local governments are likely to compete more ferociously for jobs and business development than for residential development, which they often see as a drain on public service budgets. In fact, many township leaders throughout the suburbs, observing the impacts of new residential development on the quality of life in their communities, now express a sense of having been overwhelmed by a tidal wave of development they did not control. They could not construct schools, roads, water systems, and sewer systems fast enough to accommodate new growth, causing overcrowding. Since new households arriving in their subdivisions usually cost more in public services than they contribute in taxes, township leaders in growing communities must scramble to secure their share of new office parks, malls, and other commercial developments that pay higher taxes and require fewer services. The price of accepting these large land uses is higher levels of road congestion and loss of open space. The townships are simply too small to serve as reasonable units for planning, so decisions about building subdivisions, malls, and office parks and laying down roads, water pipes, and sewer pipes are made by private developers. After those private decisions are made, township governments scramble to deal with the consequences.

Having watched this process over several decades, advocates for smart growth recognized in the 1990s that without external pressure, local governments were unlikely to band together into larger territorial units that would be appropriate for planning future development patterns. So they shifted their focus to state government, which controls some of the main levers affecting land development. State government agencies spend huge dollars on highways, water and sewer facilities, public school buildings, and incentives to developers locating plants and offices. Smart growth advocates reasoned that state leverage on these expenditures could be employed to induce greater cooperation among local governments. So activists began lobbying state government to use its power in just that fashion.

A leader in these efforts is a nonprofit organization formed in the 1990s called 10,000 Friends of Pennsylvania, modeled on an organization that helped design Oregon's progressive land use laws in the 1970s. While the organization's leadership is located in Philadelphia, it has sought allies across the state to pressure state government for laws and administrative rules that encourage compact forms of new development, protect open space, reduce traffic congestion and air and water pollution, and revitalize older town centers. Their most important victory to date was the Pennsylvania legislature's adoption in 2000 of two bills (Acts 67 and 68) that enabled—although they did not require—municipal governments to create joint planning bodies with neighboring townships. These laws represented significant progress because they removed some obstacles to multimunicipal planning, offered state incentives to townships that plan cooperatively with their neighbors, and provided a legal framework for voluntary tax base sharing to spread out both the positive and negative fiscal impacts of land use decisions.

To encourage municipalities to design joint plans for their combined land areas, the legislation offered to shield these multimunicipal planning efforts from costly "curative amendment" lawsuits. The new laws said that individual communities that plan jointly with their neighboring communities do not necessarily have to provide for every land use within each participating town. A developer who sues a township now has to prove that a particular land use is being systematically excluded from *all* of the towns cooperating in a multimunicipal planning district, not just the particular township where the development would be built.

Across the Delaware River in New Jersey, advocates for smart growth have also focused their efforts at the state level. For several decades, the New Jersey Office of State Planning has been encouraging development within designated growth areas that comprise about one-third of the state's land area, while trying to protect the remainder of the state against rampant development. Yet sometimes even a state government generally committed to smart growth principles can stumble. In what appeared to be a well-intentioned move to promote smart growth, the New Jersey legislature passed a "fast track" bill in 2004 to expedite permits for developers who wanted to build inside the designated growth areas. The bill would have given the state government only forty-five days to determine whether a developer's application met environmental requirements; if the state failed to act within those forty-five days, the permit would automatically be granted. Alarmed environmentalists began working immediately to repeal the measure. They argued that persuading developers to channel their building into large designated growth areas should not entitle them to build at *any* location within those growth areas, since within those larger zones, open space is at a premium and one can find many parcels that are environmentally sensitive. Critics of the law doubted the state's ability to process applications within the forty-five-day period, and therefore they foresaw many permits being granted by default for inappropriate locations. Within a matter of months, the governor acceded to critics and suspended the law.

It remains to be seen whether and how New Jersey state leaders will try to resurrect their efforts to channel new development into designated growth areas, or how many Pennsylvania townships will implement multimunicipal agreements and how ambitious their plans will be. One thing is clear: without impetus from the state level, local government leaders on both sides of the Delaware River would likely remain within their limited local boundaries, buffeted by market forces beyond their control.

Conclusion

Early in this chapter, we described two schools of research that have systematically investigated how Americans choose where to live. Peter Rossi and subsequent sociologists have explained residential moves as motivated by a desire for more and better living space at an affordable cost. They have focused especially on changes in family circumstances as reasons prompting people to move. Economist Charles Tiebout and his followers have concluded that movers seek to optimize the balance of costs versus advantages when they choose particular housing units. Movers, they contend, can best be understood as consumers comparing the whole package of services, amenities, and taxes conferred by different locations.

As noted earlier, the two schools of thought are not mutually exclusive. On balance, our analysis suggests that, although there is some evidence that households choose where to live in ways consistent with a value proposition, most of our results indicate that the life cycle explanation is the stronger one. Respondents to our survey cite good schools as important to them, but in our aggregate analysis of movement among the region's communities, measures of school quality did not account for migration, once other factors had been taken into account. Lower taxes did have an impact, but it was the weakest of all of those factors that were statistically significant.

Both Rossi and Tiebout see consumers performing a kind of cost-benefit calculation. Our study of greater Philadelphia leads us to suggest that for many homeowners, a critical element of that cost-benefit calculation is people's view of the home as an investment asset. If households were viewing their housing choice simply as a way to accommodate their daily living needs at the best price, many more might be choosing affordable neighborhoods that exist throughout large parts of this region. Yet demand for homes in many affordable neighborhoods is low. Rather than carefully balancing costs against services, many consumers are buying the most expensive house possible. That choice—to spend more than one has to spend—reflects the tendency to treat the home purchase as an investment decision.

In the recent housing "bubble," several forces have driven higher demand and prices in most metropolitan areas. Key among these are the commitment to home ownership as the single dominant national housing policy since 1950, the rapid increases in housing values that were sustained after the inflationary period of the 1970s, an apparent decrease in residential stability over time, and the increased use of home equity as an income supplement. Homeowners have increasingly treated their houses as investments—with a market value that could be cashed in to trade up in housing value or used as collateral to borrow funds for a variety of purposes. They have been encouraged to take this view by the U.S. tax code, which has granted deductions for mortgage interest and real estate taxes. The growth of the mortgage refinance industry has also facilitated the view of houses as investment assets. As a result, many household moves are influenced by expectations regarding a return on one's investment.

We found in this chapter that the faster-growing communities in the region have been those with the higher-priced housing. One way to look at that relationship would be to assume that high demand for homes was causing values to appreciate. However, the reverse may also be true—in other words, the pattern of rapidly appreciating prices attracted homebuyers hoping to benefit from that upward trend. The appreciating values in some communities persuade people to buy as much housing as they could afford.

Treating one's home as an investment has implications for household behavior in other realms. For example, it may affect the attitude adopted by community members toward land use and environmental controls. Research in greater Philadelphia has examined which types of suburban communities are most likely to enact regulations governing new development (e.g., requiring large lot sizes or requiring developers to share the cost of new infrastructure). Researchers found that municipalities with higher home values and higher-income residents have a greater tendency than do less affluent places to enact such land use regulation as a way of enhancing the value of homes in the community.[31]

Chapter 4 suggested that a desire to protect housing values may also lead suburban residents to support rising educational spending even though it increases their tax burden, on the assumption that good schools reinforce the value of homes in the community. It was interesting to note in Chapter 4 how many suburban school children attend private schools, even in suburbs whose public schools are well funded and highly regarded. Is it irrational for families to choose to live in suburbs whose tax rates support high-performing schools, yet also pay tuition to send their children to private schools? One plausible explanation is that they choose to live in a well-funded public school district, even though the district does not serve their own children, because they believe good public schools bolster the value of their home as an asset. Similarly, the investment mentality adopted by many homeowners may lead them to support taxation for other public amenities (parks, recreation, libraries) that enhance the immediate environment surrounding their homes. However, we know of no evidence that treating one's home as an investment fosters a sense of collective responsibility beyond the homeowner's immediate community. Some observers have even argued that homeownership substantially reduces people's willingness to contribute to the welfare of the larger society, because households are so burdened by mortgage debt that they resist paying federal or state taxes at a level that would support more generous social welfare programs.[32]

It is worth remembering that large segments of the region's population do not reap the tax advantages and other benefits of owning an appreciating asset, either because they are renters or because they own homes in declining neighborhoods where property values are stagnating. Their circumstances give them different policy preferences from the region's middle-class and upper-middle-class homeowners. They have less incentive to support increasing local taxes, since they are not benefiting from rising property values.

The differences in the fortunes, and therefore in the interests, of different groups in the region are increasingly reflected as differences between communities, with the wealthy, the well housed, and the well educated separating themselves from less advantaged citizens. The story of the last half-century is a story of the sorting of social and racial groups across a regional landscape of 353 local governments. We have argued that this fragmenting of public authority into hundreds of small units has exacerbated inequalities in access to jobs, housing, and education. In the final chapter of the book, we will focus on the changing nature of social action, as more nongovernmental institutions take responsibility for addressing the inequalities we have described.

6

WHO TAKES RESPONSIBILITY FOR ADDRESSING INEQUALITY?

⁓

The opportunity gaps separating different locations across the region are likely to widen unless they are addressed by public policies. In Chapter 1 we argued that differences between places exacerbate differences in the quality of life for the region's population. In our chapter-by-chapter examination of the distributions of employment, housing, and education, we have paid particular attention to efforts being made to overcome the inequalities in our regional landscape. Looking for those public and private actors who are currently addressing the region's uneven development, we have been struck by how many of them work in the third sector.

Policy research on urban development has traditionally focused on local government as the agent of change. In the period following World War II, local governments became increasingly involved in the physical redevelopment of cities. Our previous book on Philadelphia devoted a chapter to this postwar redevelopment process, showing that during the 1960s, Philadelphia had one of the nation's most active city governments using federal funds to retrofit the downtown area to accommodate the economic shift from a manufacturing to a service economy. Federal legislation encouraged local governments to form partnerships with profit-making investors to rebuild stagnant central cities. Typically local government took responsibility for purchasing and clearing land, rezoning, and offering tax abatements to private developers to build on the land.

That is hardly surprising, since local government officials are essentially stewards of *places*. They have a strong stake in sustaining the vitality of the places they govern. Their political interests are served by bringing investments into their jurisdictions, especially investments that bolster the value of places. After all, their budgets for public services depend on locally generated taxes. This is true for both urban and suburban officials. They possess powers that are crucial to making and remaking places, particularly the power of eminent domain, which allows them to transfer land from one use to another. In earlier chapters, we have seen several examples of the priority that local political leaders place on bolstering places, from the clearing and reconstruction of older neighborhoods to providing tax abatements that lure corporate tenants to occupy new office buildings, refurbishing aging commercial strips, and competing for malls, office parks, and other tax-producing commercial development. Local government has long been an important initiator of such ventures, as the discussion of the Neighborhood Transformation Initiative in Chapter 3 illustrated.

Now, however, the organizational field has become more complex, with a wider variety of actors beyond local government playing important roles. In their efforts to transform places, local governments have increasingly turned to organizations outside of government to carry out place-based development projects. We were struck by how numerous and how important these nongovernmental organizations are.

The Expanding Role of the Third Sector

Opportunities for redevelopment often occur at a scale smaller than local government or larger than local government boundaries. Rather than trying to adjust the formal boundaries to match these varying problem scales (an approach that regional government advocates have been unsuccessfully touting for decades), metropolitan activists are spawning a host of nonprofit organizations to tackle public issues. These efforts arise from either the inability or the unwillingness of local and state political actors to tackle the issues produced by changing social and economic conditions. In this chapter, we examine how different kinds of regional nonprofits seek to address the region's developmental issues.

Business Improvement Districts

Among the fastest-growing of the nongovernmental bodies taking responsibility for revitalizing older urban areas are business improvement districts (BIDs). In Chapter 2 we saw that BIDs have worked to improve commercial districts like Center City and West Philadelphia. But BIDs have been used in both the city and suburbs. About a dozen Philadelphia neighborhoods have business improvement districts, known in Philadelphia as "special service districts." Not content with the public services provided by local government, the residents and businesses in those locations have organized to tax themselves above the normal tax level in order to provide desired services at a higher level than they are receiving from municipal government. They focus on trash collection, street maintenance, security patrols, maintaining open spaces, operating shuttle buses, and funding sidewalk beautification. Although they start with "clean and safe" activities, these nongovernmental, nonprofit authorities often branch out into planning and economic development functions as well. It is estimated that in 2002, Philadelphia's BIDs spent approximately $20.4 million to pay for services that supplemented local government services. When spread across the territory they covered, the average expenditure per block was $23,000.[1]

Such special service districts exist not only in the strongest commercial districts (Center City; West Philadelphia, adjacent to the University of Pennsylvania and Drexel University; and City Line Avenue, where the city abuts a major suburban commercial strip) but also in a number of less vital neighborhood strips like the aging industrial neighborhoods of Germantown and Frankford. BIDs are appearing in the suburbs as well. Collingswood, which pioneered this approach in South Jersey in 2000, now has multiple districts, while Audubon, Haddon Township, and Haddonfield have created BIDs of their own.

Neighborhood Development Organizations

In residential areas, community nonprofit organizations began to multiply in the 1970s to take responsibility for a range of neighborhood improvements—establishing town watches to supplement police efforts, business associations to upgrade retail strips, housing committees to lure investment back to declining markets, and social services for children and families. These community organizations were born out of a sense that the city's neighborhoods "must either be satisfied with reduced services or devise ways of providing them."[2] Nonprofit community organizations are typically funded by a combination of foundation grants, city pass-throughs of federal Community Development Block Grant (CDBG) funds, bank donations in response to the Community Reinvestment Act, and a variety of other smaller sources.

As in other cities, Philadelphia has seen many of these grassroots organizations falter and even disappear for lack of adequate funding, management, or community support. Particularly during the 1980s when federal funding for inner-city redevelopment shrank dramatically, many community-based organizations (CBOs) of the 1970s went out of business. Those that survived were disproportionately the community development corporations (CDCs) operating with strong business models to build and rehabilitate housing units, train and support small business owners, and operate day care centers, youth programs, and other services. Philadelphia now contains several dozen strong, sophisticated CDCs and hundreds of other smaller, struggling nonprofits working to sustain disadvantaged communities.

Although community-based organizations are often seen as grassroots vehicles to pressure local governments and even oppose them, today's neighborhood nonprofits are likely to have strong links to local government agencies and officials because they depend heavily on allocations of CDBG funds and on the government's power of eminent domain. They are typically responsive to politicians. Indeed, many CBOs have evolved into political support associations resembling both partisan ward organizations and consultants who expect contracts and grants as a normal aspect of their operation; they partake in a set of "ossified relationships of obligation and reward" that characterize city government.[3] As partners cooperating with local governments, CBOs play an important role, even those whose annual production of housing and commercial ventures is small. They serve as signals to for-profit investors that ventures in disadvantaged neighborhoods can be successful. A study comparing the strength and diversity of nonprofit community development corporations in several large U.S. cities concluded that in cities with rich networks of CDCs, banks and other private capital sources participated the most in financing community projects.[4]

Community Development Financial Institutions

Crucial to the success of nonprofit networks in attracting private sector investors are the Community Development Financial Institutions (CDFIs), which help banks and other financial institutions mitigate the risks they take when they invest in disadvantaged neighborhoods. CDFIs are nonprofit organizations that help to match investors with worthwhile development projects in neighborhoods that those investors would typically bypass. CDFIs acquire pools of working capital from foundations, corporations, the government, and individual investors, and then use the capital to stimulate businesses and projects that create opportunity for low-income households. Beyond the investment dollars, CDFIs typically provide planning and technical assistance. In order to accomplish this, they rely on detailed data analysis and often first-hand knowledge of conditions in the disadvantaged communities where they make investments.

It is this analytical capacity possessed by a Philadelphia CDFI that led Mayor Street to entrust the important analytical work underpinning his

Neighborhood Transformation Initiative to The Reinvestment Fund (TRF) rather than assigning the work to governmental staff members. The mayor judged that in the course of making its investment choices over two decades, TRF had developed sufficient information and analytical capacity relating to the city's neighborhoods to be able to identify which areas of Philadelphia could benefit from different renewal strategies. Based on this work, The Reinvestment Fund also became one of the principal partners devising reinvestment strategies for Camden, New Jersey. Using funds from the Ford Foundation and William Penn Foundation, TRF collected and analyzed detailed information about the neighborhoods in Camden and worked with city and state officials to decide where and how the state's investments could best be targeted.

This same CDFI has also exercised a public planning role by acting as a conduit for distributing tax credits like the federal government's New Market Tax Credits. As an intermediary, TRF has been assigned by the U.S. Treasury Department the responsibility for selecting projects to benefit from over $100 million worth of federal tax credits supporting projects in low-income areas. Under earlier urban renewal programs, the city government would have been exercising such judgments. But in the new policy environment, it is a nonprofit CDFI that often decides how governmental subsidies should be divided among projects like new supermarkets serving disadvantaged neighborhoods, inner city commercial and apartment buildings, and a retail and movie complex.

Foundations

Although much of their work is conducted out of public view, foundations are increasingly exerting influence over the region's future. Several Philadelphia foundations have large enough endowments to invest tens of millions of dollars in major development projects. Even smaller foundation grants can have important impacts, especially because foundations have the flexibility to decide quickly where and how to spend their money.

One of the most dramatic impacts foundations have made on Philadelphia's development in recent years results from a cultural initiative pursued by a coalition of three local foundations. The Pew Charitable Trusts, the Annenberg Foundation, and the Lenfest Foundation joined forces to move an important cultural institution, the Barnes Foundation, from its suburban location into downtown Philadelphia. The Barnes Foundation is home to one of the finest collections of impressionist paintings in the world, and the three foundations decided to use it to revitalize the Benjamin Franklin Parkway, the monumental boulevard that connects City Hall with the Philadelphia Art Museum. The three foundations promised to raise $150 million to keep the financially troubled Barnes Foundation solvent, but only if the museum's trustees would relocate the institution to the downtown site. Once the museum made the controversial decision to accept the foundations' bargain, its trustees had to spend years defending their decision against lawsuits that contended the move would violate the will of the founder, Albert Barnes, who had specified that he wanted the collection to remain in the suburban structure he built for it. Ultimately the Barnes trustees prevailed, in partnership with the three foundations.[5]

Philadelphia's foundations also have been active in public school reform. Several foundations weighed in during the 1990s to pursue changes in the district's instructional approach. They sought greater continuity in curriculum from grade to grade, uniform standards for student achievement in each grade, and the breakup of the larger, more impersonal schools into smaller units. For example, the Pew Charitable Trusts funded the Philadelphia Schools Collaborative in the early 1990s to promote high school restructuring. They gave the district money to experiment with breaking the larger school buildings into smaller school units, each with its own budgets, staff allocations, and decision-making powers. The reactions of veteran school administrators ranged from caution to outright opposition. In another initiative that appeared to bypass district structures, the Pew foundation commissioned the Philadelphia Education Fund (a private nonprofit organization) to develop standards for measuring whether student performance was improving. Once developed by the nonprofit consultant, the standards were presented to the school board in 1996 with an implication that if the board rejected the standards, Pew's money might not be forthcoming in the future.

At about the same time, in the mid-1990s, another large Philadelphia institution, The William Penn Foundation, invested substantial sums in a plan to divide the massive school system into twenty-two "clusters"—formal groupings of schools that included one neighborhood high school and its feeder elementary and middle schools. The purpose was to provide continuity for children from K to 12th grade. Key to the new structure were small learning communities at all grade levels. In 1995 the foundation granted almost $14 million to the school district to test whether the new cluster arrangement would produce higher student performance. But as it turned out, the foundation was testing an arrangement that subsequently was abandoned by the district, not because it was proven ineffective, but simply as a cost-cutting measure.

By far the largest foundation initiative in the public schools was the Annenberg Foundation's gift of a $50 million challenge grant, to be administered through a business coalition, Greater Philadelphia First. The district had to match the foundation grant with $100 million raised from other public and private sources. This led an influential columnist to write critically about the effect that the Annenberg Foundation money had in redirecting public funds within the district; the critic called it "a very big, very undemocratic tail wagging a democratic dog." This "checkbook democracy," he lamented, allowed the foundation to call the shots for a democratic institution like the school board.[6]

Quasi-public Corporations

Another institution outside of government employed for major redevelopment projects is the quasi-public corporation. This is not a new phenomenon in Philadelphia. Alternately labeled "corporations" or "authorities," these organizations have proliferated since the mid-twentieth century. Typically, quasi-public corporations are run by boards of directors that combine elected officials with business leaders. They represent what has come to be known in the urban development field as "public-private partnerships." Their proponents argue that by placing major capital investment programs under the control of such boards, the projects can be operated independently of the political process. Having no direct political accountability, project managers in these organizations are free to use financial and technical criteria to make operating decisions. Since civil service protections do not extend to employees of such independent corporations, their managers have more flexibility than political officials in hiring, promoting, and firing staff. And the clarity of their mission, when compared with the complex functions performed by general-purpose government, makes it easier to evaluate their performance.

On the New Jersey side of the region, the Cooper's Ferry Development Corporation in Camden is an example. It has worked since its inception in 1984 to develop the Delaware River waterfront. Its board includes political officials from the city, county, and state of New Jersey as well as religious leaders and representatives from business and the community. To advance its mission of waterfront development, Cooper's Ferry developed a master plan that included offices, marinas, restaurants, a hotel-conference center, apartments, and a museum. With the master plan in hand, it pursued individual projects one by one, rather than seeking a single developer to transform the whole waterfront. Over the years, Camden acquired the New Jersey State Aquarium, the Tweeter Center (concert arena), Campbell's Field for baseball, and the Battleship New Jersey Museum. On occasion, when its master plan has been opposed by other political forces in Camden, Cooper's Ferry has fought back fiercely. For example, in the mid-1990s, a newly elected mayor moved to pull the development corporation's vision for the city into line with his own: "No nonprofit, private entity can come to this city and have free rein over everything they choose to have without coordination." The head of Cooper's Ferry Development Corporation shot back, "In most cities, it's not the expectation that the mayor is the hands-on, day-to-day coordinator of the development process," and cited Philadelphia as an example, "Mayor Rendell has his vision but it's groups like the Philadelphia Industrial Development Corporation and Penn's Landing that go out and implement that vision."[7]

That frustrated reference was to Penn's Landing Corporation, a nonprofit created to oversee development along the Philadelphia side of the Delaware River. It was created in 1970 to maintain and improve the Delaware River waterfront. It receives half a million dollars of subsidy each year from the city government, to which it adds income from grants from other sources. The organization stages festivals and other public events, maintains the boat basin, and leases waterfront land for many purposes. Its board contains some of the region's key business and political figures.

More than any other quasi-public corporation in the city, this one demonstrates that giving such bodies the responsibility for major public assets does not guarantee that projects can be brought to rapid and successful conclusion. In its thirty-year history, the Penn's Landing Corporation has repeatedly tried and failed to establish a unified plan for one of the city's most valuable tracts of land. Instead of implementing its own master plan, as did Cooper's Ferry on the New Jersey side, Penn's Landing Corporation has tried to lure a series of megadevelopers, each time expecting the outsider to supply the master vision for the tract. While across the United States cities have reclaimed their waterfronts as major civic assets, with new parks, museums, housing, and entertainment, Philadelphia has so far failed to realize the ambitions of five successive mayors who have tried to transform the waterfront.

State Intervention in the Region

Not only has Philadelphia's governance shifted more functions into the public-private partnerships described above, but local governments have also seen significant power shifting upward to the state level. Since the early 1990s, both Pennsylvania and New Jersey state governments have been taking a more aggressive posture with respect to the lagging older cities. A good example is state-level influence on the waterfront developments just described, exerted through the actions of the Delaware River Port Authority (DRPA), which was formed in the mid-twentieth century and governed by eight commissioners each from Pennsylvania and New Jersey. This congressionally sanctioned interstate authority was initially created to oversee the operation of toll bridges that connect Philadelphia to New Jersey across the Delaware River, a mission it pursued for decades in obscurity. In the 1990s, however, its job expanded to include regional economic development, a function normally assigned to local or state governments. Funded by bridge tolls instead of taxes, DRPA had a revenue stream larger than it needed to cover the cost of maintaining the bridges and the high-speed rail line that takes commuters from New Jersey towns in and out of Philadelphia every day. So the governments of New Jersey and Pennsylvania jointly decided in 1992 to begin spending the DRPA's surplus funds on a variety of projects that would boost economic development in the greater Philadelphia region.

Some of the agency's investments resemble classic economic development projects (e.g., investments to help resurrect the Philadelphia Navy Yard after it was decommissioned as a defense installation or to help expand the Philadelphia Convention Center). DRPA has also become the major patron of the two development corporations described above—Penn's Landing and Cooper's Ferry. However, DRPA has surprised observers by investing many dollars in tourism, entertainment, and cultural institutions. Large grants have subsidized the Franklin Institute science museum, the Please Touch children's museum, the National Constitution Center, Camden's minor league baseball stadium, the effort to bring the Battleship New Jersey to Camden's waterfront, a tramway linking tourist attractions on the Camden and Philadelphia waterfronts, and even ice skating rinks and beautification projects. This unexpected emphasis on tourism and culture attracted media attention and drew opposition from critics who argued that commuters paying bridge tolls were unwillingly subsidizing these public projects. Such critics could do little more than complain, however, since DRPA was not accountable to the public for its decisions.

By taking other state actions, state officials have overridden local opposition. In fact, both Pennsylvania and New Jersey governments have gone so far as to take over important local functions, placing portions of local government in receivership as a condition of sending more state money to the cities. This has happened on both sides of the Delaware River. As the financial conditions of Philadelphia, Camden, Chester, and other older cities have worsened, local government managers have faced widening gaps between revenues and expenditures. State governments have stepped in to help close those gaps, but they have demanded more state control over local budgets.

The first major instance occurred in Philadelphia in the early 1990s when ballooning deficits threatened to bankrupt the city government. To solve the crisis, the state government in 1991 created the Pennsylvania Intergovernmental Cooperation Authority (PICA), a body whose twin functions were to raise money through the sale of bonds and to impose discipline on the city's budgeting process. PICA borrowed money to meet the city's cash needs, while the city accepted an additional 1 percent sales tax on goods sold within the city and agreed to divert a part of the city wage tax to repay PICA's debt. PICA gained the right to review annually the city's five-year budget plans and the right to audit virtually every branch of Philadelphia government in order to assure itself that the city was sticking to the austerity plan. That bargain had significant consequences for the city, particularly affecting labor relations. The agreement with PICA obligated Philadelphia's mayor to advise PICA before approving any labor contracts or any other expenditure that would exceed $1 million. While it stopped short of making PICA a party to the city's labor negotiations, it gave PICA a powerful influence over labor contracts.

State officials have also chosen also to take control of one of the region's most important development assets, the Pennsylvania Convention Center. Philadelphia had opened this new convention center in 1993, after ten years of start-and-stop planning and political wrangling. At the cost of one-half billion dollars, the centerpiece of the city's hospitality industry was initially governed by a nine-member board appointed by a combination of the city government, the suburbs, and the governor. During its first decade of operation, complaints plagued the facility, mostly about high labor costs, surly workers, and fights about which union was entitled to do which jobs on the exhibit floor. In June 2002 a formal report disclosed that because of labor and management problems, only 17 percent of the groups whose conventions had met in Philadelphia during the previous year said they would return. Frustrated about being asked for hundreds of millions more to expand the convention center when labor conflicts remained unresolved, the state legislature removed control of the convention center from the city's hands. They did so by simply expanding the size of its governing board with new members appointed from outside the city, thereby diluting the city's voting power. With the state's majority firmly established, the governor and legislative leaders proved agreeable to spending $630 million more from state funds for a major expansion to add 50 percent more exhibit space.

Even more dramatic than the above examples was Pennsylvania's takeover of local schools. When Philadelphia's school superintendent threatened in 1998 to close down the city schools if the state failed to cover an estimated $85 million deficit, the majority leader of the state House of Representatives (the same politician who engineered the takeover of the convention center) immediately moved to enable a state takeover. He drafted legislation authorizing the state secretary of education to declare any district "distressed" if it failed to budget appropriately and thus deprived children of their education. This sweeping legislation would allow the governor to appoint a district superintendent, strip the local board of education of its powers, forbid strikes by the teachers' union, and it would allow the state-run district to bring in outside contractors. Although Philadelphia was not the only city targeted by this legislation, it was clearly the trigger for state action.

One might expect representatives from the Philadelphia region unanimously to have rejected this assault on local control of the public schools. Yet among the city legislators, five Republicans and three Democrats voted *in favor*

TABLE 6.1   VOTES CAST FOR ACT 46 ALLOWING THE STATE
GOVERNMENT TO TAKE OVER PHILADELPHIA SCHOOLS,
1998

	Voting Yes	Voting No
Legislators from city	8	24
Legislators from suburbs	39	6

Source: *Pennsylvania Legislative Journal of the General Assembly, for the House of Representatives and for the Senate.*

of the state takeover. Table 6.1 shows how the legislative delegation from greater Philadelphia, including members of both houses, voted on the takeover bill. Note the strong support for the bill from the suburbs surrounding Philadelphia. This shows how weakly the suburbs supported the Philadelphia district management.

Although Philadelphia's fiscal crisis precipitated the takeover legislation, Philadelphia was actually not the first district in the region to be taken over by the state. Instead, an impoverished school district in the Philadelphia suburbs became the first. With only about 5,000 enrolled students, that suburban district may have appeared easier to tackle. The Chester Upland district, including the aging industrial city of Chester located on the Delaware River, was producing some of the state's lowest test scores. In 2000 the state appointed its own Board of Control to oversee the district, which then contracted with several companies—Edison Schools, LearnNow, and Mosaica—to operate its schools. The state teachers' union opposed the takeover, and many local officials and school advocates opposed hiring profit-making firms to manage their schools. Nevertheless, the Board of Control moved ahead. State oversight does not appear to have improved district operations. In fall 2004 a state report on continuing budget problems suggested that even the state-appointed board was guilty of "gross overspending" and "mismanagement."[8]

If turning around Chester Upland proved more complicated than it first appeared, the Philadelphia district, with over 200,000 pupils, presented state officials with an even more difficult takeover target. Although they were armed by the legislature with broad powers to intervene, state administrators initially seemed reluctant to step into Philadelphia. They gave the mayor three years following the landmark takeover legislation to negotiate with state officials. Mayor Street took his time negotiating with the governor for the best possible terms he could obtain for the city: the state agreed to annually provide millions of additional dollars in return for greater control over the city schools. In late 2001 Philadelphia became the largest school district in the United States ever taken over by a state. The district has since been run by a five-member School Reform Commission made up of three members picked by the state and two picked by the city.

Across the Delaware River, the city of Camden has been experiencing a similar loss of power to the state government of New Jersey. In Chapter 3, we described a $175 million relief plan for Camden that provided funds to expand the city's colleges and hospitals, demolish abandoned buildings, rehabilitate housing, build parks, and improve roads and other infrastructure. In exchange for giving Camden the $175 million, the state government gained sweeping control over the city. That control is held by a state-appointed chief operating officer whose decisions supercede even the elected mayor's authority. The chief operating officer has broad power extending even to changing the municipal code and city ordinances.

At the same time the state imposed its control over economic redevelopment, the New Jersey legislature dictated that Camden's nine-member elected school board would be supplemented by members appointed by the governor and Camden's mayor. Further, the school board would give the governor a veto over its actions. The school board challenged the state action in a lawsuit, claiming the state was taking control of Camden's schools without going through the normal procedures required to take over a school district. But as in Philadelphia's school takeover, Camden's Mayor Gwendolyn Faison favored the arrangement as the only way to secure for her city the resources it badly needed. The actions of the two city mayors illustrate that while the prospect of state takeovers appears draconian, it actually serves the interests of at least some local leaders. As is the case with quasi-public corporations, business improvement districts, neighborhood nonprofits, and other organizations discussed in this chapter, local political leaders have sometimes gained political advantages by ceding authority to other entities, including state governments.

Perhaps the most troubling feature of this trend of states taking over major local institutions and processes is that state legislatures are arenas in which cities have steadily lost power, as population has shifted to the suburbs. States are gaining direct decision-making authority at a time when they have less sympathy for and less day-to-day knowledge about urban conditions.

Who Takes Responsibility for Moving People to Opportunity?

Compared with their commitment to reviving older places, local governments have a much weaker stake in moving people to opportunity. Political power is territorially based, and local elected officials typically invest little energy in encouraging their constituents to seek opportunities elsewhere. Even state governments have taken a weaker role than we might expect because legislators representing the advantaged areas are focused on maintaining whatever competitive edge their communities possess, while they see little to gain by incorporating disadvantaged residents into their constituencies. Suburban legislators, who outnumber the legislators representing the urban centers of the region, are seldom enthusiastic about accepting affordable housing or welcoming school pupils from poorer districts into their schools. As we saw in Chapter 3, even strong judicial actions like the series of Mt. Laurel court decisions have not succeeded in dispersing inner-city residents to the suburbs. However, other players outside of local government have emerged in the metropolitan area to promote this agenda. Below we look at the organizations beyond local governments that are leading such initiatives in four areas: transportation, workforce development, affordable housing, and promoting educational choice.

Serving Low-Income Commuters on Public Transportation

We saw in Chapter 2 that the region's public transit authority, the Southeastern Pennsylvania Transportation Authority (SEPTA) has expended considerable effort to find ways to accommodate commuters who travel from the urban centers of the region to entry-level jobs in the suburbs. Since transporting low-wage workers to suburban jobs is a common interest shared by the city and the suburbs, reverse commuting programs have enjoyed support from both the suburban and city representatives who sit on SEPTA's governing board. That city-suburban agreement within the SEPTA board is an exception to the pattern of competition and conflict that usually characterize relationships between the city and suburban counties.

As Chapter 2 explained, SEPTA has partnered with suburban Transit Management Associations (TMAs) to operate shuttle buses and vans that transport riders from SEPTA stations to their ultimate suburban destinations in office parks or shopping malls. TMAs represent an interesting form of nonprofit member-controlled organization, intended to provide custom-tailored transportation routes serving particular collections of workplaces—for example, commercial districts, medical centers, and office or industrial parks. They get their funds from businesses and the federal government. As small nongovernmental organizations, they can move nimbly to adjust services to rapidly changing employment patterns in the suburbs. This kind of partnership between a regional authority and private nonprofit TMAs exemplifies the organizational networks beyond local governments that are needed to promote mobility strategies.

A completely different approach to transportation problems of the working poor is being taken by a nonprofit family services agency in suburban Montgomery County. As we saw in Chapter 2, owning an automobile dramatically increases a household's chances of escaping poverty because it provides access to jobs that may be virtually inaccessible by public transit, especially in the suburbs. A national nonprofit lending program called Ways to Work[9] has a local affiliate in the Philadelphia suburbs. Ways to Work is a community development financial institution based in Milwaukee that has secured a pool of capital from foundations, banks, and government sources. It disperses the money to affiliated organizations in twenty-five states. Those local affiliates take loan applications from low-wage workers who are raising at least one child and who have poor credit or no credit at all. All loans must be transportation related (i.e., to buy or repair a car that is required to take the borrower to work). The amounts are small (up to $3,000) and must be repaid within two years. Across the United States, Ways to Work has grown large enough to have approved over $20 million in loans.

Workforce Development

Watching its economic dominance waning in the region, Philadelphia officials are wary of ceding autonomy to regional bodies that are likely to be dominated by powerful suburban neighbors. An example is the city's resistance to joining a regional workforce investment board (WIB), as described in Chapter 2. Although Pennsylvania's governor called for the city and surrounding suburban counties to create a single-region WIB, that never happened because advocates for Philadelphia feared the city would suffer when competing against the suburbs for jobs, funds, and support. This turf protection is predictable behavior on the part of local government officials; it illustrates the reason why initiatives to train workers and provide mobility to opportunities across boundaries are more likely to come from nongovernmental than governmental actors.

A promising approach to regional workforce planning is represented by a project undertaken through Philadelphia's third sector. Philadelphia was one of six cities selected by the Annie E. Casey Foundation in 1995 for the foundation's Jobs Initiative. The foundation's goal was to identify models for training and employment that might be replicated nationally. In Philadelphia the foundation granted funds to The Reinvestment Fund (TRF), a nonprofit intermediary described earlier in this chapter. Rather than limiting its work to the central city, TRF formed a regional coalition of over 100 employers, transportation groups, unions, CBOs, and educators to identify the main workforce problems facing the region. The group identified customer service and information technology as two job categories in demand by employers in all parts of the region. In response to those findings, TRF incubated two new programs: one to train entry-level job seekers with customer service skills and another to increase opportunities for high school and community college students for IT careers.

Reflecting its role as an intermediary rather than a service provider, TRF chose not to implement these initiatives on its own, but rather to recruit two strong nonprofit organizations (Jewish Employment and Vocational Services and the United Way of Southeastern Pennsylvania) to undertake them. Additional investments went to other existing nonprofits, for example, to experiment with Project STRIVE, a nationally recognized model for short-term training emphasizing "soft skills" and to a worker-owned private company called Home Care Associates. Since TRF is an investor in many small- and medium-sized companies throughout the region, it has coordinated workforce development efforts with its business portfolio. Always seeking to combine other funding sources with its own investments, the intermediary has found foundation dollars particularly important: "Private foundation funding is flexible. It's critical for leveraging public funding."[10]

In Camden, the sizeable state expenditures for workforce development are having only limited success because of the fragmentation among job training programs. Many smaller community-based providers are unaware of the state funding available for job training. The frustrated director of the Latin American Economic Development Association recommended that "there should be a clearinghouse all nonprofits should be able to access."[11] As in other regions of the country, it is this fractured institutional picture that creates the need for intermediary organizations like TRF to assume responsibility for planning and coordinating region-wide efforts.[12]

Housing

Since we observed previously that the governmental picture in the region is highly fragmented, it is perhaps not surprising that there is no coordinated governmental planning for affordable housing in the region. Although HUD requires all counties and municipalities to develop housing plans in order to receive federal housing money, the region's local and county governments have independently developed their plans: "As a result, affordable housing in Southeastern Pennsylvania is guided by 13 consolidated plans, six public housing authority plans, five county comprehensive plans, and up to 238 municipal comprehensive plans."[13]

The fact that local politicians do not typically promote movement across jurisdictional boundaries is obvious from our discussion of Section 8 vouchers in Chapter 3. Consider the controversy engendered by dispersing Section 8 tenants into working- and middle-class neighborhoods within the city of Philadelphia. When Section 8 programs have introduced outsiders into neighborhoods where they were unwanted, local politicians whose districts were affected immediately called for a halt to dispersing Section 8 tenants. We can only imagine how much more contentious would be the reaction to dispersing Section 8 tenants from the inner cities of Philadelphia and Camden to the suburbs. Without any actual instances of such transfers across district boundaries, there is no evidence to report. There is virtually no "portability" of housing vouchers from cities into suburbs because suburban housing authorities prefer to allocate scarce affordable units to people on their local waiting lists. Realistically, the only way to increase housing mobility from the core cities to the suburbs would be to create many more affordable housing units in the suburbs. As we saw in Chapter 3, some nonprofit organizations are working to do just that. But their impact so far has been limited.

One way to assess the rate at which the suburbs are creating affordable opportunities is to examine the number of low-income units being created through the Low Income Housing Tax Credit program (LIHTC), the national program established in 1986 to issue federal tax credits to investors who put money into acquiring, rehabilitating, or constructing new housing targeted to lower-income households. Each state receives a tax credit of $1.75 per person that the state can allocate to encourage investment in affordable housing projects. Any local government or nonprofit organization or for-profit company may apply for tax credits to subsidize affordable housing. Most often, applications come from partnerships of these different groups collaborating on development projects. The LIHTC program has become the single most important federal-state tool for producing low-income housing across the United States, and tax credits are used in a majority of low-income developments these days. Table 6.2 shows that from 1987 to 2004, the LIHTC program supported the creation of almost 14,000 low-income housing units in the greater Philadelphia region. Almost two-thirds (61 percent) of those units were located within the core cities of Philadelphia and Camden. Seventeen years worth of LIHTC deals in each of the suburban counties produced low-income units numbering only in the hundreds (the exceptions being Burlington and Camden counties). Yet the qualified households currently on Section 8 waiting lists in those same suburban counties number in the thousands. A 2005 report estimated that there were 1,500 households on the waiting list in Bucks County and around 3,000 households each in Chester and Delaware counties.[14] Since county housing authorities are allowed by federal law to give preference to applicants from their own waiting list over applicants coming from the central city, it is impossible to imagine affordable housing units in the suburbs opening up to the city's Section 8 tenants any time soon.

TABLE 6.2   LOW-INCOME HOUSING UNITS BUILT WITH
LOW-INCOME HOUSING TAX CREDITS, 1987–2004

Philadelphia	7,343
Camden	1,060
Bucks County	223
Chester County	865
Delaware County	987
Montgomery County	401
Burlington County	1,132
Camden County (outside the city of Camden)	1,259
Gloucester County	269
Salem County	207
Total	13,746

Source: U.S. Department of Housing and Urban Development, Low Income Housing
Tax Credit Database, accessible at www.huduser.org/datasets/lihtc.html#data.

School Choice through Charters

In Chapter 4 we described the immense challenges facing the school districts
of Philadelphia, Camden, Chester, and other urban centers of the region.
While many advocates have stressed the need to invest more dollars to revitalize these older school districts, a growing chorus of voices favors breaking the
geographic link that has historically tied enrollments to neighborhood
schools. That position is explicitly part of the federal No Child Left Behind
Act, which stipulates that students in "failing" schools should be offered a
chance to transfer. Yet there is significant distance between the federal law and
its implementation on the ground. We reported in Chapter 4 that within
Philadelphia, despite the fact that two-thirds of the district's schools have ratings low enough to make their students eligible for transfers, few transfers take
place and few families even request transfers. That is not because people in
this region regard neighborhood schools as sacrosanct. (Consider the very
high enrollments in private schools in this region.) The low transfer rate results instead from a lack of alternatives. State laws do not require, nor even encourage, interdistrict transfers of pupils. So suburban school officials are
under no obligation to accept students transferring from the cities. Nor are
districts with failing schools eager to send students to other districts, since the
sending district would be required to transfer funds to the receiving schools to
help pay for the newcomers.

Rather than attempting the impossible (i.e., trying to move students
across city-suburban boundaries), advocates for school choice have focused
their energy on promoting charter schools as alternatives to the neighborhood public school. Advocates for charters stress that by giving these third-
sector organizations greater flexibility than traditional schools enjoy, the
community can expect in return more innovative and effective approaches

to education. In Philadelphia, for example, dozens of charters offer diverse curricula ranging from a focus on architecture and design to computer technical skills, multicultural education, foreign languages, aviation, and many other emphases.

More than other policy areas considered in this book, education highlights the tension between government actions that advance public purposes versus actions that create private opportunities and benefits. Schools have always provided opportunities for individual students to acquire skills and knowledge in pursuit of their own personal development, while at the same time serving larger social and economic purposes like producing the next generation of workers, citizens, consumers, and community members. Some arguments in favor of school choice seem to reduce educational policy to serving only the first of those purposes (i.e., promoting individual rights, expressed in consumer choices). The argument in favor of expanding choice through *charters* (as opposed to vouchers to be used at private schools) is that this organizational form combines the best elements of both governmental institutions and private entities. It is created by, and accountable to, governmental authorities, while adopting many features of the marketplace. Since the third sector is particularly suited to function as a bridge between the government sector and the market, most charter schools (though not all) are nonprofits. For many observers, of course, debates about the virtues of particular organizational forms are secondary to the more central question of whether charters can deliver better academic results for the pupils and families they serve. As we saw in Chapter 4, we do not yet have enough evidence to answer that question.

Why Is Responsibility Shifting Away from Local Governments?

In these policy realms, the role of local governments is being eclipsed by networks of nongovernmental organizations for several reasons. One is that local governments have so often proven incapable of cooperating effectively with each other to address conditions that spill across their boundaries. For the reasons explained in Chapters 2 and 5, relations among municipalities are more often marked by competition than collaboration. Effectively responding to trends like reverse commuting, lack of housing choice, or sprawl requires cooperation across boundaries. Nongovernmental bodies have found it easier to pursue such cooperation than have political officials.

A second important reason for the shift of responsibility away from local governments is money. As federal funds to promote physical redevelopment projects passing through city governments have shrunk, local governments have found it impossible to replace those intergovernmental transfers out of their own budgets. Although borrowing is an option, it is closely regulated by the state government. Local governments are permitted to borrow only up to a ceiling set in accordance with their tax collections. In cities like Philadelphia, fiscal stress has meant the local government is often functioning at the upper limit on its borrowing and therefore has an incentive to assign responsibility for costly projects to outside entities. Outside organizations often find it easier to obtain financing for development projects than does the city government itself. Independent entities can borrow for large projects without having the debt count against the municipality's total indebtedness. So even when the city government can no longer borrow money for major development projects, independent entities may legally borrow. The city has often used quasi-public corporations deliberately to circumvent the debt limit.[15]

Yet another explanation for local governments ceding functions to other entities is that labor unions are increasingly seen as posing insurmountable problems to local governments. As sources of campaign contributions and campaign workers have waned in the city, construction unions and public employee unions have gained influence because of their generous campaign contributions and other forms of support in local elections. Local politicians must struggle to accommodate the interests of organized labor, whereas nonprofit organizations and state government are less beholden to unions.

The power of the construction trades in Philadelphia comes into play in many development projects, especially large ones that involve significant numbers of construction jobs. Like other big cities, Philadelphia has seen major political struggles over securing construction contracts and jobs for women and minorities.[16] In the past thirty years, a number of forces have converged—including economic restructuring, the loss of jobs from cities, and the rise of minority political leaders—to make hiring preferences a powerful political issue at the local level. Political pressures for set-asides are difficult for politicians to manage because construction unions and developers—groups that typically contribute significant sums to campaigns—often oppose hiring preference legislation. Local politicians see public struggles over hiring preferences as no-win situations that they can dampen by assigning development responsibility to nongovernmental organizations like the ones described in this chapter. Moving the projects outside of government is less trouble than disrupting established patterns of money raising and patronage. Writing about union issues he faced while a government official, a former director of Philadelphia's Office of Housing and Community Development described the advantages of assigning Community Development Block Grant (CDBG) dollars to neighborhood nonprofits in order to avoid running afoul of the federal Davis-Bacon Act, a law stipulating which federally funded redevelopment projects must pay union-scale wages to construction workers: "The fact that Davis-Bacon requirements don't apply to any CDBG-funded housing development ventures or to small-scale rental ventures (fewer than eight units) gives cities a lot of latitude in structuring opportunities for Davis-Bacon-free construction work."[17]

In other instances as well, local governments have shifted responsibility to other bodies in order to reduce the power of public employee unions. Pennsylvania's takeover of the Philadelphia schools, of the city's finances through PICA, and of the convention center were all prompted in part by the perception that local government was incapable of standing up to intransigent unions. In the case of the schools, Philadelphia's school managers shared the view of many state government officials that the teachers' union was the main obstacle to measures that would improve school performance—for example, introducing performance rewards for teachers, extending each school day by an hour or more, and giving back to school principals the right to decide which teachers would be employed in which school buildings (a right that previous union contracts had ceded to the teacher seniority system). The legislation passed by the state legislature dramatically undercut the union's bargaining position, giving the School Reform Commission the power to unilaterally impose many work rules (like assigning teachers to particular schools) and barring the teachers from striking. In practice, the school managers who took over the Philadelphia district in 2001 did not choose to invoke most of these draconian provisions of the state law, preferring to negotiate changes with the teachers' union. But there is no doubt that the teachers' weaker bargaining position prompted its 20,000 members to accept changes they would not have previously entertained, like giving the school district more power over how teachers are assigned to schools.

Similarly, the move to establish state control over the Pennsylvania Convention Center was motivated by a view shared by the facility's managers and state politicians that the unions' unwillingness to cooperate was driving away exhibitors. Management wanted the carpenters, teamsters, and other laborers to work for the convention center instead of working for independent trade show contractors. Although Philadelphia's mayor spent months trying to persuade union leaders to accept some changes in the work rules to create a more unified workforce, he was unsuccessful. State politicians (including several Philadelphia legislators) drove a much harder bargain with the unions. They threatened not only to take control of the convention center but also to replace the workforce with direct state employees. That threat, which labor leaders labeled "draconian" and "disrespectful," was enough to pressure the unions into accepting new work rules that reduced labor costs being charged to exhibitors, eliminated arguments over work tasks, and gave the Pennsylvania Convention Center Authority the right to supervise workers. That episode illustrated clearly that organized labor gets a far less sympathetic hearing in the state capitol than in city hall.

Such high-stakes, dramatic standoffs as the state takeover of the school district and convention center are not the only way that unions are losing ground in public services. Just as important as these highly publicized confrontations are the many years of contracting public services out to nongovernmental providers, many of whom employ nonunion labor. This is true of nonprofit as well as for-profit providers. For example, the dozens of job training agencies that are part of the region's workforce development network operate independently in both the nonprofit and for-profit sectors. Within the welfare-to-work system, government funds are channeled to a host of independent organizations to train workers, place them in jobs, coach them, and provide support the workers may need in order to stay on the job. These contracting agencies seldom employ unionized workers. Thus, one factor driving the movement toward privatizing more government services is that contractors' labor costs are generally lower than government's labor costs. Another example of this cost difference is the Transit Management Associations (TMAs) that supplement the mass transit services offered by SEPTA. While SEPTA workers are unionized, the TMAs employ nonunion labor to drive the vans and buses that take commuters from transit stations to their suburban workplaces.

An important reason for the rise of third-sector organizations to manage large-scale development projects is that they provide a vehicle for powerful suburban interests to protect their stake in the central city's future development. If suburban economic and political elites once believed they could sustain their prosperity even while the central city stagnated, they no longer hold that view. Recognizing that the region will only succeed in the global marketplace if it maintains a strong port, airport, convention center, cultural district, and other centrally located assets, suburban leaders have increasingly sought to influence the building and maintenance of those core assets. Since they cannot directly control city government, they find third-sector organizations to be useful institutions that give them some influence over the city's development priorities. Third-sector institutions provide these external stakeholders with some leverage over the physical redevelopment of the core city, "allowing them to reconfigure urban space to meet the region's needs."[18]

What Is the Downside of This Decentering of Governance?

This chapter has described how state-level actors as well as a broad range of nonprofits are assuming responsibility for the region's development. They represent the kinds of public-private partnerships that are touted by civic leaders and urban scholars as the new way to get things done in metropolitan regions. Many analysts have welcomed the decentering of public authority at the local level, believing that a broad array of organizations serving public purposes will be more responsive to citizen preferences than government could be, especially in big cities. More than local governments, these partner organizations are able to identify and address specific needs and preferences. They can focus on solving particular problems and build solutions that are tailored to particular community contexts.

For example, neighborhood-based associations are sometimes seen as the urban analogues to the privatized suburbs that sit beyond the city limits. For decades, observers have remarked on the ability of suburban governments to cater to the relatively narrow range of needs and preferences expressed by their homogeneous populations. Every township struggles to secure the revenues it needs in order to satisfy the demands of the citizens living within its boundaries. The advantage of this system has been to provide suburban residents with service "packages" that suit their lifestyles and service preferences. Historically, residents of large cities have had less opportunity to tailor public services to their community preferences. Working within the third sector, community residents can secure amenities and services they may not get from the government.

However, these advantages of public-private partnerships must be balanced against some important disadvantages. One is that the work of all the independent organizations operating in the realms of economic development, housing development, and public education cannot easily be coordinated. Consider the quasi-public corporations that control many of the most important development projects in the region. Almost twenty years ago, a civic watchdog organization cautioned Philadelphia's leaders that by entrusting important development functions to these bodies, the city was trading a certain amount of public accountability for more effective project management: "The existence of separate authorities inevitably leads to increased complexity of government, diffuses accountability, and adds to the number of interagency negotiations needed to accomplish a governmental purpose."[19]

The examples of Penn's Landing Corporation and Cooper's Ferry Development Corporation, described earlier in this chapter, illustrate the problem that city administrations face coordinating the efforts of the quasi-public corporations. Because each quasi-public corporation is set up with a specific assignment, a separate staff, and its own financing mechanisms, these agencies tend to operate on their own, only intermittently seeking to coordinate their efforts with those of other agencies and sometimes actively resisting attempts by a mayor, city planning commission, or city council to bring them into line. Recently, the long-standing director of the highly successful Cooper's Ferry Development Corporation in Camden stressed the importance of maintaining his autonomy from elected political leaders. Without an independent, nongovernmental agency, he said, "The vision would not have been sustained . . . it would have died every time a mayor was indicted."[20] What he did not acknowledge was that the proliferation of quasi-public corporations like his own makes it harder to achieve rational city planning.

In a similar vein, relying on community-based organizations to lead neighborhood revitalization efforts may dilute the impact of citywide planning. A former housing director of Philadelphia, when describing his working relationship with community nonprofit developers, acknowledged that he sometimes had difficulty predicting whether the projects these groups proposed would actually get built. To deal with the uncertainty about which of the community groups would complete its planned developments, the city government committed far more dollars to support initial proposals than it could actually deliver, calculating that only a fraction of the community proposals would ever come to fruition.[21] Not knowing in advance which projects would succeed, the city spent its housing dollars to produce a pattern of development that was ultimately determined, not by any comprehensive plan, but by which nonprofits could get their projects up and running. While perhaps necessary to deal with the contingencies of funding, that approach could hardly be labeled "strategic planning."

Education is another arena in which the proliferation of providers poses a coordination challenge. An independent evaluation of the Philadelphia School District's "diverse provider model" examined the district's relationships with dozens of nonprofit and profit-making organizations as school managers. According to the evaluator, the arrangement is hindered by confusion about roles and responsibilities and is short on accountability, relying more on developing trusting relationships with partners instead of enforcing strict performance standards.[22]

The accountability problems that frequently arise in these new styles of local governance arrangements contribute to another drawback—namely, that placing more public functions outside the governmental arena erodes democratic control. Actually, that may be one strong reason prompting local politicians to use the third sector for important projects. While downtown business interests favor investing the city's scarce resources in large-scale redevelopment, populists in city council have often questioned the development agenda, stalling major projects like the convention center. One way to minimize the impact of these debates on the redevelopment program is to put that program outside the reach of normal political processes.[23]

For example, earlier we saw that some of the subsidies handed out by the Delaware Regional Port Authority (DRPA) have drawn significant criticism, particularly expenditures for tourism and culture. Critics have pointed to DRPA's closed decision-making process, impervious to democratic influences because the authority is run by appointees who do not need to consult the electorates of Philadelphia, Camden, or any municipalities in the region. Without electoral accountability, critics charge, the process is dominated by backroom dealing, checked only by newspaper reporters who periodically expose cronyism and waste. In a scathing editorial criticizing the DRPA's process for spending $40 million on various economic development projects, the *Philadelphia Inquirer* asked rhetorically:

> How was this huge pot to be spent? Would applications be solicited and vetted at public hearings? Would citizens, elected officials, business leaders and advocates get to weigh in publicly on how to best use this fund? Nah. Decisions would be made behind closed doors by a small committee of players ... The players represented the Penn's Landing Corp. and the Philadelphia Industrial Development Corp., the two quasi-public agencies charged with disbursing the money.[24]

In recent times, the Penn's Landing Corporation has made closed-door decisions about allocating a waterfront site to casino developers, a controversial prospect. As a nonprofit corporation, it has refused to open its voting sessions to the public, even though it has received substantial tax dollars over the years to manage city-owned land. The state "sunshine" law that requires most city and state agencies to hold open meetings does not apply to nonprofit organizations. The head of a Philadelphia civic watchdog group admitted that the corporation "might not necessarily be doing anything wrong ... but at the very least, we can't have any confidence in all of it because it all seems to be happening in the dark."[25]

The complaints voiced about DRPA and the Penn's Landing Corporation could be applied to virtually all of the different types of organizations that are partnering with local government. Neighborhood nonprofit organizations, special service districts, and quasi-public corporations all represent decision-making forums beyond the direct control of the electorate. Granted, they may respond to local citizens, businesses, and other interests within the areas they serve. But the broader public of voters and taxpayers does not exercise democratic control over the nonprofits that have assumed a significant share of the burden for sustaining and improving the quality of life in communities. Foundations, by their very nature, are politically unaccountable. That can be an advantage, freeing them from some of the unproductive, even unsavory, forces that drive decisions in the political arena. But it can also lead foundations to pursue reforms that lack permanence because they are not rooted in political realities. As we saw earlier in this chapter, that problem plagued a number of the school reform efforts promoted by Philadelphia foundations during the 1990s.

Consider the case of special services districts that exist to improve the quality of services in commercial areas. City governments officially create them to provide extra services without burdening the city treasury. Although in theory, the city's elected government exercises influence over these bodies, the city's dependence on them makes it unlikely they will be terribly closely monitored and regulated. When their efforts displace crime or other problems into adjacent areas of the city or when their marketing campaigns draw business away from other commercial strips, there is little chance that city government will move to curtail those activities. Questions have even arisen about whether special services districts are truly accountable to the property owners who pay their assessments. Such complaints get worked out, if at all, through private mediation outside the bounds of electoral institutions.[26]

We are not implying that third-sector organizations operate completely outside the political system. Far from it. The boards that govern these hybrid organizations routinely include members appointed by, and directly accountable to, powerful politicians at the local and state levels. Yet these links between board members and their political sponsors do not produce broad public accountability for the actions taken by the organizations. Decisions to spend money, enter into contracts, and hire employees are less open to scrutiny than decisions taken by departments of government. This leaves open the opportunity for political sponsors to use the organizations for patronage purposes. Since they sit outside local government, they are not regulated by civil service guidelines for hiring. Nor is their contracting governed by standard municipal rules about bidding contracts.

Neighborhood nonprofits are often closely linked to politicians but not necessarily within a framework of democratic electoral politics. Community-based organizations often deal with political patrons via informal relationships that lack public transparency. Rather than openly competing for resources in public forums, neighborhood organizations are more likely to link to individual politicians through personal connections, hoping to benefit from sponsorship by those political patrons. This pattern of patronage doled out by powerful individual politicians has become more entrenched in Philadelphia as the city's political parties have atrophied (a subject we discussed in our first book about Philadelphia). For instance, any developers trying to build within the city, whether nonprofit or for-profit, must secure endorsement for their work from the city council member who represents the district in which the project is located. One outspoken executive of a private development firm described it this way: "it's like there are ten townships in Philadelphia: the Township of Nutter, the Township of O'Neill, the Township of Blackwell . . . ," referring to city council members.[27]

The most celebrated local example of nonprofit ties to political sponsors is the case of a powerful state senator, Vincent Fumo, who represents a district that includes South Philadelphia. In 1998 Senator Fumo played a central role in the state government's negotiation of the terms under which PECO Energy Company would relinquish its monopoly and begin competing against other utility companies. As part of those negotiations, the senator persuaded PECO to make large contributions to two new nonprofit organizations. The first nonprofit, to which PECO promised $11 million, spurred development projects ranging from urban farming to computer training for members of a local carpenters' union and renovation of a homeless shelter. The second nonprofit, which received $17 million from PECO, funded charter schools, street cleaning, fixing up buildings, and other local projects. When these unpublicized side payments by the utility were discovered by investigative news reporters, critics protested against the senator using his political office to channel corporate funds to nonprofits he established in his district. Senator Fumo was unapologetic: "They (the critics) shouldn't be mad at me. They should be calling their own state senator and saying, 'Hey, what are you doing to help us out in our neighborhoods?' "[28] Such instances of politicians creating nonprofit organizations that they control has led many observers to worry about the lack of transparency and accountability when nonprofits are employed as arms of government.

This book has portrayed a region that is decentering and has balkanized into hundreds of small, separate jurisdictions that offer their residents widely differing opportunities to work, live, and educate their children. In this regional landscape, the patterns of privilege tend to reinforce each other, creating multiple barriers to households with lower incomes and augmenting the advantages enjoyed by the affluent. Working to redress those inequalities, a vast network of third-sector organizations now pursues objectives that neither the government nor the marketplace has been able to accomplish. They rebuild declining neighborhoods, help disadvantaged residents find alternative schools for their children, provide affordable housing, or give transportation options to get workers to inaccessible jobs. They serve as vehicles to mobilize regionwide interests in support of development goals that are too ambitious to be accomplished by one, or even several, local governments. Some nonprofit organizations operate as an arm of government, receiving substantial funding from taxpayers; others mobilize resources completely outside of the sphere of government. Whichever is the case, the invention of these new institutional forms comes with a political price: to the extent that they displace local governments as the drivers of development, they erode local democratic control over the region's future. This is occurring at the same time that state government is exerting more direct influence over important local institutions and development projects, further eroding local control. This is especially true for the core cities of Philadelphia and Camden, whose school districts and redevelopment agendas are dominated by state actions.

Regional Solutions for Regional Problems?

We have painted a picture of a region that offers residents dramatically different opportunities for employment, housing, and education, based on where they live. This theme, which we explored at the scale of the city in our previous book, *Philadelphia*, is equally useful for analyzing patterns across a wider spatial scale.[29] People and firms who have chosen against the city for their place of business or residence continue to reflect the forces of decentralization that we noted in the earlier work. The economic, social, and political divisions that were a core theme earlier show evidence of both persistence and change as we have expanded our analysis to the regional level.

The inequalities that characterize the region are the legacies of past divisions and the effects of cumulative advantage and disadvantage. Consider the city of Camden, designated in late 2004 the nation's "most dangerous city" by Morgan Quitno Corporation, a company that publishes an annual reference book compiling statistics for murder, rape, robbery, aggravated assault, burglary, and auto theft. Not far from Camden sits the New Jersey township of Moorestown that ranked first in the nation on *Money Magazine's* 2005 list of the 100 best places to live in the United States. The publisher said about Moorestown, "It's an all-American town, a true community offering a rich life that draws people who grew up there back home to raise their own families."[30]

The stark inequalities documented within this volume pose a problem not only to people of conscience who think it is fundamentally unfair for families to raise children in places that provide vastly different levels of education, safety, air quality, social networks, and a dozen other requirements for a healthy upbringing. These inequalities should also trouble the growing number of people concerned about the region's prospects for growth. In Chapter 1, we acknowledged a shift in the urban policy literature, which is now placing a decreasing emphasis on distributional justice while putting greater stress on the capacity of urban public institutions to deliver public services in ways that attract and retain residents and employers. Questions about how to structure urban regions more fairly are being replaced with questions about how to make urban regions more competitive in the global economy. However, in *Regions that Work: How Cities and Suburbs Can Grow Together,* Manuel Pastor and his coauthors made the case that regional leaders need not sacrifice equity in order to gain competitiveness. In fact, Pastor and colleagues cautioned civic and political leaders that if they want to improve their regions' prospects for economic growth, they need to address the kinds of distributional inequalities this book has documented for the greater Philadelphia region.[31] Studying growth and poverty in seventy-four U.S. metropolitan areas, they focused on statistical relationships between income growth and various measures of poverty, equity, and residential segregation. They found that rising inequality in urban regions is associated with slowing economic growth, while reductions in inequality are associated with positive growth. Their study, while it demonstrated a statistical association between distributional equity and economic growth, could not fully explain the reasons for this finding. They offered several intriguing suggestions, including the possibility that when the communities within a metropolitan area are more equally positioned, they may cooperate more easily to address problems and recover from economic shocks or they may invest more in health, education, and human capital in general.[32] It may also be the case that place-based disadvantages, left unaddressed, create an increasing drag on the regional economy because they reproduce increasing levels of disadvantage and social problems, which require rising social expenditures.

Overcoming the twin problems of social inequality and stagnating growth requires collaboration among the leaders of the region's many communities. As we noted in the introduction to this book, analysts like Myron Orfield and Neal Peirce have argued forcefully that revitalizing cities and maintaining the competitiveness of metropolitan regions will depend on cities and suburbs cooperating to plan their shared future.[33] Like many other advocates for regionalism, Orfield and Peirce have urged elected local officials to take cooperative action to rationalize the distribution of benefits and costs of development across metropolitan areas. Is such intergovernmental collaboration likely to occur in an environment where basic differences in quality of life and opportunity appear to be dividing communities, not bringing them together? We see forces moving to apply new resources and new institutional frameworks to the problems of uneven development. The initiative is not coming from elected local leaders. On a number of important issues states can function as a harmonizer of interests among the many units of local government, helping the region to function as an economic unit. As a higher-level authority, states can address the inequalities of tax base as well as the negative spillovers that local governments may impose on each other. They can help fund large-scale projects and infrastructure whose benefits spread across multiple localities and whose costs should not exclusively burden one jurisdiction. At the local level, much of the action is shifting to vehicles outside of local governments. These nongovernmental institutions form an increasingly thick network across the region, mobilizing money and political support that would not be available to traditional institutions of government. To a great extent, they operate independently of one another, without the rational planning and coordination desired by many proponents of regionalism. The emerging pattern is one of regionalism by default, not by design. This is not exactly the rational reform movement that Neal Peirce, Myron Orfield, and other advocates for regionalism had in mind. Yet this piecemeal approach represents the most likely path to regionalism in greater Philadelphia.

While we are not prisoners of our past, it is instructive to revisit the Philadelphia that Sam Bass Warner wrote about in his landmark history of Philadelphia titled *The Private City*.[34] He saw the emergence of nongovernmental institutions and approaches to addressing the common good as a characteristic of most of the periods of Philadelphia's development through its industrial peak and the beginning of its postindustrial reshaping. In Warner's account, the important nongovernmental organizations were the city's profit-making businesses (e.g., the ones that operated omnibus lines in the 1830s, horse car lines in the 1850s, and later electric streetcars). And the most important civic actors were businessmen (downtown merchants, utility and railroad owners, bank directors, and real estate developers) who "defined themselves as amateurs, helping out for a brief time"[35] in order to pursue public projects. Rather than entrusting their government with responsibility for charting the city's course and exercising their influence through democratic politics, Philadelphians saw the private realms of family, community, and business as the important arenas for action: "No powerful group had been created in the city which understood the city as a whole and wanted to deal with it as a public environment of a democratic society."[36]

The emergence of the nonprofit sector resonates with Warner's portrayal of limited local government that gives expression to localized economic and social agendas. Yet today's third-sector leaders do not see themselves as amateurs or short-term participants entering the public arena only to promote specific projects. On the contrary, the region's civic infrastructure now includes hundreds of nonprofits that are permanent, well-financed, and professionally managed organizations. Some have direct access to large amounts of tax revenues to sustain their operations, and many are staffed by career professionals. As these localized and specialized organizations are carrying responsibility for many dimensions of community life, simultaneously state agencies are taking on other functions that state officials see as crucial to the region's future, especially its economic prospects. The scale at which public responsibility is exercised is both broadening and narrowing simultaneously, as the postmodern metropolis confronts the problem of uneven development.

APPENDIX 1

Constructing the Community Typology

Thirteen variables were used: five housing, six socioeconomic, and two household characteristics. The housing variables were percent of units built before 1940, percent of units built after 1995, percent vacant, percent detached single units, and percent owner occupied; the socioeconomic variables were percent African American, percent with less than a high school education, percent with a bachelor's degree or better, percent of persons less than 150 percent of the poverty line, percent working outside municipality of residence, and percent males unemployed; the household variables were percent of families with children under eighteen and percent of families which were female headed. Although we have spent considerable effort trying to improve the typology using measures of taxation, land use, and density, the alternatives proved statistically and intuitively inferior.

Communities were defined differently for the city and suburbs. To define communities in the city, we used the twelve planning analysis districts that the Philadelphia Planning Commission has historically used in its work; in the suburbs, the communities are the municipalities.

The validity of the typology was assessed three different ways: (1) its criterion validity was assessed using a variety of measures such as the percentage of households with incomes above $75,000; (2) the classifications were analyzed through a very different statistical methodology—a multiple discriminant analysis—using the same thirteen variables with and without random elimination of observations (the initial analysis correctly classified 91.8 percent of the cases; the random elimination analysis correctly classified 88.7); and (3) between the 2004 and 2005 reports, we sent the results of the 2004 cluster analysis to our Project Advisory Committee, county planning officials, and other regional specialists for comment. As a result, we reclassified 5 of the 364 communities for 2005, reflecting instances where group quarters distorted the classification, where there was a U.S. Census Bureau locational error, and where in a couple of instances census data did not reflect the situation "on the ground."

APPENDIX 2

North American Industrial Classification System (NAICS) Coding for Industrial Classification

Industry	NAICS
Agricultural-mining-construction	113110–115310, 211111—213115, 233110—235990, 562910
Advanced technology manufacturing	312221, 322110, 322291, 324110, 325110–325998, 331311, 332991–332995, 333120–333298, 333313–333315, 333411–333412, 333611–333912, 333921–333924, 333993– 333994, 333999, 334111–334612, 335311–335314, 335991, 336111–336213, 336312, 336330–336350, 336399–336419, 336992, 339111–339114
Other manufacturing	311110–312210, 312229–321999, 322121–323122, 324121–324199, 326111–326211, 326220–331222, 331312–332919, 332996– 333112, 333311–333312, 333315–333319, 333414–333518, 333913, 333991–333992, 333995–333997, 334613–335228, 335911–335932, 335999, 336214–336311, 336321–336322, 336360–336391, 336510–337920, 339115, 339911–399980, 511110–511199, 512230
Transportation-communication-utilities	221111–0221330, 481111–487210, 487990, 488111–488390, 488490–493190, 513111–513330, 561510, 561520, 561599, 562111–562920, 562998, 621910, 713930
Wholesale	421110–422990
Retail	441110–454390, 722110–722410
Finance-insurance-real estate	521110–531390, 533110, 541191, 551111, 551112, 812220, 813211, 813990

Industry	NAICS
Advanced technology services	511210, 513340–513390, 514191, 514210, 532420, 541511–541519, 541310, 541320, 541330, 541360–541380, 541511–541611, 541613–541618, 541690, 541710, 541720, 541820, 541910, 541940, 561110, 561210, 611710, 811212
Business services	512210–512220, 512240, 512290, 514110, 514199, 514199, 522320, 532210, 532291, 532299, 532310, 532411, 532412, 532490, 541110, 541199, 541211, 541214, 541219, 541340–541350, 541410–541490, 541612, 541620, 541810, 541830–541890, 541922, 541930, 541990, 561310–561499, 561591, 561611–561621, 561710, 561720, 561790– 561990, 812320, 812921, 812922
Consumer services	326212, 339116, 487210, 488410, 512110–512199, 512290, 532111–532120, 532220, 532220, 532230, 532292, 532490, 541213, 541430, 541921, 561622, 561730, 561740, 562991, 611410–611699, 621111–621610, 621991, 621999, 623110, 623210, 623311, 624410, 711110–711510, 712190, 713110, 713120, 713210–713920, 713940–713990, 721110–721310, 811111–811211, 811213–812210, 812310–812332, 812910, 812930, 812990
Nonprofit organizations	514120, 611110, 611210, 611310, 622100–622310, 623220, 623312–623990, 624110–624310, 712110–712130, 813110, 813212–813920, 813930, 813940, 813990
"Meds"	325411, 325412, 325413, 325414, 339111, 339112, 339113, 339114, 339115, 339116, 421450, 421460, 422210, 524114, 621111, 621112, 621210, 621310, 621320, 621330, 621340, 621391, 621399, 621410, 621420, 621491, 621492, 621493, 621498, 621511, 621512, 621610, 621910, 621991, 621999, 622110, 622210, 622310, 623110, 623210, 623220, 623311, 623312, 623990, 813212
Tourism	481111, 481112, 483112, 483114, 485510 ,485999, 487110, 487210, 487990, 512131, 512132, 561510–561999, 711110–722410

APPENDIX 3

Lowest- and Highest-Achieving Districts: Organizational and Housing Characteristics

District	SAT Score	Pupil-Teacher Ratio	Education Expenditure per Pupil	Percent Lived in Different Home, 1995	Percent Moved within Same Town	Mean Mortgage Amount	Percent Post 1995 Owner-Occupied Housing	Percent Post Renter-Occupied 1995 Housing
Lowest Twenty SAT Scores								
Chester-Upland	724	16.2	$11,774	42.8%	51.2%	$66,682	0.2	5.5
Camden	763	11.2	$15,274	44.3%	67.9%	$54,101	1.9	0.0
William Penn	812	16.2	$9,789	32.0%	12.2%	$87,452	0.8	0.2
Philadelphia	828	18.9	$8,020	38.1%	72.7%	$105,195	0.5	2.0
Southeast Delco	844	15.5	$8,686	34.9%	19.2%	$73,355	0.3	0.5
Willingboro	856	12.3	$11,608	28.7%	0.0%	$122,648	0.5	0.0
Bristol Borough	874	14.5	$10,036	31.8%	34.7%	$111,425	1.9	0.4
Morrisville Borough	905	15.0	$11,028	41.2%	25.7%	$137,078	3.9	1.0
Pennsauken	906	14.3	$10,778	35.3%	25.3%	$105,719	1.3	0.5
Burlington City	916	10.5	$13,716	38.5%	36.4%	$128,505	32.9	8.5
Bristol Township	921	15.0	$10,867	31.2%	19.1%	$132,781	1.2	1.5
Penns Grove–Carney's Point Regional	925	11.9	$11,696	36.6%	29.7%	$87,735	1.8	1.0
Norristown Area	926	13.6	$11,211	42.1%	28.2%	$125,019	1.9	0.8
Pottstown	928	15.5	$9,799	40.3%	49.7%	$92,117	0.4	2.1
Glassboro	929	12.6	$11,271	47.0%	15.8%	$128,999	7.8	2.5
Paulsboro	930	13.5	$10,522	44.7%	44.0%	$85,594	1.2	2.9
Coatesville Area	930	15.8	$9,920	35.8%	13.5%	$137,196	11.1	4.3
Pemberton	934	11.4	$15,391	39.0%	1.3%	$120,964	5.0	7.0
Gloucester City	934	10.0	$14,835	34.1%	45.7%	$78,915	1.4	1.3
Ridley	935	14.5	$9,412	29.8%	4.9%	$112,228	1.6	0.2
TOTAL	886	13.9	$11,282	37.4%	29.9%	$104,685	3.9	2.1

Highest Twenty SAT Scores

District	SAT Score	Pupil-Teacher Ratio	Education Expenditure per Pupil	Percent Lived in Different Home, 1995	Percent Moved within Same Town	Mean Mortgage Amount	Percent Post 1995 Owner-Occupied Housing	Percent Post 1995 Renter-Occupied 1995 Housing
Kennett Consolidated	1073	16.6	$9,629	45.9%	9.6%	$258,890	18.2	1.0
Cheltenham	1074	14.0	$12,457	40.4%	1.7%	$166,485	1.0	0.4
Central Bucks	1076	18.8	$8,374	43.1%	3.5%	$213,330	22.1	5.7
West Chester Area	1078	16.2	$10,157	48.5%	6.2%	$227,600	12.4	10.1
Great Valley	1085	15.1	$11,562	47.2%	3.8%	$233,056	15.6	18.5
Wissahickon	1089	15.2	$11,965	39.9%	7.4%	$235,388	11.3	1.8
Council Rock	1094	14.0	$10,392	35.1%	2.0%	$275,728	9.6	4.8
Cherry Hill	1106	14.5	$11,594	33.3%	8.0%	$167,415	2.8	5.6
Eastern Camden County Regional	1107	14.8	$11,324	40.7%	3.9%	$167,835	9.1	13.3
New Hope–Solebury	1109	14.1	$12,784	49.5%	3.1%	$304,741	22.0	1.9
Lower Moreland	1114	15.2	$11,337	26.6%	0.0%	$243,982	2.0	6.7
Jenkintown	1118	11.9	$14,431	35.0%	13.4%	$148,520	0.0	0.0
Wallingford-Swarthmore	1126	13.8	$10,691	34.4%	11.8%	$211,494	1.5	5.0
Unionville–Chadds Ford	1132	15.1	$10,325	40.6%	0.0%	$294,557	16.1	3.9
Tredyffrin-Easttown	1149	14.4	$11,561	41.9%	2.7%	$282,180	6.0	1.2
Upper Dublin	1152	15.7	$9,577	32.3%	1.3%	$216,222	4.8	2.0
Haddonfield	1153	13.9	$10,579	35.2%	27.1%	$261,334	1.2	8.9
Moorestown	1162	14.4	$10,861	41.4%	0.0%	$298,210	12.7	4.3
Radnor Township	1176	13.0	$12,765	50.1%	14.8%	$365,321	2.5	0.9
Lower Merion	1184	12.7	$16,411	39.3%	2.9%	$260,397	1.5	0.6
TOTAL	1118	14.7	$11,439	40.8%	5.2%	$204,520	8.6	4.8

Sources: New Jersey, Pennsylvania Departments of Education, 2001–2004; *Common Core of Data, 2001–2004*, National Center for Educational Statistics.; U.S. Bureau of the Census, 1990 Census of Population and Housing, summary tape file 3; U.S. Bureau of the Census, 2000 Census of Population and Housing, summary file 3; Federal Financial Institutions Examination Council, Home Mortgage Disclosure Act Data, 2002–2004.

NOTES

INTRODUCTION

1. C. Adams, D. Bartelt, D. Elesh, I. Goldstein, N. Kleniewski, and W. Yancey, *Philadelphia: Neighborhoods, Division, and Conflict in a Postindustrial City*. Philadelphia: Temple University Press, 1991.

2. C. Harris and E. L. Ullman, "The Nature of Cities," *The Annals* 242 (1945): 7–17.

3. M. Orfield, *Metropolitics: A Regional Agenda for Community and Stability*. Washington, D.C.: Brookings Institution and Lincoln Institute of Land Policy, 1997; also M. Orfield, *American Metropolitics: The New Suburban Reality*. Washington, D.C.: Brookings Institution Press, 2002.

4. D. Rusk, *Cities Without Suburbs*, 2nd edition. Washington, D.C.: Woodrow Wilson Center Press, 1995; also D. Rusk, *Inside Game, Outside Game: Winning Strategies for Saving Urban America*. Washington, D.C.: Brookings Institution Press, 1999.

5. B. Katz, "Reviving Cities: Think Metropolitan," Policy Brief No. 33. Washington, D.C.: Brookings Institution, 1998.

6. D. Hayden, *Building Suburbia: Green Fields and Urban Growth, 1820–2000*. New York: Pantheon Books, 2003; R. Lewis, ed., *Manufacturing Suburbs*. Philadelphia: Temple University Press, 2004.

7. G. Frug, *City Making: Building Communities without Building Walls*. Princeton, NJ: Princeton University Press, 1999, p. 7.

8. S. B. Warner, *The Private City: Philadelphia in Three Periods of Its Growth*. Philadelphia: University of Pennsylvania Press, 1968, p. 4.

9. Ibid.

10. N. Peirce, *Citistates: How Urban America Can Prosper in a Competitive World*. Washington, D.C.: Seven Locks Press, 1993.

11. Orfield, *Metropolitics* , p. 9.

12. State Representative Nicholas Micozzie quoted in L. S. Ditzen, "The Apostle of St. Paul," *Philadelphia Inquirer*, July 9, 1997.

13. Advisory Commission on Intergovernmental Relations, *Urban America and the Federal System*. Washington, DC: U.S. Government Printing Office, 1969; R. L. Bish and V. Ostrom, *Understanding Urban Government: Metropolitan Reform Reconsidered*. Washington, D.C.: Enterprise Institute for Public Policy Research, 1974; S. Greer, *Governing the Metropolis*. New York: John Wiley, 1962.

14. T. Swanstrom, "What We Argue About When We Argue About Regionalism," *Journal of Urban Affairs*, 23, no. 5 (2001): 479–496, p. 482.

15. W. Barnes and L. Ledebur, *The New Regional Economics: The U.S. Common Market and the Global Economy*. Thousand Oaks, CA: Sage, 1998; A. D.Wallis, "Regions in Action: Crafting Regional Governance under the Challenge of Global Competitiveness," *National Civic Review* 85, issue 2 (Spring-Summer 1996): 15–24.

16. M. Weir,"Coalition Building for Regionalism," in *Reflections on Regionalism*, ed. B. Katz. Washington, D.C.: Brookings Institution Press, 2000, pp. 127–153.

17. J. Powell, "Addressing Regional Dilemmas for Minority Communities," in *Reflections on Regionalism*, ed. B. Katz. Washington, D.C.: Brookings Institution Press, 2000, pp. 218–246, 222.

18. N. Brenner, "Decoding the Newest Metropolitan Regionalism in the USA: A Critical Overview," *Cities*, 19 (2002): 3–21, p. 8; S. Clarke and G. Gaile, *The Work of Cities*. Minneapolis: University of Minnesota Press, 1998.

19. D. Norris. "Prospects for Regional Governance under the New Regionalism," *Journal of Urban Affairs*, 23, no. 5 (2001): 557–571, pp. 561–562.

20. Brenner, "Decoding the Newest Metropolitan Regionalism in the USA," p. 5.

21. We gratefully acknowledge the support of The William Penn Foundation, whose investment allowed us to build the MPIP.

22. P. Dreier, J. Mollenkopf, and T. Swanstrom. *Place Matters: Metropolitics for the 21st Century*, 2nd ed. Lawrence: University Press of Kansas, 2004, p. 269.

23. P. Dimond, "Empowering Families to Vote with Their Feet," in *Reflections on Regionalism*, ed. B. Katz. Washington, D.C.: Brookings Institution Press, 2000, pp. 249–271, 249.

24. E. Goetz, *Clearing the Way: Deconcentrating the Poor in America*. Washington, D.C.: Urban Institute, 2003, p. 2.

CHAPTER ONE

1. H. Gillette, *Camden After the Fall: Decline and Renewal in a Post-Industrial City*. Philadelphia: University of Pennsylvania Press, 2005.

2. P. Kerkstra and D. Mastrull, "Writing a Second Act for Norristown," *Philadelphia Inquirer*, November 25, 2003, p. A1.

3. John Gattuso, Senior Vice President of Liberty Property Trust, quoted in H. Holcomb, "Liberty is Staying Suburban While Opening Office in Town," *Philadelphia Inquirer*, November 8, 2001.

4. P. Levy, introduction to *The State of Center City 2005*. Philadelphia: Philadelphia Center City District, 2005.

5. Ibid.

6. P. Dreier, J. Mollenkopf, and T. Swanstrom. *Place Matters: Metropolitics for the 21st Century*, 2nd ed. Lawrence: University Press of Kansas, 2004, p. 98.

7. X. de Souza Briggs, ed., *The Geography of Opportunity: Race and Housing Choice in Metropolitan America*. Washington, D.C.: Brookings Institution Press, 2005, p. 5.

8. G. Galster, "Identifying Neighborhood Thresholds: An Empirical Exploration," *Housing Policy Debate* 11, no. 3 (2000): 701–732.

9. Dreier, Mollenkopf, and Swanstrom, *Place Matters,* p. 4.

10. M. Fellowes and B. Katz, "The Price is Wrong: Getting the Market Right for Working Families in Philadelphia." Washington, D.C.: Brookings Institution, April 2005.

11. Dreier, Mollenkopf, and Swanstrom, *Place Matters,* p. 28.

12. B. Katz, *Back to Prosperity: A Competitive Agenda for Renewing Pennsylvania.* Washington, D.C.: Brookings Institution, December 2003.

13. R. Ewing, R. Pendall, and D. Chen, *Measuring Sprawl and Its Impact.* Washington, D.C.: Smart Growth America, 2002. Available online at www.smartgrowthamerica.org.

14. The index is computed by finding the percentages of the metropolitan area's White and Black populations that fall into each census tract. For each tract, the absolute value of the difference between these two percentages is found and the differences are summed over all tracts and divided by two. The result is called the "index of dissimilarity" and ranges in value between 0 and 100. It has the value 0 when Whites and Blacks are represented in each tract in the same percentages as in the metropolitan area, and it has the value 100 when all Whites live in one set of tracts and all Blacks live in a completely different set of tracts.

CHAPTER TWO

1. For an account of these changes, see chapter 2 , Economic Erosion and the Growth of Inequalityin C. Adams, D. Bartelt, D. Elesh, I. Goldstein, N. Kleniewski, and W. Yancey, *Philadelphia: Neighborhoods, Division, and Conflict in a Postindustrial City*. Philadelphia: Temple University Press, 1991.

2. The definitions for advanced technology manufacturing and services are based on industry expenditures on research and development and the percentage of employees in engineering and technical occupations. See M. Boretsky, *The Threat to U.S. High Technology Industries: Economic and National Security Implications*. Washington, D.C.: U.S. Dept. of Commerce, International Trade Administration, 1982; L.A. Davis, *Technology Intensity of U.S. Output and Trade*. Washington, D.C.: U.S. Dept. of Commerce, Office of Trade and Investment Analysis, 1983; and A.M. Lawson, "Technological Growth and High Technology in U.S. Industries," in *Industrial Economics Review*, Washington, D.C.: U.S. Department of Commerce, 1982. Alternative but similar definitions do not appear to significantly change the industries so identified. See A. Markusen, P. Hall, and A. Glasmeier, *High Tech America*. Boston: Allen and Unwin, 1986.

3. S. Sassen, *The Global City*. Princeton, N.J.: Princeton University Press, 1991; also S. Sassen, *Cities in a World Economy*. Thousand Oaks, CA: Pine Forge Press, 1994.

4. We use *Zip Code Business Patterns*, a U.S. Census Bureau data set that provides the finest geographic resolution over the longest available time period, 1994–2004. Work with *Zip Code Business Patterns* revealed occasional anomalous and inexplicable fluctuations in employment in adjacent years in particular zip codes. To reduce the effect of these anomalies, we averaged the data for 1994–1995 and 2003–2004 when comparing zip codes.

5. I. Harkavy and H. Zuckerman, *Eds and Meds: Cities' Hidden Assets*. Washington, D.C.: Brookings Institution, 1999, p. 6.

6. C. Adams, "The Meds and Eds in Urban Economic Development," *Journal of Urban Affairs* 25, no. 5 (2003): 571–588; R. Florida, *The Rise of the Creative Class: And How It's*

Transforming Work, Leisure, Community and Everyday Life. New York: Basic Books, 2002; M. J. Waits, D. Henton, and W. Fulton, "Meds and Eds: The Key to Arizona Leapfrogging Ahead in the 21st Century," Arizona Biomedical Collaborative. Retrieved July 17, 2005, from http://www.abor.asu.edu/special_editions/Med_Ed/Meds_Eds.pdf.

7. I. Harkavy and H. Zuckerman, *Eds and Meds: Cities' Hidden Assets.* Washington, D.C.: Brookings Institution, 1999.

8. Adams, "The Meds and Eds in Urban Economic Development."

9. E. Hoover, *An Introduction to Regional Economics.* New York: Alfred A. Knopf, 1971.

10. SRI International, *Gaining the Lead in the Global Economy, Vol. II.* Philadelphia: Greater Philadelphia First, 1995.

11. A list of the North American Industrial Classification System (NAICS) codes used to define these sectors is given in Appendix 2.

12. D. Elesh, S. Hakim, and W. Stull, *What Temple Means to Southeastern Pennsylvania and the State.* Social Science Data Library. Philadelphia: Temple University, 1998.

13. "Penn and the Region: An Economic Impact Study," Philadelphia: University of Pennsylvania, 1997. Retrieved January 30, 2005, from http://www.upenn.edu/almanac/v46/n10/econ-study.html.

14. "The University of Pennsylvania Economic and Fiscal Impact Report," Philadelphia: Econsult Corporation, 2006. Econsult defined the Philadelphia region as including New Castle County, Delaware, and Cecil County, Maryland, in addition to the nine counties we have used here.

15. "The Economic and Fiscal Impacts of Temple University," Philadelphia: Econsult Corporation, 2004. Differences between the scope and methods of the earlier and later studies of the impacts of both Penn and Temple make comparisons hazardous. While it is clear that there has been significant growth, the differences do not allow their quantification.

16. This figure includes 8,978 jobs directly created by the Temple University Health System; it does not include any jobs generated by the expenditures of the health system. Were that estimate available, the job total would clearly be materially higher. We thank Thomas Healey and Patricia Finley of Temple's Office of Policy, Planning, and Institutional Research for this information.

17. We are grateful to Timothy Walsh, Temple's director of institutional research, for this information. The data exclude Temple's campus in Japan.

18. U.S. Office of Travel and Tourism Industries, *2004 Inbound Travel.* Washington, D.C.: Department of Commerce, 2006. Retrieved 20 January 2006 from tinet.ita.doc.gov/cat/f-2004-45-561.html.

19. M. Stoll, *Job Sprawl and the Spatial Mismatch between Blacks and Jobs.* Washington, D.C.: Brookings Institution, 2005.

20. J. Garreau, *Edge City.* New York: Doubleday, 1991; A. Liez, *Land Use in Pennsylvania: An Analysis of Changes to Pennsylvania's Municipalities Planning Code in 2000.* Philadelphia: PennEnvironment, 2001.

21. The U.S. Census Bureau extensively revised the definitions of metropolitan areas in 2002. The new definition does away with the concept of primary metropolitan areas employed here and by the Census of Governments. In 2000, Chicago had 299 municipalities, Los Angeles, 88, and New York, 52.

22. G. Galster, R. Hanson, M. Ratcliffe, H. Wolman, S. Coleman, and J. Freihage, "Wrestling Sprawl to the Ground: Defining and Measuring an Elusive Concept," *Housing Policy Debate* 12, no. 4 (2001): 681–717.

23. Galster, Hanson, Ratcliffe, Wolman, Coleman, and Freihage use the urbanized area as the basis for their analysis because they wish to avoid dealing with the rural fringe that is part of many metropolitan counties. Urbanized areas are defined as areas with a minimum population density of 1,000 persons per square mile.

24. R. Lang, *Edgeless Cities: Exploring the Edgeless Metropolis*. Washington, D.C.: Brookings Institution Press, 2003.

25. Garreau, *Edge City*, p. 9.

26. Zip codes clearly vary in size, but when we map jobs per square mile, we find the same diffuse spread of jobs near major roads.

27. Lang, *Edgeless Cities*.

28. Lang examines twelve of the thirteen largest metro areas in 2000; he substitutes Denver, the nineteenth largest area, for Seattle, the thirteenth.

29. G. Pivo, "The Net of Mixed Beads: Suburban Office Development in Six Regions," *Journal of the American Planning Association* 56, no. 4 (Autumn 1990): 457–469.

30. Galster Galster, Hanson, Ratcliffe, Wolman, Coleman, and Freihage, "Wrestling Sprawl to the Ground."

31. Interview with Thomas Kenyon, president of New Jersey Planning Officials, August 1, 2005.

32. Interview with Brody Bovero, associate planner, Upper Merion Township, September 21, 2005.

33. Ibid.

34. Percentage from *American Community Survey*, U.S. Census, 2005.

35. D. Smith, *The Delaware Valley Life Science Workforce: An Analysis of Current and Future Needs*. Philadelphia: Center for Healthcare Research and Management, Temple University, 2003.

36. For a discussion of this issue for low-income households, see T. Sanchez, Q. Shen, and Z.Peng, "Transit Mobility, Jobs Access and Low-Income Labour Participation in US Metropolitan Areas," *Urban Studies* 41, no. 7 (June 2004): 1313–1331. Our examination of cross-lagged correlations of auto ownership and income in *Panel Survey of Income Dynamics* data (a nationally representative, longitudinal survey of families begun in 1968) indicates that auto ownership more strongly affects income than vice versa, but this is an area requiring further research.

37. All data relating to motor vehicle ownership and incomes come from tabulations of the U.S. Census's *Public Use Microdata Sample (PUMS) 5%* file for the Philadelphia metropolitan area for 2000. The age restriction is to eliminate those who are likely to be retired. Without that restriction, the percentage of households without a vehicle is 16.3.

38. D. Elesh, C. Adams, M. Mattson, D. Bartelt, and J. Freely, "The Metropolitan Philadelphia Indicators Project," presented at the American Sociological Association, Philadelphia, August 13, 2005.

39. J. Elliot, "Social Isolation and Labor Market Insulation: Network and Neighborhood Effects on Less-Educated Urban Workers," *Sociological Quarterly* 40, no. 2 (1999): 199–216; N. Lin, "Social Status and Status Attainment," *Annual Review of Sociology* 25 (1999): 467–487; L. Falcon and E. Melendez, "Racial and Ethnic Differences in Job Searching in Urban Areas," in eds. A. O'Connor, C. Tilly, and L. Bobo, *Urban Inequality: Evidence from Four Cities*. New York: Russell Sage Foundation, 2001, pp. 341–371; R. Kleit, "Job Search Networks and Strategies in Scattered-Site Public Housing," *Housing Studies* 17, no. 1 (2002): 83–100.

40. M. Granovetter, "The Strength of Weak Ties," *American Journal of Sociology* 78, no. 6 (1973): 1360–1380; also M. Granovetter, *Getting a Job: A Study of Contacts and Careers*. Chicago: University of Chicago Press, 1995.

41. This point was nicely illustrated by a National Public Radio interview of a shrimp fisherman in a Louisiana town demolished by hurricane Katrina, which also destroyed his livelihood. As he put it, "when all the people you know are shrimpers, how are you going to find another job?"

42. We replicated the analysis of Figure 2.12 in national data and found an even stronger trend for prime working-age males to be either unemployed or out of the labor force.

43. J. Schmitt, *Labor Markets and Income Inequality in the United States Since the End of the 1970s*. Washington, D.C.: Center for Economic and Policy Research, 2005; U.S. Bureau of the Census, "Historical Income Inequality Tables," Washington, D.C.: U.S. Department of Commerce, 2005. Retrieved January 5, 2007, from www.census.gov/hhes/www/income/histinc/ineqtoc.html.

44. The ratios were computed from the U.S. Census, *1% Public Use Microdata Sample (PUMS) 1% file, for* 2000, for the Philadelphia metropolitan area for persons aged 25–64 and who worked in 1999.

45. Adams, Bartelt, Elesh, Goldstein, Kleniewski, and Yancey, *Philadelphia*, chapter 4.

46. E. Birch, "Having a Longer View on Downtown Living." *Journal of the American Planning Association* 68, no. 1 (Winter 2002): 5–21, p. 16.

47. F. Kummer, "Logo Spells First Start for Rte. 130 Towns," *Philadelphia Inquirer*, August 19, 2004, p. B1.

48. R. Briggs and L. Kamb, "Firm Hears of Tax Breaks and Chooses Not to Leave," *Philadelphia Inquirer*, April 16, 1999, p. C1.

49. D. Campbell, "Tax-Free Zone is OKd for U.S. Steel," *Philadelphia Inquirer*, May 29, 2004, p. B1.

50. David Sciocchetti, executive director of Chester's Economic Development Authority, quoted in D. Campbell, "Tension Over Tax Deals: Opportunity Zones Are Stirring Battles in the Suburbs, Too," *Philadelphia Inquirer*, March 10, 2004, p. A1.

51. H. Brubaker, "Where Are All the Jobs Promised?" *Philadelphia Inquirer*, April 4, 2004, p. E1.

52. Andy Paravis quoted in D. Mastrull and P. Kerkstra, "Renewal Advocates Gaining Allies" *Philadelphia Inquirer*, November 23, 2003, p. B18.

53. These three state assistance programs for businesses were the Opportunity Grant Program, the Infrastructure Development Program, and the Pennsylvania Industrial Development Authority's Low Interest Loan Program.

54. D. Bellafiore, S. Herzenberg, M. Myer, and A. Rothrock, *Economic Development Subsidies in Pennsylvania: Do They Fuel Sprawl?* Harrisburg, PA: Keystone Research Center, 2003, table 15.

55. "Executed BEIP Grants: From 6/1/1996 to 1/31/2008," New Jersey Economic Development Authority, 2006. Retrieved February 4, 2006, from http://www.njeda.com/pdfs/BEIP_Activity_Chronological.pdf.

56. J. Nowak, "Neighborhood Initiative and the Regional Economy," in eds. J. Blair and L. Reese, *Approaches to Economic Development*. Thousand Oaks, CA: Sage Publications, 1999, pp. 149–156, 153.

57. N. Gorenstein, "Blue Route's Popularity Drives Volume Predictions Off Map," *Philadelphia Inquirer*, August 24, 1993, p. A1.

58. Bruce Toll quoted in A. Colton, "Singin' the Blue Route Blues—The Opening of the Blue Route," *Philadelphia Magazine*, December 1991, p. 57.

CHAPTER THREE

1. P. Dreier, J. Mollenkopf, and T. Swanstrom, *Place Matters: Metropolitics for the 21st Century,* 2nd ed. Lawrence: University Press of Kansas, 2004, p. 77.

2. H. Gillette, *Camden After the Fall.* Philadelphia: University of Pennsylvania Press, 2006.

3. It is also the case that the census estimates of value are derived from self-reported data by householders to a census questionnaire item, whereas the *State of the Nation's Housing* estimates come from actual sales as reported through the National Association of Realtors. We accept the sales estimates (showing an overall increase of 12.9 percent from 1990 to 2003).

4. S. Malpezzi and R. Green, *A Primer on U.S. Housing Markets and Housing Policy.* Washington, D.C.: Urban Institute Press, 2003.

5. W. Lucy and D. Phillips, *Tomorrow's Cities, Tomorrow's Suburbs.* Chicago: American Planning Association, 2006.

6. National Low Income Housing Coalition. *Out of Reach, 2005.* Washington, D.C., 2005. Online at www.nlihc.org/oor/oor2005.

7. There are differences in the minimum wage and in Supplemental Security Income (SSI) payments in the two states: in 2005 New Jersey had a $6.15/hour minimum wage and a $183/month SSI payment, while Pennsylvania had a $5.15 minimum wage and a $174/month SSI payment.

8. Research for Democracy, *Blight Free Philadelphia.* Philadelphia: Temple University Center for Public Policy, October 2001, p. 7.

9. Ibid., p. 21.

10. R. Suarez, "How We Live: Philadelphia," *The News Hour,* PBS, October 2, 2002. Transcript at www.pbs.org/newshour/bb/entertainment/july-dec02/hwl_10-2.html.

11. M. A. Hughes, "Dirt into Dollars: Converting Vacant Land into Valuable Development," *Brookings Review,* June 1, 2000.

12. McKinsey and Company, *A Path Forward for Camden.* Baltimore: Annie E. Casey Foundation, June 13, 2001, p. 7.

13. Ibid.

14. Nora Lichtash quoted in K. Gregory, "There Goes the Neighborhood," *Philadelphia Weekly,* January 26–February 1, 2005, pp. 2024.

15. L. Freeman and F. Branconi, "Gentrification and Displacement: New York City in the 1990s," *Journal of the American Planning Association* 7, no. 1 (2004): 19–52.

16. Metropolitan Philadelphia Policy Center, *Flight or Fight: Metropolitan Philadelphia and Its Future.* Philadelphia: Metropolitan Philadelphia Policy Center, 2001; see also B. Katz, *Back to Prosperity: A Competitive Agenda for Renewing Pennsylvania.* Washington, D.C.: Brookings Institution, 2003.

17. W. Lucy and D. Phillips, *Confronting Suburban Decline.* Washington, D.C.: Island Press, 2000, p. 21.

18. The Reinvestment Fund, *Choices: A Report on the State of the Region's Housing Market.* Philadelphia: The Reinvestment Fund, 2001; see also The Reinvestment Fund, *Choices in Pennsylvania—Developing a Rational Framework for Housing Investment in Pennsylvania.* Philadelphia: The Reinvestment Fund, 2003; and Metropolitan Philadelphia Policy Center, *Flight or Fight.*

19. J. Gertner, "Chasing Ground," *New York Times Magazine*, October 16, 2005.

20. Robert Toll quoted in B. Fernandez,"Bob Toll's Housing Developments Lure Buyers, Irk Locals," *Philadelphia Inquirer*, October 5, 2003.

21. B. Fernandez, "Cashing in on housing boom," *Philadelphia Inquirer*, April 16, 2006.

22. Based on a housing calculator developed by the Fannie Mae Foundation and on the median mortgage amounts actually written between 2000 and 2004.

23. Metropolitan Philadelphia Indicators Project, *Where We Stand: Community Indicators for Metropolitan Philadelphia*. Philadelphia: Temple University, 2004, p. 38.

24. The data presented in Figure 3.5 refer to applicant logs maintained by banks and mortgage companies, which are reported every year to the Federal Financial Institution Examination Council (FFIEC) as part of Home Mortgage Disclosure Act annual reporting requirements.

25. C. Adams, D. Bartelt, D. Elesh, I. Goldstein, N. Kleniewski, and W. Yancey, *Philadelphia: Neighborhoods, Division, and Conflict in a Postindustrial City*. Philadelphia: Temple University Press, 1991.

26. I. Goldstein, *The Wrong Side of the Tracts*. PhD dissertation. Philadelphia: Temple University Department of Sociology, 1985.

27. K. Temkin, J. Johnson, and D. Levy, "Sub-prime Markets, the Role of GSEs, and Risk-based Pricing." Washington, D.C.: Department of Housing and Urban Development, 2002.

28. E. Gramlich, "Subprime Mortgage Lending: Benefits, Costs and Challenges," remarks to the Financial Services Roundtable Annual Housing Policy Meeting, Chicago, May 21, 2004.

29. Standard and Poor's (2000) estimates that loans with loan-to-value ratios of 95% are three times riskier than loans with loan-to-value ratios of 80%. Loans with loan-to-value ratios of 100% are four times riskier than loans with 80% loan-to-value ratios.

30. Temkin, "Sub-prime Markets, the Role of GSEs, and Risk-based Pricing;" see also J. Weicher, "The Home Equity Lending Industry: Refinancing Mortgages for Borrowers with Impaired Credit." Indianapolis,IN: Hudson Institute, 1997.

31. C. Bradford, "Risk or Race? Racial Disparities and the Subprime Refinance Market." Washington, D.C.: Center for Community Change, 2002. Although imperfect, these computations relied upon the list of lenders HUD has identified as engaged in the subprime and manufactured housing market. Available at www.huduser.org/datasets/manu .html.Retrieved April 2, 2008.

32. I. Goldstein, "Mortgage Foreclosure Filings in Pennsylvania." Philadelphia: The Reinvestment Fund, 2005.

33. Fannie Mae Foundation, *The Growing Demand for Housing*. Washington, D.C.: Fannie Mae Foundation, 2002.

34. J. Carr and L. Kolluri, "Predatory Lending: An Overview," in *Financial Services in Distressed Communities: Issues and Answers*. Washington, D.C.: Fannie Mae Foundation, 2001; see also K. Engel and P.McCoy, "A Tale of Three Markets: The Law and Economics of Predatory Lending," *Texas Law Review* 80, no. 6 (2002): 1255–1381.

35. For example, in the conventional prime market, "points" are of basically two types: (1) origination fees charged by the lender to the borrower to make the transaction, and (2) discount fees charged up front to reduce the interest rate. In the sub-prime predatory market, there is generally no such distinction and points are simply fees exacted by the lender from the borrower *because they can.*

36. I. Goldstein, *Foreclosures in Philadelp*hia. Philadelphia: The Reinvestment Fund, 2006.

37. The Reinvestment Fund, "Mortgage Foreclosure Filings in Pennsylvania." Philadelphia: The Reinvestment Fund, 2005.

38. Fannie Mae Foundation, *Growing Demand for Housing*, p. 9.

39. H. Lax, M. Manti, P. Raca, and P. Zorn, "Subprime Lending: An Investigation of Economic Efficiency," *Housing Policy Debate* 15, no. 3 (2004): 533–571.

40. A. White, "Risk Based Mortgage Pricing: Present and Future Research," *Housing Policy Debate* 15, no. 3 (2004): 503–531, p. 509.

41. J. Caskey, *Fringe Banking: Check-Cashing Outlets, Pawnshops and the Poor*. New York: Russell Sage Foundation, 1994; see also M. Barr, "Banking the Poor," *Yale Journal on Regulation* 21, no. 1 (2004). While the presence of branch locations is generally considered an important factor in the extent to which people in a community avail themselves of traditional banking services, there is evidence to suggest that other factors, such as convenience, impact the extent to which people utilize those services.

42. C. L. Mansfield and A. White, "Literacy and Contract," *Stanford Law and Policy Review* 13, no. 2 (2002).

43. M. Samuels and D. Elliott, *The Costs of Sprawl in Pennsylvania*. Philadelphia: Ten Thousand Friends of Pennsylvania, 2000.

44. Katz, *Back to Prosperity*.

45. T. Ferrick, "As Blight Relief Sits, Dream Persist," *Philadelphia Inquirer*, September 19, 2001.

46. Details can be found at www.phila.gov/ohcd/brewerytown.htm.

47. Larry Eichel, "Rising from Ruins: Why Public Housing, Once the Scourge of the City, Now Is a Vital Part of its Life and its Future," *Philadelphia Inquirer*, December 4, 2005.

48. I. Saffron, "Philadelphia Housing Authority Changes the Architecture of Low-Income Housing," *Philadelphia Inquirer*, April 21, 2005.

49. J. Milkman, "Revitalizing our Small Cities and Boroughs," Discussion Paper. Philadelphia: 10,000 Friends of Pennsylvania, 2003.

50. N. Smith, P. Caris, and E. Wyly, "The Camden Syndrome and the Menace of Suburban Decline," *Urban Affairs Review* 36, no. 4 (2001): 497–531.

51. J. Goering, J. Feins, and T. Richardson, "What Have We Learned about Housing Mobility and Poverty Deconcentration?" in *Choosing a Better Life? Evaluating the Moving to Opportunity Social Experiment*, eds. J. Goering and J. Feins. Washington, D.C.: Urban Institute Press, 2003, pp. 3–36.

52. S. Popkin, L. Buron, D. Levy, and M. Cunningham, "The Gatreaux Legacy: What Might Mixed-Income and Dispersal Strategies Mean for the Poorest Public Housing Tenants?" *Housing Policy Debate* 11, no. 4 (2000): 911–942.

53. G. Galster, P. Tatian, and R. Smith, "The Impact of Neighbors Who Use Section 8 Certificates on Property Values," *Housing Policy Debate* 10, no. 4 (1999): 879–917.

54. Mayor John Street quoted in L. Fleming, "PHA Will Limit Sec 8 Aid," *Philadelphia Inquirer*, February 14, 2003.

55. PHA Web site, http://www.pha.phila.gov/housing/Housing_Choice/index.html. Retrieved April 2, 2008.

56. Liz Hersh, Executive Director of the Housing Alliance of Pennsylvania, quoted in Fleming, "PHA Will Limit Sec 8 Aid."

57. B. Katz and M. A. Turner, "Who Should Run the Housing Voucher Program? A Reform Proposal," *Housing Policy Debate* 12, no. 2 (2001): 239–262.

58. J. Shields, "Tough Sell for First-Time Homebuyers," *Philadelphia Inquirer*, March 2, 2005.

59. N. Calavita, K. Grimes, and A. Mallach, "Inclusionary Housing in California and New Jersey: A Comparative Analysis," *Housing Policy Debate* 8, no. 11 (1997): 109–142, p. 112.

60. Ibid., p. 129.

61. E. Goetz, *Clearing the Way: Deconcentrating the Poor in Urban America*. Washington, D.C.: Urban Institute Press, 2003, p. 252.

62. Ibid.

CHAPTER FOUR

1. K. Goyette, "School Quality," in *Where We Stand: Community Indicators for Metropolitan Philadelphia*, Metropolitan Philadelphia Indicators Project. Philadelphia: Temple University, 2006.

2. J. Coleman et al., *Equality of Educational Opportunity*. Washington, D.C.: U.S. Government Printing Office, 1966.

3. To make sure our calculations were not reflecting only one-year aberrations for individual school districts, we averaged SAT scores, both locally and nationally, over three succeeding test years, 2002–2004.

4. T. Haas, "Top Schools," *Philadelphia Magazine*, September 2005, pp. 79-81.

5. In Pennsylvania, this is the percent falling "below basic," indicating inadequate academic performance that reflects little understanding and minimal display of skills included in the Pennsylvania Academic Content Standards. The comparable performance category in New Jersey is "partially proficient."

6. SAT scores were available for 111 of the 183 districts. Comparison of the districts for which SAT data were available with those for which it was not available revealed that the former were substantially larger (average size: 45,313 versus 7,392), more affluent (average percent of households making $75,000 or more: 33 versus 30), better educated (percent with BA or better: 30 versus 21), but not substantially more African American (percent African American households: 10 versus 9). These differences suggest that the analysis may underestimate the true effects of the socioeconomic variables.

7. Pennsylvania Department of Education, "2003–2004 Disaggregated Assessment Results: Grade 11 District Level Disaggregated Data," accessible online at http://www.pde .state.pa.us/a_and_t/cwp/view.asp?A=3andQ=107474. Unfortunately, there were no suburban school districts with as many as fifty Latino 11th graders, so we could not do a similar comparison between White and Latino test scores.

8. D. Mezzacappa and A. Emeno, "Promises Unfulfilled," *Philadelphia Inquirer*, May 16, 2004, p. A1.

9. D. Card and J. Rothstein, "Black-White Test Scores: Neighborhoods, Not Schools, Matter Most," Working Paper No. 12078. Cambridge, MA: National Bureau of Economic Research, March 2006.

10. J. Holme, "Buying Homes, Buying Schools: School Choice and the Social Construction of School Quality," *Harvard Educational Review* 72 (2002): 177–205.

11. S. E. Black, "Do Better Schools Matter?" *Quarterly Journal of Economics* 114 (1999): 577–599; W. T. Bogart and B. A. Cromwell, "How Much Is a Neighborhood School Worth?" *Journal of Urban Economics* 47 (2000): 280–305; L. Barrow and C. E. Rouse, "Using Market Valuation to Assess Public School Spending," Working Paper. Cambridge, MA:

National Bureau of Economic Research, 2002; C. Hilber and C. Mayer, "Why Do Households without Children Support Local Public Schools?" Working Paper.:Philadelphia: Federal Reserve Bank of Philadelphia, 2002; T. Kane, D. Staiger, and G. Sammis, "School Accountability Ratings and Housing Values," *Brookings-Wharton Papers on Urban Affairs,* 2003, pp. 139–170.

12. A. Molnar, W. Farrell, J. Johnson, and M. Sapp, "Research, Politics, and the School Choice Agenda," *Phi Delta Kappan* 78 (1996): 240–244; P. E. Peterson, "A Report Card on School Choice," *Commentary* 104, no. 4 (October 1997): 29–34, 36–39; J. P. Viteritti, "A Way Out: School Choice and Educational Opportunity," *Brookings Review* 17, no. 4 (1999).

13. D. Hardy, "No Child Provisions Lagging in the Region," *Philadelphia Inquirer,* June 19, 2005, p. B1.

14. K. Bulkley and J. Fisler, "A Decade of Charter Schools: From Theory to Practice," *Educational Policy* 17 (2003): 317–342.

15. Research for Action, *Adequate Yearly Progress: Where Philadelphia Public Schools Stand,* Philadelphia: Research for Action, 2004.

16. G. Miron, C. Nelson and J. Risley, "Strengthening Pennsylvania's Charter School Reform," Kalamazoo: Western Michigan University, October 2002, p. 147.

17. C. Lubienski, "Innovation in Education Markets: Theory and Evidence on the Impact of Competition and Choice in Charter Schools, "*American Educational Research Journal* 40 (2003): 395–443.

18. S. Saporito and A. Lareau, "School Selection as a Process: The Multiple Dimensions of Race in Framing Educational Choice," *Social Problems* 46 (1999): 418–435.

19. J. B. Cullen, B. A. Jacob, and S. D. Levitt, "The Impact of School Choice on Student Outcomes: An Analysis of the Chicago Public Schools," Working Paper No. 7888. Cambridge, MA: National Bureau of Economic Research, 2000.

20. "Report Card on the Schools," *Philadelphia Inquirer* March 7, 2004.

21. J. B. Toll and M. S.Gillam, eds., *Invisible Philadelphia: Community through Voluntary Organizations.* Philadelphia: Atwater Kent Museum, 1995, pp. 711–713.

22. H. Lankford and J. Wyckoff, "The Effects of School Choice and Residential Location on the Racial Segregation of K–12 Students," Working Paper. Albany: State University of New York, 1997; R. Wrinkle, J. Stewart, and J. L. Polinard, "Public School Quality, Private Schools, and Race," *American Journal of Political Science* 43 (1999): 1248–1253; S. Saporito, W. Yancey, and V. Louis, "Quality, Race, and the Urban Education Marketplace Reconsidered," *Urban Affairs Review* 37 (2001): 267–276.

23. T. Dee, "Competition and the Quality of Public Schools," *Economics of Education Review* 17 (1998): 419–427; F. Hess and D. Leal, "Quality, Race and the Urban Education Marketplace," *Urban Affairs Review* 37 (2001): 249–266.

24. C. Lubienski and S. T. Lubienski, "Re-examining a Primary Premise of Market Theory: An Analysis of NAEP Data on Achievement in Public and Private Schools," Occasional Paper No. 102. New York: Teachers College Columbia University, National Center for the Study of Privatization in Education, 2005.

25. D. Neal, "The Effects of Catholic Secondary Schooling on Educational Achievement," *Journal of Labor Economics* 15 (1997): 98–123; D. Figlio and J. A. Stone, "School Choice and Student Performance: Are Private Schools Really Better?" Discussion Paper No. 1141-97. Madison: University of Wisconsin Institute for Research on Poverty, 1997; D. D. Goldhaber and E. R. Eide, "What Do We Know (and Need to Know) about the Impact of School Choice Reforms on Disadvantaged Students?" *Harvard Educational Review* 72 (2002): 157–176.

26. Paul Vallas quoted in S. Snyder, "Schools Seek Ways to Allow Public-to-Catholic Transfers," *Philadelphia Inquirer*, October 17, 2003, p. B1.

27. D. Epple, D. Figlio, and R. Romano, "Competition between Private and Public Schools: Testing Stratification and Pricing Predictions," Working Paper No. 7956. Cambridge, MA: National Bureau of Economic Research, 2000.

28. E. A. Hanushek, "The Impact of Differential Expenditures on School Performance," *Educational Researcher* 18, no. 4 (1989): 45–65.

29. B. J. Biddle and D. C. Berliner, "What Research Says about Unequal Funding for Schools in America," Los Alamitos, CA: *Policy Perspectives,* 2003. Accessible online at www .WestEd.org/online_pubs/pp-03-01.pdf. In 2002, Pennsylvania and New Jersey both provided less than 40 percent of K–12 public school expenditures, in comparison to 41 percent in Connecticut, 44 percent in Virginia, 45 percent in Massachusetts, 46 percent in New York, and 67 percent in Delaware. See Education Commission of the States, "Highlights of State Education Systems," Denver: Education Commission of the States, October 2002.

31. G. Ritter, "School Finance Reform in New Jersey: A Piecemeal Response to a Systemic Problem," *Journal of Education Finance* 28 (2003): 575–598.

32. C. Gewertz, "A Level Playing Field," in *Education Week*, January 6, 2005. Accessible online at www.edweek.org/ew/articles/2005/01/06/17atrisk.h24.html. Despite gains made by Abbott districts, in 2008 the governor and legislature acted to discontinue Abbott funding and instead spread enhanced state funds to all districts, based on the number of children who need extra help. Abbott supporters went back to court to challenge this action, and their lawsuit is pending.

33. S. Snyder and D. Mezzacappa, "Schools' $80 Million Bet," *Philadelphia Inquirer*, April 24, 2005, p. A1.

34. M. MacIver and D. MacIver, "Which Bets Paid Off? Preliminary Findings on the Impact of Private Management and K–8 Conversion Reforms on the Achievement of Philadelphia Students," paper presented at the annual meeting of the American Political Science Association, Washington, D.C., September 1-4, 2005, p. 11.

35. E. Useem, *Learning from Philadelphia's School Reform: What Do the Research Findings Show So Far?* Philadelphia: Research for Action, September 2005.

36. B. Gill, R. Zimmer, J. Christman, and S. Blanc, "State Takeover, School Restructuring, Private Management, and Student Achievement in Philadelphia." Santa Monica, CA: Rand Corporation, February 1, 2007.

37. P. E. Peterson, *School Reform in Philadelphia: A Comparison of Student Achievement at Privately-Managed Schools with Student Achievement in Other District Schools*, Cambridge, MA: Program on Education Policy and Governance, Harvard University, 2007.

38. Metropolitan Philadelphia Indicators Project, *Where We Stand: Community Indicators for Metropolitan Philadelphia*. Philadelphia: Temple University, 2004, p. 32.

39. H. Sheffer, "Graduate Philadelphia: The Challenge to Complete," Philadelphia: Pennsylvania Economy League and Philadelphia Workforce Investment Board, June 2005.

40. Ibid., p. 3.

CHAPTER FIVE

1. G. Sirmans and D. Macpherson, *The Value of Housing Characteristics*. Washington, D.C.: National Association of Realtors, December 2003.

2. G. Sirmans, G. MacDonald, and D. Macpherson, *The Value of Housing Characteristics: A Meta-Analysis*. Washington, D.C.: National Association of Realtors, May 2005.

3. P. Rossi, *Why Families Move*. Glencoe, IL: Free Press, 1955. Other researchers following Rossi who have contributed to this line of research include J. Logan, "Industrialization and the Stratification of Cities in Suburban Regions," *American Journal of Sociology* 82, no. 2 (1976): 333–348; W. Frey, "Central City White Flight: Racial and Nonracial Causes," *American Sociological Review* 44 (1979): 425–448; J. L. Goodman, Jr., "Reasons for Moves out of and into Large Cities," *Journal of the American Planning Association* 45 (1979): 407–416; W.A.V. Clark and J. Burt, "The Impact of Workplace on Residential Relocation," *Annals of the Association of American Geographers* 70 (1980): 59–67; P. Rossi and A. Shlay, "Residential Mobility and Public Policy Issues: Why Families Move Revisited," *Journal of Social Issues* 38 (1982): 21–34; J. S. Adams, *Housing America in the 1980s*. New York: Russell Sage Foundation, 1987.

4. Rossi, *Why Families Move*, p. 9.

5. C. Tiebout, "A Pure Theory of Local Expenditure," *Journal of Political Economy* 64 (1956): 416–424.

6. Other researchers who have added to the literature on Tiebout's proposition include V. Ostrom, C. Tiebout, and R. Warren, "The Organization of Government in Metropolitan Areas: A Theoretical Inquiry," *American Political Science Review* 55 (1961): 831–842; D. Epple and A. Zelenitz, "The Implications of Competition among Jurisdictions: Does Tiebout Need Politics?" *Journal of Political Economy* 89 (1981): 1197–1217; S. Rose-Ackerman, "Tiebout Models and the Competitive Ideal: An Essay on the Political Economy of Local Government," in *Perspectives on Local Public Finance and Public Policy*, ed. J. Quigley. Greenwich, CT: JAI Press, 1983, pp. 23–46; G. Zodrow, *Local Provision of Public Services: The Tiebout Model after 25 Years*. New York: Academic Press, 1983; N. Topham and R. Ward, "Property Prices, Tax and Expenditure Levels and Local Fiscal Performance," *Applied Economics* 24, no. 11 (1992): 1225–1232; T. Luce, "Local Taxes, Public Services, and the Intra-metropolitan Location of Firms and Households," *Public Finance Quarterly* 229, no. 2 (1994): 139–167.

7. Metropolitan Philadelphia Indicators Project, *Where We Stand: Community Indicators for Metropolitan Philadelphia*. Philadelphia: Temple University, 2004, pp. 90–91.

8. U.S. Bureau of the Census, *American Housing Survey*, 2004.

9. Metropolitan Philadelphia Indicators Project, *Philadelphia Metropolitan Area Survey*. Philadelphia: Temple University, 2003, 2004, and 2005.

10. Unfortunately, we lack data on property assessments.

11. While we offered a list of reasons, respondents could give any additional reason they chose to.

12. J. Gyourko, and A. Summers, "Philadelphia: Spatial Economic Disparities," in *Sunbelt/Frostbelt*, ed. J. R. Pack. Washington, D.C.: Brookings Institution Press, 2005, pp. 110–139, 132–133.

13. M. Orfield, *Metropolitics: A Regional Agenda for Community and Stability*. Washington, D.C.: Brookings Institution Press, 1997, p. 9.

14. The measure of job access is what geographers term a population or job potential measure. For a given municipality, it is calculated by taking the distance between the geographic center of that municipality (called its centroid) and the centroid of some other municipality and dividing that distance into the number of jobs in the "other" municipality. This calculation is repeated for all other municipalities and the results summed to give the job potential for the original municipality. The larger the job potential value, the larger the number of jobs that are close to the original municipality. The procedure is then repeated to give job potential measures for each municipality in the region.

15. Tax data come from the New Jersey Department of Community Affairs and Pennsylvania Department of Community and Economic Development. School expenditure data are from the New Jersey and Pennsylvania Departments of Education. The Metropolitan Philadelphia Indicators Project made the two states' data comparable; details on calculations are available from www.temple.edu/mpip. SAT scores are also from the New Jersey and Pennsylvania Departments of Education.

16. The percentage of African American is a computed variable from which the effect of the percentage of persons in group quarters has been removed because it distorted the overall percentage.

17. D. Massey and N. Denton, *American Apartheid: Segregation and the Making of the Underclass*. Cambridge, MA: Harvard University Press, 1993.

18. Because we have the survey respondents' addresses, we can characterize them by attributes of the communities in which they live, such as average SAT scores, school expenditures, and taxes. Sample size issues limit the extent of the analysis that is possible, but we can determine whether the municipal-level analysis masks processes visible at the household level. Because we asked how long respondents lived in their present community, we can define movers in terms of whether they had moved within the past five years (comparable to the census time period) as well as whether they had moved in the past decade.

19. Metropolitan Philadelphia Indicators Project, *Where We Stand: Community Indicators for Metropolitan Philadelphia*. Philadelphia: Temple University, 2005.

20. Gyourko and Summers, "Philadelphia: Spatial Economic Disparities," p. 111.

21. D. Miller, *The Regional Governing of Metropolitan America*. Boulder, CO: Westview Press, 2002.

22. H. Holcomb,"Move a Little, Benefit a Lot," *Philadelphia Inquirer*, November 24, 2004, p. E1.

23. Robert Cormack, Executive Director, Bucks County Economic Development Corporation, quoted in H. Holcomb, "Big Obstacles to Promoting Area's Growth," *Philadelphia Inquirer*, November 9, 2004, p. E14.

24. Center City District, "The Impact of Keystone Opportunity Improvement Zones in or Adjacent to Center City," Philadelphia: Center City District, January 14, 2004.

25. T. Infield and A. Emeno. "Anti-tax Fervor Appears on the Wane," *Philadelphia Inquirer*, October 30, 2005, p. A1.

26. Center for Opinion Research, *Lower Merion Township Resident Survey*, Lancaster, PA: Franklin and Marshall College, September 2004.

27. Jean Bolger quoted in Infield and Emeno, "Anti-tax Fervor Appears on the Wane."

28. T. Hester and J. Donohue, "Property Taxes Soar 29% in 4 Years," *Star Ledger*, January 15, 2006.

29. W. Fischel, *The Homevoter Hypothesis*. Cambridge, MA: Harvard University Press, 2001.

30. R. Strauss and T. Nechyba, "Community Choice and Local Public Services: A Discrete Choice Approach," *Regional Science and Urban Economics* 28, no. 1 (1998): 51–73.

31. J. Gyourko and A. Summers, "Land Use Regulations" in Metropolitan Philadelphia Indicators Project, *Where We Stand: Community Indicators for Metropolitan Philadelphia*. Philadelphia: Temple University, 2006, pp. 11–18.

32. J. Kemeny, *The Myth of Home Ownership*. London: Routledge, 1981; J. Kemeny, *Housing and Social Theory*. London: Routledge, 1992.

CHAPTER SIX

1. L. Hoyt, "Do Business Improvement District Organizations Make a Difference?" *Journal of Planning Education and Research* 25:2 (2005) 185-199, p. 187.

2. D. Bartelt, "Neighborhood Organizations in Philadelphia," in *Invisible Philadelphia*, eds. Jean Barth Toll and Mildred S. Gillam. Philadelphia: Atwater Kent Museum, 1995, p. 465.

3. D. Bartelt, "Workforce Systems Change in a Politically Fragmented Environment," in *Workforce Development Politics*, ed. R Giloth. Philadelphia: Temple University Press, 2004, pp. 102–139, 105, 131.

4. W. Bogart, "Civic Infrastructure and the Financing of Community Development," Working Paper. Washington, DC: Brookings Institution, May 2003.

5. J. Anderson, *Art Held Hostage: The Battle over the Barnes Collection.* New York: W. W. Norton and Co., 2003.

6. R. Byers, "Big Donor Aims to Call Shots," *Philadelphia Daily News*, February 13, 1996, p. 3.

7. Mayor Arnold Webster quoted in E. Rouse, "Competing Visions of Camden Waterfront Strike at Its Renewal," *Philadelphia Inquirer*, July 14, 1996, p. B1.

8. D. Mezzacappa, "State Report Criticizes Chester Upland Schools," *Philadelphia Inquirer*, October 8, 2004, p. B1; D. Mezzacappa, "Control of Chester Schools in Court," *Philadelphia Inquirer*, November 29, 2005, p. B1.

9. Ways to Work can be accessed online at http://www.waystowork.com.

10. Margaret Berger Bradley of The Reinvestment Fund quoted in J. Rubin, M. Seltzer, and J. Mills, "Financing Workforce Intermediaries," in *Workforce Intermediaries for the 21st Century*, ed. R. Giloth. Philadelphia: Temple University Press, 2004, pp. 293-313, 298.

11. Alfonse Castillo quoted in K. Ritter, "A Disconnect on Camden Jobs," *Philadelphia Inquirer*, July 1, 2005.

12. R. Giloth, Robert. "Workforce Intermediaries: Partnerships for the Future," *Economic Development Quarterly* 17, no. 3 (August 2003): 215–219, p. 217.

13. The Reinvestment Fund, *Choices: A Report on the State of the Region's Housing Market.* Philadelphia: The Reinvestment Fund, December 2001, p. 46.

14. Housing Alliance of Pennsylvania, "Waiting List for Affordable Apartments Tops 50,000 Statewide," Glenside, PA: Housing Alliance of Pennsylvania, April 2005.

15. Pennsylvania Economy League, "A Review of Philadelphia's Authorities," Report No. 566. Philadelphia: Pennsylvania Economy League, October 1989.

16. R. Beauregard, "Local Politics and the Employment Relation: Construction Jobs in Philadelphia," in *Economic Restructuring and Political Response*, ed. R. Beauregard. Thousand Oaks, CA: Sage Publications, 1989, pp. 149–179.

17. J. Kromer, *Neighborhood Recovery: Reinvestment Policy for the New Hometown.* New Brunswick, NJ: Rutgers University Press, 2000, p. 182.

18. C. Adams, "Urban Governance and the Control of Infrastructure," *Public Works Management and Policy* 11, no. 3 (2007): 164–176.

19. Pennsylvania Economy League, "A Review of Philadelphia's Authorities," p. viii.

20. Thomas Corcoran quoted in I. Saffron, "One Man's Waterfront Vision," *Philadelphia Inquirer*, November 7, 2004, p. B3.

21. J. Kromer, *Neighborhood Recovery*, p. 77.

22. E. Useem, "Learning from Philadelphia's School Reform: What Do the Research Findings Show So Far?" Occasional Paper. Philadelphia: Research for Action, 2005.

23. R. Friedland, F. F. Piven, and R. Alford. "Political Conflict, Urban Structure and the Fiscal Crisis," *International Journal of Urban and Regional Research* 1, no. 3 (1977): 447–471.

24. Editorial, "How to Win Friends and Wield Influence," *Philadelphia Inquirer*, March 20, 2004.

25. Zack Stahlberg quoted in M. Gelbart and J. Sullivan, "A Powerful Agency Does Its Work in the Dark," *Philadelphia Inquirer*, December 18, 2005.

26. R. Briffault, "Business Improvement Districts: A Government for Our Time?" *Columbia Law Review* 99 (1999): 365–477.

27. Vice President Robert Rosenthal, Westrum Development Corporation, quoted in I. Saffron, "Archaic Zoning Laws Inhibit Growth," *Philadelphia Inquirer*, June 5, 2005.

28. State Senator Vincent Fumo quoted in C. McCoy and M. Cattabiani, "Fumo Lauds His Deal with PECO," *Philadelphia Inquirer*, January 30, 2004, p. A1.

29. National centers of public policy discussion, such as the Brookings Institution, have increasingly analyzed the regional contexts of urban development and have often featured Philadelphia to illustrate trends in housing, economic development, and the effects of changing demographics on the state and the region, most recently in their analysis of the decline of inner-ring suburbs. See R. Puentes and D. Warren, *One-Fifth of America: A Comprehensive Guide to America's First Suburbs*. Washington, D.C.: Brookings Institution , February 2006.

30. T. Kalwarski, "Best Places to Live," *Money Magazine*, August 1, 2005.

31. M. Pastor, P. Dreier, E. Grigsby, and M. Lopez-Garza, *Regions that Work: How Cities and Suburbs Can Grow Together*. Minneapolis: University of Minnesota Press, 2000.

32. Ibid., p. 117.

33. M. Orfield, *Metropolitics: A Regional Agenda for Community and Stability*. Washington, D.C.: Brookings Istitution and Lincoln Institute of Land Policy, 1997; N. Peirce, *Citistates: How Urban America Can Prosper in a Competitive World*. Washington, D.C.: Seven Locks Press, 1993.

34. S. B. Warner, *The Private City*, Philadelphia: University of Pennsylvania Press, 1968.

35. Ibid., p. 214.

36. Ibid., p. 223.

Index

Author Biographies

Carolyn Adams is Professor of Geography and Urban Studies at Temple University and the author of numerous works focusing on Philadelphia, especially its nonprofit sector.

David Bartelt is Professor of Geography and Urban Studies at Temple University, and the author of several articles and monographs that deal with the evolution of housing and community development in Philadelphia.

David Elesh is Associate Professor of Sociology and Director of the Social Science Data Library at Temple University. He has published numerous articles on the consequences of economic and technological change on urban areas and currently focuses on households' choice of community and the sources of metropolitan political fragmentation.

Ira Goldstein is Director of Policy and Information Services for The Reinvestment Fund. He is the author of a recently completed Ford Foundation funded study of predatory lending entitled "Lost Values: a study of predatory lending in Philadelphia."

3685 010